C

MW01090050

Candy Cummings

The Life and Career
of the Inventor of the Curveball

STEPHEN ROBERT KATZ

McFarland & Company, Inc., Publishers
Jefferson, North Carolina

This book has undergone peer review.

LIBRARY OF CONGRESS CATALOGUING-IN-PUBLICATION DATA

Names: Katz, Stephen Robert, 1945– author.
Title: Candy Cummings : the life and career of the inventor
of the curveball / Stephen Robert Katz.
Description: Jefferson, North Carolina : McFarland & Company, Inc., Publishers, 2022. |
Includes bibliographical references and index.
Identifiers: LCCN 2022002069 | ISBN 9781476680378 (paperback : acid free paper) ∞
ISBN 9781476644592 (ebook)
Subjects: LCSH: Cummings, William Arthur, 1848-1924. |
Pitching (Baseball)—History. | Baseball—United States—
History—19th century. | Pitchers (Baseball)—
United States—Biography. | BISAC: SPORTS &
RECREATION / Baseball / History
Classification: LCC GV865.C86 K37 2022 | DDC 796.357092 [B]—dc23/eng/20220224
LC record available at https://lccn.loc.gov/2022002069

BRITISH LIBRARY CATALOGUING DATA ARE AVAILABLE

ISBN (print) 978-1-4766-8037-8
ISBN (ebook) 978-1-4766-4459-2

Front cover: Pitcher William Arthur "Candy"
Cummings in the early 1870s

Printed in the United States of America

*McFarland & Company, Inc., Publishers
Box 611, Jefferson, North Carolina 28640
www.mcfarlandpub.com*

To my wonderful wife, Alice.
The light of my life.

Table of Contents

Acknowledgments

Baseball history is a social science. Men and women all over the country and abroad are involved in studying, researching, writing about, and even teaching the manifold aspects of our national pastime, including its history. Many of them are members of the Society for American Baseball Research (SABR), an organization of over 6,000 people worldwide interested in the many different facets of the game, of which history is one. Some are active researchers and writers, but most are just plain fans who like to read and talk about baseball. I've been a member since 2015. Over these seven-plus years, the SABR website, its numerous publications, and its members who write about the game and contribute to SABR discussion groups have enriched my knowledge of the history of our national pastime. I'm particularly grateful to the several SABR members who responded, either directly or through the SABR online discussion groups, to my queries concerning various matters dealt with in this book.

My sincere gratitude goes to those who provided me with images used in this book and helped in other ways in bringing the book to fruition. Among them are (in alphabetical order): Kate Avard, general manager, Valley Blue Sox, Holyoke, Massachusetts; Tasha Caswell of the Connecticut Historical Society; Suzanne Durand, proprietor of Photography by Suzanne, at Gilbertville, Massachusetts; John Horne, coordinator of Rights and Reproductions at the National Baseball Hall of Fame and Museum; Leslie Landrigen of the New England Historical Society; David Roland, president, and Darla Jarvis, membership chair, of the Isaac Cummings Family Association; Mark Rucker, of the Rucker Archive; Michael Salmon, librarian of the LA84 Foundation; Craig Simmons, chairman of the Ware, Massachusetts, Cemetery Commission; and Jane Stewart of NewsBank, Inc.

I also extend my great appreciation to Gary Mitchem, senior editor, and Lisa Camp, executive editor, at McFarland & Company, for shepherding me through this process with patience and cordiality, and to the staff at McFarland for their work in making this book a reality.

Of the several libraries that I made use of in the course of my research, I would like to acknowledge, in particular, the New York Public Library and its Rare Books Division. They managed to provide me with materials even during their shutdown in the pandemic of 2020.

Most of all, I convey my boundless gratitude to my dear wife, Alice Rosengard, for her unwavering support and encouragement, and for her candid advice and editorial suggestions.

Preface

As a kid, I was not a great baseball player, although I've always loved the game. I've never, to my recollection, successfully thrown a curveball. I never wore a big league or even a college baseball uniform. But I have two things in common with Candy Cummings: We were both born in the small central Massachusetts town of Ware (although nearly a century apart), and we both moved away from Ware when we were young boys. That hardly makes us blood brothers. However, in a way, it is our shared Ware background that has led me to write about his life and career.

The Cummings family has a long tradition in Ware. They've been there since the 1700s, and there are two streets in town bearing the name Cummings, roughly in the areas where long-past generations of Cummingses had their homesteads. The most famous of them was William Arthur Cummings. He was a baseball player in the formative days of the game and became one of the earliest major leaguers. Given the nickname "Candy" because of the excellence of his pitching, he made his mark as the inventor of the curveball. His contributions to the sport earned him election to the National Baseball Hall of Fame in Cooperstown, New York.

Folks in Ware are well aware of Candy Cummings and his legacy to the game of baseball. Visitors from out of town occasionally stop at the town's small public library, asking for directions to Candy Cummings' grave, and the staff are only too happy to oblige.

So, as someone who was born in Ware and retains an abiding affection for the town, I knew about Candy Cummings. I also knew about another, more recent major leaguer from Ware, Billy Jo Robidoux, who was a slugger with the Milwaukee Brewers, Chicago White Sox, and Boston Red Sox between 1985 and 1990. What I didn't know, until recently, was that there were *five more* major league baseball players from this small town in rural Massachusetts. I became aware of this while writing my first book, which was not about baseball at all, but was about my own roots in Ware.

As I was researching that book, I came across the name of a young woman, Beatrice Giard, who had been a clerk in my grandfather's men's clothing store in Ware in the 1920s. Further exploration led me to another member of Ware's Giard family, Joe Giard, a major league ball player who was on the 1927 New York Yankees—arguably the greatest team in baseball history.

I wondered how many other major leaguers could possibly come from this one small town, and I soon discovered that there have been seven. I was so astounded by this that I became determined to tell their stories. The result was my book *Ware's Boys of Summer: The Stories of Seven Major League Baseball Players from One Small Central Massachusetts Town*. Candy Cummings, the first of Ware's major leaguers, is in the book's leadoff spot.

While researching Candy Cummings for that book, I was struck by the fact that there existed no published comprehensive account of his life and career; there were only brief—and not always accurate—entries for Cummings in biographical compilations of baseball players. The more I learned about Cummings, the more I found that these sketches didn't do justice to the man or to his contributions to the game of baseball.

Candy Cummings was an important figure in 19th-century baseball; one of his era's top hurlers, he was the creator of the pitch that transformed the game—the curveball. Over the course of his career he witnessed, and was a part of, many of the developments in the game as it began evolving into our national pastime. Cummings was also an interesting man, a blue-blood with roots in New England extending back to the time of the Pilgrims, and educated at a fine boarding school. His distinctive personality and character were molded by his Congregationalist upbringing.

The full story of Candy Cummings had to be told, and I became determined to tell it.

Author's Notes

Baseball Team Names

The names of modern major league baseball teams follow a consistent and established pattern: the name of the city (or, in four cases, the state) where the team has its home, followed by the team's appellation, essentially a nickname; for example, Boston Red Sox, or Los Angeles Dodgers. (The club based in Anaheim, California, has added a second city to its name for marketing reasons; officially, it's the Los Angeles Angels of Anaheim, more commonly referred to as the Los Angeles Angels.) These aren't necessarily the teams' formal, corporate names, but are their "official" names as used by the teams themselves, Major League Baseball, the press, and the public. Often, major league teams are referred to informally simply by their city alone, or by the team nickname, for example, "Chicago," or "the White Sox."

How teams were referred to in the 19th century has been the subject of some discussion among baseball historians. It is generally known that team names weren't so conveniently and consistently configured then as they are today. During much of the amateur era, from the earliest organized squads in the 1840s into the 1860s, teams were typically formed or sponsored by social clubs, and they went by the name of the club, without a nickname or city designation. An example is the famed Knickerbocker Base Ball Club of New York. Organized in 1845, it was known as the Knickerbocker club, or simply the Knickerbockers, not the New York Knickerbockers. In Brooklyn, the Excelsiors Base Ball Club, formed in the mid–1850s, was commonly referred to as the Excelsiors, not the Brooklyn Excelsiors. In the mid-19th century, there was really no need to mention the city. Baseball teams tended to be clustered in regions or metropolitan areas in the East, and competition was mainly local.

In the 1860s and 1870s, teams began to acquire nicknames from common usage by the sporting press or the fans. Some of these nicknames reflected a feature of the team's uniform. For example, in 1875 and 1876, Candy Cummings played for the Hartford Base Ball Club in Hartford,

Connecticut. It was popularly called the Dark Blues, based on the color of the team uniform trimming and stockings. Similarly, the Cincinnati Base Ball Club, formed in 1866, became known as the Red Stockings. Teams were also referred to in a shorthand manner simply by the cities that they represented, in the plural, such as "the Bostons."

In addition, I have found many instances in which, from the late 1860s onward, newspapers referred to baseball teams in much the same way as they are today. For example, the Red Stockings of Cincinnati were often referred to in the press as the Cincinnati Red Stockings; the Athletic club of Philadelphia was called the Philadelphia Athletics, and so on.

In this book, I refer to teams in a variety of ways, all consistent with naming patterns I've found in newspapers of the period.

References to Baseball Associations

During much of the period covered by this book, baseball was organized into various associations of players and clubs, many with similar names, and some overlapping in time. To avoid the editorial infelicity of repeating the full name of an association each time I mention it, I will often use shorthand references. I give below a guide to the shorthand designation(s) used for each association.

International Association of Professional Base Ball Clubs: International Association, the Association, or IA.
(In 1879, the International Association changed its name to the National Base Ball Association. As it succeeded the IA, I refer to it as the Association.)
League Alliance: no shorthand reference; full name used.
Massachusetts Association of Base Ball Players: Massachusetts Association.
Massachusetts State Association: State Association.
National Association of Base Ball Players: NABBP.
National Association of Junior Base Ball Players: no shorthand reference; full name used.
National Association of Professional Base Ball Players: NAPBBP, National Association, or NA.
National Base Ball Association: NBBA, or the Association.
National League: the League, or NL.
New England Association of Base Ball Players: no shorthand reference; full name used.
New England Association of National Base Ball Players: no shorthand reference; full name used.
New England Base Ball Association: New England Association.

1

Origins

"God never gave him any size, but he's the candy."

That's how Bob Ferguson, manager of Hartford's Dark Blues baseball team from 1875 to 1877, described his prized pitcher, Candy Cummings.[1] In those days, "candy" was slang for "the best."

It was an apt description.

A lanky 5' 9", weighing under 120 pounds in his playing days, Candy Cummings didn't look like an athlete—let alone one who would end up in the Baseball Hall of Fame. Even by the standards of the 19th century, most professional ball players were considerably heftier than he was.[2]

Despite his scarecrow-like physique, this right-hander was one of the best pitchers of his era. In most of his seasons as a professional ball player, he figured among the top five or ten big league pitchers in nearly every statistical category recorded on baseball-reference.com. In several of those categories, he was number one. And he did it with style. Tim Murnane, a highly respected sportswriter and the baseball editor of the *Boston Globe* from the 1880s into the 1900s, once said of Cummings, "I never saw a more graceful ball player or one with more confidence in himself in a ball field."[3] Murnane was in a position to know. A big-league ballplayer himself before becoming a scribe, his in-uniform career paralleled that of Cummings, and he had even faced Cummings in games. Murnane was not alone in his assessment. Sam Crane, also an ex-ballplayer and baseball writer contemporary of Murnane, called Cummings "the most graceful pitcher I think I ever saw."[4]

Groomed on the sandlots of 1860s Brooklyn, New York—the "crucible of baseball"—Cummings went on to play at the dawn of the professional game and in what many consider the first major league. Later, he was chosen to be the first president of baseball's first minor league.

But he is best remembered as the inventor of what would become a staple of any pitcher's arsenal: the curveball.

Candy Cummings' story begins in the small central Massachusetts town of Ware. Set nearly in the geographic center of the state, Ware lies at the western edge of a geological feature known as the Central Uplands. This swath of elevated terrain, formed by the wearing away of ancient mountain ranges over millions of years, runs down the state's midsection. Etched into the landscape of the region are many streams and rivers.[5]

The largest of them is the Ware River, which flows through the town's present commercial and residential center. Once teeming with salmon, the river was an important source of food for the Quaboag Indians, a tribe of the Nipmuck group. They inhabited the area before it was settled by colonists of European ancestry. The Quaboag called the river Nenameseck, or a variation thereof, a word in their Algonquian dialect that referred to the place where they fished. By the river's falls, located in the present-day downtown commercial district, the Indians erected weirs—basket-type barriers—to trap the salmon. The word "weir," derived from Old English, was pronounced "ware" by the colonial settlers. "Ware" became the name of the river and eventually of the town that grew along its banks.[6]

The early settlers of this raw territory were a rugged, unpolished lot. Strongly individualistic, they had come as immigrants from abroad or from more settled regions of New England, seeking opportunity or escaping misfortune. Most were farmers, tilling the shallow and rock-strewn soil—a legacy of the glaciation in North America during the Ice Age. Eventually, basic production operations, such as grist mills and sawmills, were established along the town's waterways. Later, small-scale industries emerged, such as iron smelting, leather tanning, and brick making; small factories were built to produce straw goods, boots and shoes.[7]

In the 1820s came the textile mills that would become the mainstay of the town's economy for the next century and a half. They were among the mills that were springing up all over New England, thanks to a revolutionary new process, brought to the region from England, for harnessing water power to produce textiles. By the mid–1800s, large factories producing woolen and cotton goods had established themselves alongside the Ware River—near the falls that had been fished by the Quaboag Indians—and were in full swing. Their growing hunger for labor attracted large numbers of immigrant workers from French-speaking Canada, Poland, Ireland, England, and elsewhere.[8] In 1837, the town had two cotton mills and two woolen mills, in addition to the smaller manufacturing facilities.[9] By 1850, Ware's population had ballooned from 1,154 to 3,785, largely because of the mills, which were the town's largest employers.[10] With all this economic activity going on, Ware had, by the end of the 19th century, become the most thriving town in the county.[11]

This town of textile mills, small manufacturing, and agriculture was the Ware into which William Arthur Cummings was born on October 18, 1848.[12] He was the second of 12 children brought into the world by William

Brackenridge Cummings and his wife, Mary Parker (Clark), between 1846 and 1873, a span of 27 years. Two of those children—their third and tenth— died in infancy; two others did not survive beyond ages four and eight, respectively.[13]

The Cummingses were one of Ware's oldest and most prominent families. Their genealogy extends back to medieval Scotland, and before that, probably to northern France or Lombardy in the north of Italy.[14] Isaac Cummins, a direct ancestor of William Arthur, was the first of the Cummings lineage to come to America. Born in 1601, Isaac was from County Essex in the east of England. He, his wife, and his son were among the Puritans who, discontented with the governance and practices of the Church of England, migrated to America during the Great Migration of the 1620s and 1630s. Isaac arrived in the mid-1630s, probably landing at Salem, which was then the most important port of the Massachusetts Bay Colony. He and his family made their way to Ipswich, less than 15 miles to the north, where they settled; later, Isaac purchased farmland in nearby Topsfield.[15] Today, descendants of Isaac can be found in all 50 states of the United States as well as the United Kingdom and Canada.

Service to community and church was in the DNA of the Cummings line. In Topsfield, Isaac was a grand-juryman—then an appointed judicial position—and moderator of the Town Meeting. A member of the Congregational church, he served as its deacon for many years. Isaac died in Topsfield in 1677.[16]

After their arrival in New England, the Puritans established Congregationalism as their religion. Eager to free themselves from the "Popish practices" of the Church of England—with its ceremonies and its rigid hierarchical governance—they set up a "purified" system of churches with a simple order of worship, organized and governed by the free and voluntary consent of believers. Central to Congregationalist doctrine was that "the Congregation, rather than the presbyters, or the bishops, or the pope, can be trusted to decide what it ought to do."[17] Congregationalists extended this principle to their civic affairs; it was a seed of democratic precepts "that government derives its legitimacy from the voluntary consent of the governed, governors should be chosen by the governed, rulers should be accountable to the ruled, and constitutional checks should limit both the government and the people."[18]

With these rights came social and moral obligations to play a part in carrying out God's work on Earth. Congregationalists were the first to send missionaries to Indians in North America, as well as to foreign lands. And they were prominent and forceful soldiers in the anti-slavery and abolitionist movements of the 19th century.

Education was of fundamental importance to Congregationalists; it was their "unfaltering belief that neither state nor church is secure unless the people have knowledge."[19] From them came the idea of public school systems. And Congregationalists founded renowned New England colleges such as Yale, Harvard, Dartmouth, Bowdoin, Amherst, and Williams.

Successive generations of Isaac Cummings' descendants were Congregationalists. The principles of their faith would help shape the character of William Arthur "Candy" Cummings.

Three generations after Isaac, the first of William Arthur's ancestors arrived in Ware. They were Jacob Cummings and his wife, Martha—William Arthur's great-great-great-grandparents—who came from Killingly, Connecticut, around 1740.[20] Jacob, a farmer, was one of Ware's founders. He was among 33 freeholders who, in 1742, petitioned the colonial legislature of Massachusetts Bay province—the General Court—to establish the area that they inhabited as a separate self-governing precinct, and to grant them the necessary authority to establish their own house of worship. Acceding to their request, the General Court created Ware River Precinct, also referred to as Ware River Parish, which eventually became the Town of Ware. The designation "parish" was used in relation to the district's ecclesiastical affairs, "precinct" for governmental and other secular matters.

Shortly after the establishment of the precinct/parish, the inhabitants elected Jacob as a member of its governing body—the Committee of the Precinct—one of several public offices in which he served over the years. He presided over the organization of public worship in the parish and the establishment of the meeting house. Consistent with Congregationalist practice in the New England colonies, the meeting house served both religious and civic functions; the meetings of the inhabitants were held there, and it was the location of the First Congregational Church. Jacob was one of the first deacons of that church.

Jacob Cummings also served in the provincial army during the French and Indian War. In August 1757, he led a company of 39 militiamen (including his son, Jacob, Jr., and other Cummingses) on a 15-day march from Ware River Precinct to upstate New York to help the British regulars defend Fort William Henry against a heavy siege by French troops.

Jacob's grandson Joseph, an innkeeper in Ware, was a member of a company of Minute Men who responded to the British attack at Lexington and Concord that opened the Revolutionary War. Other members of the Cummings family also fought in the war for independence, as well as in the War of 1812 and the Civil War.[21]

Joseph Cummings, Jr., a great-grandson of Jacob—and William Arthur's grandfather—continued the Cummings tradition of public service. Once a teacher and a surveyor by trade, Joseph became deacon of the two Congregational churches then in Ware, and he served at various times as justice of the peace, county commissioner, representative of Ware in the General Court, and postmaster.[22]

William Arthur's father, William Brackenridge Cummings, was a manufacturer of bonnets and other straw goods.[23] His middle name came from another venerable Ware family; his mother, Sally, was a Brackenridge. Sally's father, William Brackenridge, was of Scottish stock. In 1727, at the age of four, he accompanied his parents, James and Sarah Breakenridge, when they immigrated to central Massachusetts from Ireland. The family settled in what became the town of Palmer, just south of Ware.

William Brackenridge moved to Ware in 1756 and held several public offices, including service with Jacob Cummings on the town's first Committee of the Precinct. He was also a member of Jacob's military unit during the French and Indian War. At the outbreak of the Revolutionary War, he resigned his commission in the King's army and raised a company of militia to fight the Redcoats.[24]

William Arthur's mother, Mary Parker (Clark) Cummings, also had distinguished parentage. Like the Cummingses and Brackenridges, Mary's father, Avery Clark—another straw-goods manufacturer—was active in Ware's municipal affairs and represented the town in the Massachusetts legislature.[25]

Leaders in government, the military, church, and community—this was William Arthur Cummings' pedigree. From such forebears he inherited his mental acuity and his ambition, perseverance, and fortitude—traits that served him well in conceiving of and developing the curveball and rising to the top among pitchers of his era.

Being in the same line of work and involved in the affairs of the town, William Brackenridge Cummings (William Arthur's father) and Avery Clark (his maternal grandfather) were, no doubt, close acquaintances. This could have been how William B. met Avery's daughter, Mary. Their relationship blossomed, and the couple married in Hartford, Connecticut, on June 20, 1845. They then returned to Ware to start a family.[26]

Six years and two toddlers later, including William Arthur, William B. and Mary P. left their small town for the big city.

2

Brooklyn

Around 1850, William Arthur's grandfather, Avery Clark, moved with his wife, Mary (Fowle), and their eight children to New York City, where Avery established a straw-goods manufacturing business.[1]

William Arthur's parents, William B. and Mary P. Cummings, followed them to the metropolitan area. In 1851, after burying their third-born, Charlie, in Ware, they took their two surviving children, Mary and William Arthur, and relocated to Newark, New Jersey.[2] The family remained there just long enough for William B. and Mary P. to produce a fourth child, Gertrude, who was born in Newark on April 4, 1852.[3] Then they moved to Brooklyn, New York.[4]

Completing the game of city-tag, Avery Clark and his family relocated to Brooklyn around 1856.[5]

Why Brooklyn? To put it simply, the city was booming. (Brooklyn would not become part of New York City until 1898.) Its waterfront on the East River, then one of the world's busiest waterways, was throbbing with activity. The Brooklyn Navy Yard had opened in 1801 and was building and servicing ships for the United States Navy.[6] Several other shipyards were located in Brooklyn. One of them, the Continental Works, built and in 1862 launched the *USS Monitor,* the Navy's first ironclad warship. With the completion of the Erie Canal in 1825, goods began to flow between the New York City area and Buffalo and to points beyond. Shipyards, docks, and warehouses sprang up along Brooklyn's East River waterfront to service the vessels and the tons upon tons of cargo of all kinds that poured into and out of the metropolis, which had become the country's industrial and commercial hub.[7]

This burst of commercial activity and the economic growth that it produced attracted a large influx of people—immigrant laborers from abroad who found work on the waterfront as well as professionals and businessmen who moved to Brooklyn from elsewhere in the northeast to participate in the rapidly growing economy. The steam ferry service begun by Robert Fulton in 1814, and other ferry services established later in the 1800s, made it easy for them to live comfortably in Brooklyn and commute to work across the East River in New York City. By 1860, 40 percent of Brooklyn's wage earners were taking the short ferry ride to and from work in New York City each day.[8] Among them was William B. Cummings, who was employed as a cashier in one of the several telegraph offices that had opened in New York City shortly after the commencement of commercial telegraph communications in 1846.[9]

Between 1840 and 1870, the population of Brooklyn increased from 36,000 to 400,000, making it the third-largest city in the United States.[10] In 1869, the *Brooklyn Daily Eagle* described the city's astonishing growth:

> Let an old resident return after an absence of twenty years and he beholds such changes, that in his wildest dreams he did not imagine—where acres of tall grain waved and nodded in the sunlight, and broad fields of corn rustled to the breeze, he would behold long rows of palatial residences; blocks of brown stone and bricks....[11]

The vast numbers of people pouring into Brooklyn from the mid–1800s onward were a boon to real estate speculators and builders. In 1869, the *Brooklyn Daily Eagle* marveled, "Buildings and dwellings have sprung up as if by magic. Long rows of brown stones and brick buildings have risen, seemingly, in the space of a single night."[12]

Many of the upscale newcomers to Brooklyn were, like William B. Cummings and Avery Clark, merchants and manufacturers from New England. New Englanders came in such numbers that they became an influential force in the affairs of the city. By the 1870s, there were more of them living in Brooklyn than there were in Boston.

In Brooklyn, these migrants established their own churches in the Congregational denomination that they had practiced in New England. The largest was the Plymouth Church, founded in 1847 in the district today known as Brooklyn Heights. A piece of Plymouth Rock is on display in the church arcade.[13]

Plymouth Church's first and longest-serving pastor was Henry Ward Beecher, the outspoken anti-slavery preacher. He was a brother of Harriet Beecher Stowe, the author of the anti-slavery novel, *Uncle Tom's Cabin*. Under his ministry, the church became active in the abolitionist movement. An important stop on the Underground Railway, the church was secretly referred to as the "Grand Depot." A nondescript door behind the pulpit and organ led down to a labyrinth of tunnels and chambers, used for hiding escaping slaves. One of baseball's most notable figures, Branch Rickey, was at one time a parishioner at the Plymouth Church. A deeply religious man, Rickey, when he was general manager of the Brooklyn Dodgers, signed Jackie Robinson and broke baseball's color barrier.

In 1847, a group of prominent New Englanders established the New England Society in the City of Brooklyn, with the aims of promoting fellowship and common interests, and providing charitable relief to indigent or unfortunate persons of New England origin.[14] The society continues to operate to this day, awarding scholarships to Brooklyn students to attend colleges and universities in New England, and celebrating the members' New England heritage.

The Cummings family lived in one of Brooklyn's newest and more desirable neighborhoods. It was within an area then known as South Brooklyn, which the *Brooklyn Daily Eagle* described as having been "but a dreary sand-hill" a mere ten years earlier.[15] Today, that section is known as Carroll Gardens. Although bounded on two sides by busy expressways, it remains a quiet, tree-lined enclave with rows of traditional, elegant brownstone residences.[16] Its name, bestowed in the mid–1960s to give it an identity separate from neighboring communities, reflects one of its distinguishing features: the spacious gardens that front each of the brownstones. "Carroll," which is also the name of a street and a park in the district, honors Charles Carroll, a signer of the Declaration of Independence from Maryland, who commanded a colonial regiment that came to the area's defense during the Revolutionary War.[17]

Until the 1840s, the area encompassing what is now Carroll Gardens was farmland and woods owned by the Bergen family, descendants of early Dutch settlers.[18] Richard Butt, one of Brooklyn's city surveyors, laid out the plan for the neighborhood in 1846.[19] His design called for the dwellings to have unusually large front gardens—over 33 feet deep—which provided "a sense of remoteness and a sunny, airy openness."[20] The houses were built of first class brick or stone and were 2½ and 3½ stories tall.[21] When the Cummings family moved there from Newark, the neighborhood was still in the process of development; 1855 maps[22] show many streets in the area with lots unoccupied by buildings. Although most of the original buildings were replaced from the 1870s onward,[23] the residences there today, with their ample front gardens, probably look much like the ones that were there in the Cummingses' time.

An 1854 advertisement of the sale of building lots in the neighborhood described the Cummingses' neighborhood:

> The superior class of improvements already made in this vicinity (whole blocks of ornamental, marble, and brown stone front houses having been erected) warrants the belief that it will continue to be, as it is now, the most elegant and desirable part of the city of Brooklyn, and comparing favorably with the aristocratic portions of the city of New York. The location has all the elements required for first class private residences. One of the lines of city railroads runs within one block.... The streets and places are all paved, and are of good width,

the latter being over 100 feet wide, are short, and will never be crowded thoroughfares…. Carroll Park, adjoining these lots, will soon be fenced and beautified, and become another ornament to this already beautiful section of the city.[24]

Typical of many neighborhoods in what are now the five boroughs of New York City, the population make-up of Carroll Gardens has changed over the years. In the latter part of the 19th century, it was home to many Irish immigrants. As they moved onward to other communities, they were gradually replaced by new arrivals from Italy who came to work on the docks and in the shipyards.[25] The infamous mobster Al Capone, born to Italian immigrants and raised in another section of Brooklyn, met his future wife—an Irish girl named Mary ("Mae") Coughlin—at a social club in Carroll Gardens; they married in a neighborhood church, St. Mary's Star of the Sea, on December 30, 1918.[26] Even today, Carroll Gardens, with its Italian markets, bakeries, and cafés, and the cadences of Italian dialects, exudes an Italian-American flavor.

During the 1860s, the Cummingses lived at several different addresses within the prosperous Carroll Gardens neighborhood. The head of the household, William B., left his position at the telegraph office in New York and went into the flourishing wallpaper and paper-hanging trade. He was a pioneer in the manufacture of wallpaper. Later, he entered the construction business, building numerous houses in the Bushwick section of Brooklyn.[27]

The Cummings family lived comfortably, with many of the upper-middle-class trappings and conventions of the period. They employed live-in servants—single women from Ireland—and for a while took a boarder, a professional singer named Eliza "Jennie" Puffer.[28] A music lover, William B. was a violinist and founded the Brooklyn Chorale.[29] He and his family no doubt attended concerts and theatrical productions at the Brooklyn Academy of Music, which opened in 1861 and became a center of the city's community life.[30]

In another practice typical of their station, William B. and Mary had their portraits painted. Executed in 1870 by John Bernard Whittaker, one of Brooklyn's foremost painters and art educators, the paintings capture the characters of the couple. They appear kindly, self-assured, and intelligent: William erect and stalwart, with barely a tinge of gray in his full, chest-length beard, and Mary motherly and nurturing, with not a hint of gray. The portraits were handed down through successive generations of William B.'s descendants. In 1961, they were donated to the public library in Ware by a great-grandson of William B. and Mary, the Rev. Edward Sumner Gray. They are still there.[31]

Continuing the Congregationalist tradition in the Cummings family, William B. and Mary P. Cummings joined the South Congregational Church, another one of the churches in Brooklyn established by

William Brackenridge Cummings and Mary Parker (Clark) Cummings, parents of Candy Cummings. Artist: John Bernard Whittaker (1836–1926). The original portraits, painted in 1870, are held by the Young Men's Library Association, Ware, Massachusetts. The photographs of the portraits shown here were taken by Suzanne Durand Photography, Gilbertville, Massachusetts.

transplanted New Englanders.[32] Located in the South Brooklyn neighborhood where the Cummingses resided, the church was said to be the inspiration of Henry Ward Beecher, pastor of the Plymouth Church. A pamphlet published on the occasion of its 90th anniversary contains the following account: "Rev. Henry Ward Beecher, standing one day on a hill in South Brooklyn overlooking the meadows and corn-fields which ran down to the sea, exclaimed, 'Here—the next Congregational church shall be built!'"[33]

Reflecting their New England Congregationalist heritage, William B. and Mary prized education. They saw to it that William Arthur—he went by the name Arthur, or "Artie" to his family and friends—was properly educated. When he reached school age, he would have attended either a private school run by a church or one of the public schools near his home.

At a public primary school, little Artie—perhaps wearing breeches and a broad bowtie and sitting at his double wooden desk shared with a classmate—would have learned reading, spelling, printing, and basic arithmetic. Graduating to the next level, grammar school, his curriculum would have included English grammar, composition, and essays; arithmetic and algebra; geography; history; and natural sciences.[34] Public schools were in session year-round, six hours a day, with three weeks off in the summer. Although they were open to all children, attendance was not compulsory—except for delinquent boys. It couldn't be, since there were only enough schools and teachers to accommodate a fraction of the children seeking admission. In 1869, fewer than half of Brooklyn's school-age children attended school.[35]

When Artie wasn't in school, he was playing baseball. In the mid–1800s, there was no better place than Brooklyn—and South Brooklyn in particular—for a youngster to learn and play the game. Dubbed the "crucible of baseball" by modern-day author Mark Pestana, the city was a baseball mecca.[36] In 1865, the *Brooklyn Daily Eagle* stated—not without bias, but also not lacking truth: "in no city of the Union is the game so popular as in Brooklyn. We are somewhat proud of this, for anything it is worth while doing it is worth while doing well."[37] And in Brooklyn, they did indeed do it well.

3

The Crucible
of Baseball and the Birth
of the Curveball

Modern baseball historians trace our national pastime to ball games played by children in England in the 18th century and earlier. The forms and names of these games varied, depending on the region of the country where they were played, and each one had certain features that also exist in the baseball of today. When English settlers came to the American colonies, they brought with them the games that they had played as children and introduced them in the communities where they put down roots. Over time, these games morphed into Americanized forms. Depending on the region, they were called "town ball," "round ball," "base ball," and other names.

In New York City and Brooklyn, and northward into upstate New York, the game was "base ball." In 1845, the Knickerbocker Base Ball Club of New York City codified the rules of baseball, modifying somewhat the game that boys in the region had been playing. Twelve years later, at the instigation of the Knickerbockers, several clubs in the New York metropolitan area banded together to form the National Association of Base Ball Players—the NABBP. The organization produced a revised and expanded set of rules of baseball based on the Knickerbocker rules of 1845.[1] This became known as the "New York game."[2]

The game played in Massachusetts and the rest of New England was called "round ball" in some areas and "town ball" in others. In May 1858, six ball clubs from Boston and vicinity formed the Massachusetts Association of Base Ball Players and adopted rules and regulations for *their* game, which they, too, called "base ball," bringing under one set of rules the numerous local variants of round ball and town ball.[3] This came to be known as the "Massachusetts game," distinguishing it from its New York cousin.

A game similar to New England's round or town ball arose in Philadelphia. Also called "town ball," Philly's version spread to much of the rest of

"A Base-Ball Match at the Elysian Fields, Hoboken" (1859). Depicted is the "New York game," an early version of baseball played in the New York and Brooklyn metropolitan area, and in some other areas, in the mid-1800s. The New York game evolved into the modern game of baseball (Library of Congress).

"Thirty or More Players (15 or More on Each Side) With a Bat and Ball Playing Town Ball, Sometimes Called Round Ball, and Subsequently the So-called Massachusetts Game of Base Ball." This early version of baseball, often called the "Massachusetts game," was played in Massachusetts and throughout New England in the mid-1800s. By the end of the 1860s, it had disappeared, replaced by the New York game. In this view, the batter, called the "striker," is in position midway between "first goal" (i.e., first base, manned by the player at the far right) and the "fourth" or "home" goal (manned by the third player from the left) (A.G. Spalding Baseball Collection. New York Public Library Digital Collections).

Pennsylvania, as well as to some midwestern states such as Illinois, Indiana, Missouri, and Ohio. A form of town ball was even reported in Montana.[4]

Much like kids today, who improvise bat-and-ball games to accommodate the space and number of players available, 19th-century youngsters getting together at the local vacant lot would often play informal ball games called "old cat." These games had nothing to do with aged felines; the name "cat" possibly came from an early version in which a piece of wood, the catapult, was hit instead of a ball to start the action. There was one, two, three, and even four old cat, depending on the number of players available.[5]

The nomenclature and geography of the versions just described should not be viewed with the precision of a lexicographer or a cartographer. In fact, there was considerable fluidity with the names given to the different variants of the game and to the geographic reach of each variant. For example, another name used for the early game of "base ball" played by boys in the New York/Brooklyn area was "town ball," which was also the name of different versions played in New England and Philadelphia.[6] Confusing matters further, New York's "base ball" or "town ball" was also called "three old cat."[7]

The popularity of the New York game spread beyond its traditional domain and began to overtake other versions of baseball. It first expanded southward, replacing Philadelphia's town ball by the early 1860s, leaving only the New York and Massachusetts games as the main forms of the sport.[8] There were big differences between the two; here are some of them:

Layout of playing field

New York game: The infield was in the form of a diamond, with four bases 90 feet apart. (The original configuration, in the Knickerbocker rules of 1845, was 42 paces from home to second base and the same number of paces from first to third base.) First, second, and third bases consisted of sand- or sawdust-filled canvas bags, painted white; "home base" was a white, "flat circular iron plate"— probably the origin of today's "home plate." The batter stood at home base. The front of the pitcher's "box"—the raised "mound" would not come until later— was 45 feet from home base.

Massachusetts game: The infield was in the form of a square, with four bases— also called "bounds" or "goals"—60 feet apart and consisting of wooden stakes in the ground. The batter, called the "striker," stood midway on the line between home and first bounds. The pitcher, or "thrower," stood 35 feet in front of the striker.

Foul balls

New York game: Balls hit wide of first or third base were foul.

Massachusetts game: There were no foul areas; a ball hit anywhere, even behind the striker, was fair.

Bounced balls

New York game: Batted balls caught on the fly or on one bounce were out. This controversial "bound catch" rule was later changed; from 1865, fair balls had to be caught on the fly—the "fly catch"—for the batter to be out. For foul balls, the bound catch rule remained until 1883.

Massachusetts game: A batted ball caught on the fly was out; a ball that hit the ground was in play.

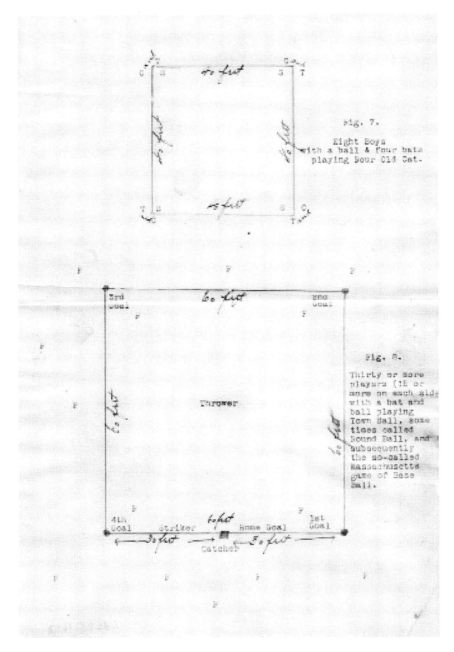

The bottom figure is a diagram of the "Massachusetts Game." At the top is a diagram of "four old cat." "Old cat" games, in their various versions, were informal ball games played in many regions (A.G. Spalding Baseball Collection. New York Public Library Digital Collections).

Putting out a baserunner

New York game: A baserunner was out when a fielder, in contact with first base, came into possession of the ball before the runner reached it, or when a runner was tagged with the ball. There was no force out of a runner compelled to advance to a base beyond first; the runner had to be tagged.

Massachusetts game: A baserunner was put out by throwing the ball at him. If it hit the runner, he was out. This was called "plugging" or "soaking." [This was also a feature of New York's early form of "base ball" until the Knickerbockers eliminated the practice in their 1845 rules.]

Of the two versions, the New York game was much more like the baseball that we know today. One big difference from modern baseball was in the pitching department. The New York game was essentially a contest between hitters and fielders, with pitchers playing only a supporting role; their job was to deliver the ball in such a manner that the batter could put it into play. As it was put in the 1867 version of the NABBP rules,[9] the pitcher must "deliver the ball as near as possible over the center of the home base, and fairly for the striker." When a batsman took his position at the plate, the umpire would ask him where he wanted the pitch; he could respond, for example, high or low, and the pitcher would have to comply. The rules strictly regulated how the pitcher propelled the baseball to the batsman: the ball had to be "pitched, not jerked or thrown, to the bat." Encompassed within these few words were requirements that the ball be delivered underhand, with the arm straight and swinging in a perpendicular motion, and with both feet on the ground—much like the pitching of horseshoes.[10] The rules of the Massachusetts game provided just the opposite, while still requiring that the ball be delivered so that the striker could put it into play: "the ball must be thrown"—i.e., overhand—"not pitched or tossed, on the side preferred by the striker, and within reach of his bat."

The Massachusetts game did not survive. For its demise, blame—or thank, depending on your point of view—a New York City watchmaker named Edward G. Saltzman. A member of New York's Gotham Base Ball Club, Saltzman brought the New York game to New England when he relocated to Boston in 1857. Not long after his arrival, Saltzman, with some colleagues, founded Boston's Tri-Mountain Base Ball Club. The Tri-Mounts decided to play baseball under the New York rules, the first club in New England to do so.[11] But as the only team around that played the New York game, they had trouble finding opponents. They finally did: the Portland Base Ball Club, from Maine, came down to play a "friendly" match—an exhibition game—against the Tri-Mountains on September 9, 1858, on Boston Common, using the NABBP rules. The Portlands traveled back to Maine happy; they defeated the Tri-Mountains, 47–42.[12]

The New York game apparently appealed to players and fans in the

Northeast. In 1860, a Boston newspaper reported that the game was "fast becoming popular in New England, and in fact over the whole country."[13] A big blow to the Massachusetts game came in October 1865, when 11 clubs from Boston and its vicinity formed the New England Association of National Base Ball Players as a branch of the NABBP and agreed to be governed by the NABBP's playing rules.[14]

In 1867, with most of the clubs in the Bay State playing under the NABBP rules, the Massachusetts Association (which had renamed itself the New England Association of Base Ball Players) disbanded.[15] By the end of the decade, the Massachusetts game had become extinct. That left the New York version as the only game standing. It was the New York game that evolved into the modern game of baseball.

So, which version of the game did young Artie Cummings play? In his senior years, he recalled having played round ball when he was a little fellow in his native town of Ware.[16] This was probably not while his family was still living in Ware, since he was only around three years old when they moved away. But the Cummingses regularly journeyed back to Ware to visit relatives and friends, and it is possible that he played round ball with some of them during those visits. In Brooklyn, however, Artie would have played the New York game, or "old cat," with his chums and schoolmates. His pitching, therefore, was underhand and straight-armed.

Prior to the Civil War, baseball was pretty much a regional sport focused on the Northeast; by war's end, it had become America's national game.

Even as the conflict raged, baseball continued to be played, but teams became depleted as their players rushed to enlist. Many clubs struggled to field squads, and some were unable to play at all for much of the four years.

Despite all the anguish, pain, hardship, and destruction wrought by the war, it had a beneficial effect on baseball. Soldiers from the Northeast, leaving behind their homes and families and going off to join the fight, brought baseball with them. They played ball in their regimental camps as a respite from the horrors of battle and the tedium of camp life; they played as prisoners in POW camps. Soldiers from other sections of the country joined in games and soon became lovers of the sport. The military authorities encouraged ball playing, as it provided the men with a way to keep fit and to stay out of trouble. The government provided baseball equipment to regiments requesting it, and even the navy provided facilities for sailors to play ball when their ships were in port.

Soldiers from all over the country who had learned baseball while serving in the military brought it home with them when their service was over. By the end of the war, the popularity of the game had grown and spread throughout the country.[17]

For much of the period from the late 1850s up to 1870, Brooklyn was at the top of the baseball world. "During the years when baseball became America's game," writes baseball historian David Dyte, "it was played best in Brooklyn."[18] The city had dozens of organized clubs taking to its ball fields, far more than its more populous neighbor across the East River.[19] All of the clubs up through the 1860s were amateur organizations; their purpose was to provide young men with healthful exercise, enjoyment, and fellowship. Professional baseball did not officially come into the picture until 1869 (although before then, ways were found to funnel cash to players).

From 1859 to 1866, and again in 1869, Brooklyn clubs were the acknowledged champions of baseball. There was no official champion in those days; the amateurs' governing body, the NABBP, didn't recognize one. In the late 1850s, the title was accorded by general consensus of the baseball community. Afterwards, the champion was considered to be the victor in a "home and home"—a best-of-three-game match—between the reigning champion and any club that considered itself good enough to challenge it.[20] These challenges and matches could occur at any time during a season, so the championship could change hands multiple times over the course of the year. Since home and home matches were not necessarily consecutive games, a championship series could begin one season and carry over into the next.

One of the Brooklyn clubs, the Continental, raised at an NABBP convention the idea of an officially sanctioned championship, arguing that it would be an additional incentive for first-class clubs to play to their highest standard, and it would provide a clear structure for determining the champion. But the proposal was not adopted. (The NABBP's little brother, the National Association of Junior Base Ball Players, did institute a championship amongst its member clubs.)[21] An article in the *New York Clipper* of April 6, 1861, put the general thinking this way: "This question of championship is too apt to lead to but an unsatisfactory and most unstable honor and position, at the best; and its too eager coveting, to many heart-burnings and undignified controversies, which detract sadly from the legitimate results of true sport—relaxation, pleasure, exercise, and health." There was also a feeling that championships would lead to betting on games, bribery, buying and selling of players, and the surrender of what was then an amateur game to one motivated by pecuniary interests.[22]

For a Brooklyn club to be acknowledged the best team in baseball, which to all intents and purposes encompassed the universe of NABBP teams, meant something. As the NABBP expanded, geographically and in numbers—from its 25 founding clubs to 80 in 1860, around 200 in 1867, and more than 400 in 1868[23]—the number of clubs that could potentially vie with the Brooklyn teams for supremacy increased.

During much of the 1860s, three Brooklyn "nines," as teams were colloquially referred to in the 19th century, dominated the field: the Atlantic, Excelsior, and Eckford clubs. The Atlantics, from the Bedford section of Brooklyn, were the powerhouse team during the first half of the decade. In 1859, Henry Chadwick, the foremost baseball journalist of the 19th century, anointed the Atlantics as the best in the country, and other writers agreed.[24]

Here is a 19th-century humorist's paean to his city's Atlantics:

> Our noble city, third in population and first in Base Ball, has been glorified in field sports by the Atlantic Club, who have whipped everything in the Ball line.
>
> As a Brooklynite I am proud of the Atlantics.
>
> There are nine of them.
>
> They are wonderfully smart fellows. Stand six feet two in their stockings, can run two miles a minute, jump over a forty foot fence, or through a knot-hole; turn a somersault and catch anything from a base ball to the measles.
>
> They are an honor to Brooklyn.[25]

The Atlantics treated their fans to two seemingly interminable winning streaks—they were undefeated from October 1857 through September 1859, and 1864 through 1865. They were recognized as baseball's champion from 1859 up to 1861, from 1864 to 1866, and again in 1868.[26] Their rivals were the Excelsior club from South Brooklyn, Artie Cummings' neighborhood.

Like other amateur ball clubs of the era, the Excelsior Base Ball Club was a social organization, composed of young gentlemen—bankers, brokers, lawyers, and clerks in professional offices—who banded together for fellowship and healthy recreation. Formed in 1854 as the "J.Y.B.B.B.C."—Jolly Young Bachelors' Base Ball Club—it took the name "Excelsior" soon afterward.[27] "Excelsior" was the official motto of New York State and a popular name for baseball clubs not only in the state but also farther afield.[28] The club's membership numbered in the hundreds, of whom only a few actually played on its teams in regular competition.

Amateur games typically took place on weekday afternoons, beginning around three or four o'clock. This posed a difficulty for many players who had full-time employment and had to leave work early to play ball. It got so bad that prospective employers were asking applicants whether they were members of ball clubs, and if they replied in the affirmative, they weren't hired.[29] Some amateur players, however, such as those with the Excelsiors, were employed at banking and professional firms, many of which closed around 3:00 p.m., making it possible for them to leave work and make it to the grounds in time. Even players who worked in lower Manhattan could clock out and scoot over to one of the several ferries back to Brooklyn. Sometimes, however, game starts were delayed due to the late arrival of a player or two. When teams went on tour, the players had to take vacation time.[30]

In 1860, the Excelsiors "stood at the head of the then existing base ball organizations of the country."[31] They actually had a better overall record than the Atlantics that year, but the Atlantics remained champions after the third and deciding game of a home and home series between the two clubs was terminated in the sixth inning when the Excelsiors' captain—with his team leading the Atlantics, 8 to 6—called his players off the field to protect them from the aggressive and threatening behavior of the fans.[32] The Excelsiors' 1860 tour of cities outside the metropolitan region—the first by any ball club—has been credited with extending the popularity of the game beyond New York and Brooklyn.[33]

With the outbreak of the Civil War, the ranks of the Excelsiors were depleted as several of their players went off to battle. From 1861—when they played no match games at all—through 1865, the club lost its dominance. But once the war ended, the Excelsiors regained some of their pre-war potency.[34]

In 1862 and 1863, the baseball crown was worn by another strong Brooklyn club, the Eckfords, from the Greenpoint, and later Williamsburg, sections of the city.[35] Also among the top clubs were the Stars; in the early 1860s, and again later that decade, they were "the crack club" in South Brooklyn.[36]

The supremacy of Brooklyn's championship clubs was recognized far beyond the Brooklyn and New York City metropolitan areas. In October 1860, when the Excelsiors played in Baltimore against a team of that city with the same name, the president of the Baltimore Excelsiors toasted the Brooklynites as "the Champion club of the United States." He was mistaken; as noted by the *New York Clipper* in its report on the event, "*the* champions are the Atlantics." Embarrassed by the *faux pas,* the eloquent president of Brooklyn's Excelsiors, in responding to the toast, begged to be excused from accepting the compliment.[37] And when they traveled to Boston, the accolade "the celebrated Excelsior base ball Club" they had received from the press in 1862 had, by 1867, ballooned to "one of the most celebrated Clubs in the United States."[38] In 1865, a Philadelphia paper referred to the then-champion Atlantics from Brooklyn as "the best organization of players west of the ocean."[39] Not to be outdone, in 1868 a paper in Leavenworth, Kansas, pronounced the Atlantics "the most famous Base Ball Club in the world."[40]

Many other baseball clubs were active in Brooklyn during the 1860s, and several of them were based in Artie Cummings' South Brooklyn. In addition to the senior clubs, there were numerous junior and youth squads, as well as teams fielded by firemen, postal workers, butchers, poulterers, bakers, and the like.

The city was baseball-mad.

Artie's father, William, was a great fan of the game. He was full of stories about the old teams in the Brooklyn and New York City area, and he claimed to know many of the players personally.[41] His enthusiasm for baseball no doubt had an influence on his son's attraction to the game, and he provided advice and encouragement to Artie as his ball-playing career progressed. William did the same for his youngest son, Edward, who in the 1890s followed in his older brother's footsteps and pitched for a few amateur clubs in Brooklyn.[42]

The official baseball season for Brooklyn's teams ran through Thanksgiving and sometimes extended into December, weather permitting.[43] But not even winter's frost could cool the ardor of Brooklynites for the game. Freezing outside? No problem—they played on ice. If a team had a player who couldn't skate to the required standard, it brought in a substitute who could. In the first such match, held on one of Brooklyn's ice-skating venues on February 4, 1861, the Atlantics glided past the Charter Oak club, 36–27, before a crowd estimated—perhaps somewhat extravagantly—at 10,000 to 15,000. Initially a novelty, such events became a feature of the seasonal calendar in Brooklyn, and they were soon emulated across the East River. And these were real games; they were played according to the NABBP rules, with variations as necessary to accommodate the unique challenges of hitting, fielding, and base-"running" on ice skates. By the late 1860s, several more clubs were lacing up their skates, and a series for the baseball-on-ice championship was instituted.[44]

With all this baseball going on around him, how could an energetic lad like young Arthur Cummings *not* be drawn into the sport? He didn't have to go far to catch a game or play in one. A short walk from the Cummings home was the attractive and green Carroll Park, a central feature of the neighborhood. It was also the location of one of Brooklyn's principal baseball venues. Originally a private garden for the benefit of the brownstones that surrounded it, the park was acquired by the city and opened to the public in 1853.[45] Adjoining the park was a group of vacant lots, where baseball diamonds were laid out; at various times in the 1860s, they were the home fields of the crackerjack Excelsiors and Stars, as well as several other South Brooklyn ball clubs. During the 1862 baseball season, there were games there every day.[46]

The Carroll Park grounds were true sandlots, albeit with clubhouses for the teams. With their hard, sandy soil, they had the distinction of hosting the opening games of the metropolitan area's baseball season each year, since they could accommodate play earlier in the spring than the soft turf at the region's other ball fields.[47] The Carroll Park grounds were eventually gobbled up by the expanding development of the neighborhood, and today, although the park itself remains, brownstones stand where the sandlot diamonds once were.[48]

It was here, in South Brooklyn, that Artie Cummings began to develop into a ballplayer—practicing throwing or hitting with a couple of his friends after school or on weekends, and joining in pick-up games on the vacant lots in his neighborhood. Some of the schools had teams,[49] and if his school had one, he likely played for it.

And it was here, in his mid-teens, that Artie Cummings first conceived of the curveball. The story, related by Cummings himself in several published sources, has become inscribed in baseball history. As he told it, the idea of making a baseball curve came to him by accident:

> In the summer of 1863, a number of boys and myself were amusing ourselves by throwing clam shells (the hard-shell variety) and watching them sail along through the air, turning now to the right and now to the left. We became interested in the mechanics of it and experimented for an hour or more. All of a sudden it came to me that it would be a good joke on the boys if I could make a baseball curve the same way. We had been playing "three old cat" and town ball, and I had been doing the pitching. The joke seemed so good that I made a firm decision that I would try to play it.[50]

In a piece he wrote in 1912, Cummings said that the clam shell incident had taken place on a vacant lot in Brooklyn, and that he and his mates were "throwing clam shells along the shore, watching the wide curves they made, first in one direction, then in another, with great curiosity."[51] But where, exactly, were they? One possibility was at Gowanus Creek, a tidal estuary of Upper New York Bay that penetrated into South Brooklyn. Once a prime source of oysters, the creek flowed right by Artie's neighborhood, so its presence was part of life for the people who lived there. Artie and his pals could have reached it with a mere five-minute walk to the east. Alongside the creek were wetlands and open areas that were undoubtedly strewn with oyster and clam shells and other marine detritus.

In 1849, the State Legislature decided to transform the creek into a navigable watercourse to meet the needs of the city's burgeoning industry for docking and storage facilities; at the same time, areas around the creek would be drained and lots laid out for eventual development of housing for the rapidly expanding Brooklyn population. The project would become the Gowanus Canal. But construction didn't begin until 1853, and then proceeded slowly. The first few years were devoted to dredging and draining areas around the creek. Work on the canal itself did not begin until after the Civil War, and it was completed only in 1869. In the summer of 1863, when, according to Cummings, the clam shell incident took place, there would have been areas by the creek where Artie and his chums might have gone and whiled away the afternoon tossing clam shells.[52]

Artie experimented and practiced every spare moment that he had out of school, trying various grips and positions, determined to make a baseball curve. "Month after month," he wrote, "I kept pegging away at my theory," even in the face of "chafing" and derision from his schoolmates looking on.[53] "I ... worked hard every minute I had out of school, determined that if it were at all possible, I would solve the problem." Getting a baseball to curve became a great challenge for Artie, and the more his friends ridiculed him, the more resolute he became: "I knew I could do it," he insisted.[54] Stick-to-itiveness, to the point of stubbornness, was a core part of Candy Cummings' makeup.

Did the clam shell incident take place, or is the story apocryphal?

Apart from Arthur's recollection, there is no direct evidence either corroborating or refuting the account. Cummings repeated essentially the same story, with some minor variations, many times over the years, and it therefore has some benefit of consistency.[55] In 1895, however, Tim Murnane, a major leaguer himself for eight seasons in the 1870s and 1880s and later the long-time baseball editor at the *Boston Globe,* put forth a different version. Recalling a conversation he'd had with Cummings 16 years previously, he quoted Cummings as saying that the inspiration for the curveball came to him while he "was pitching to some boys in the open lots outside of Brooklyn, where I lived, one afternoon, and noticed the ball would work away from their bats."[56] In a letter to Murnane in 1896, Cummings wrote that he'd gotten the idea of the curveball while throwing clam shells in Brooklyn. As far as Murnane was concerned, this settled the matter.[57]

In 1899, however, when Cummings attended the annual meeting of the National League, he was reported to have told essentially the same story as originally told by Tim Murnane. The *Washington Post* recounted it this way: In 1864, while practicing pitching with his catcher, Candy noticed that the ball would describe a wide curve whenever he applied a sharp snap of the wrist. Thinking initially that it was the wind that veered the ball, he continued to apply the twist and found he was able to make the ball curve every time.[58] Did it slip Candy Cummings' mind that he'd gotten the inspiration for the curveball from tossing clam shells? That doesn't seem likely; it's not something one would forget, especially since he'd repeated it several times previously, as recently as 1896 to the *Boston Globe's* Tim Murnane.[59] Or was his experience with clam shells, somehow omitted from the *Post's* account, what induced him to try snapping his wrist during that practice session with his catcher? After all, that delivery was illegal under the rules applicable in 1864, so something must have caused him to try it. That something was possibly his observation of the flight of clam shells as he idly tossed them with his mates on a Brooklyn lot.

Yet another version was put forth in 1910, when E.J. Edwards, for decades a widely read journalist with papers including the *Hartford Courant,* the *New York Sun,* and the *Philadelphia Press,* published an account of a chance encounter he had with Arthur in 1876, in Hartford. Edwards, whose forte was finance and not sports, quoted Cummings word-for-word—remarkably, 34 years after the event—as saying that the idea of curving a baseball first came to him when he was pitching for the Stars in Brooklyn and noticed that the ball swerved outward instead of traveling in a straight line.[60] But, as we shall see in Chapter 8, Edwards's story is so flawed that it cannot be accepted as true.

In his encyclopedic history of baseball, *A Game of Inches*, Peter Morris surveys the various renderings of Candy Cummings' "Eureka! Moment," and he finds it plausible that Cummings drew inspiration for the curveball from the throwing of clam shells. Candy, Morris reasoned, had probably seen curves thrown when he was a youngster in Massachusetts, and, once in Brooklyn, the throwing of clam shells made him believe that it might be possible to do so even under strict pitching rules of the New York game.[61]

South Brooklyn gave Artie Cummings his start in organized baseball. In 1864, at the age of 15, he joined a local junior club called the Carrolls, so named because their home ground was at Carroll Park, near Cummings' home.[62]

Many ball clubs of that era fielded more than one team—a "first nine," composed of its best players; a "second nine," made up of its less accomplished or second-string players; and, possibly, a "muffins" squad, for the club's least-skilled players. (The term "muffins" alluded to the propensity of these players to muff, or misplay, balls.) Some of the clubs also maintained or were affiliated with separate junior teams, which served to develop players for their first nines. Other junior clubs, such as the Carrolls, existed independently, not as part of a senior organization. Players on junior teams were generally teenagers, although there was no strict age demarcation between junior and senior players: there were junior squads that had players younger than their teens, and some talented youths as young as 15 were playing on senior teams.[63]

No record of any of Artie Cummings' appearances with the Carrolls has been found. However, another member of the club, James Gordon Spencer, confirmed in a letter to the *New York Times* published in its July 21, 1900, issue, that he had been a teammate of Arthur Cummings on the Carrolls.

As the summer of 1864 edged toward autumn, with the slaughter in Civil War battlefields continuing, it was time for young Artie Cummings to pack his bags, leave Brooklyn, and head off to a new school, where he would experience his first baseball triumph.

4

The Seminarian
and the Silver Ball

In the summer of 1864, 15-year-old Arthur Cummings went away to
boarding school at Falley Seminary in Fulton, New York.[1] Fulton is situated
in the far western part of the state, 12 miles from Lake Ontario. In the early
1800s, it was a small village of farmers and a few grist mills. But it grew rapidly, thanks to its location on the Oswego River—the setting for James Fenimore Cooper's novel, *The Pathfinder*—and the Oswego Canal.

Fulton's swift-flowing river provided prodigious water power, attract-
ing mills and other manufacturing enterprises, and with them an influx
of settlers. The canal, opened in 1829, linked the port city of Oswego on
Lake Ontario with the Erie Canal (which had opened four years earlier),
enabling water-borne transport from Lake Ontario to the Hudson River at
Waterford, just north of Troy, and then all the way down to New York City.
Rail service came to Fulton in the late 1840s with the completion of the
Oswego and Syracuse Railroad. At Syracuse—25 miles to the south—the
O&S joined two main rail lines: the Syracuse, Binghamton & New York Rail
Road to New York City, and the New York Central to the New York metrop-
olis as well as to Buffalo and Lake Erie. The canals and railroads opened up
commerce between Fulton and distant population centers and markets. By
1877, Fulton ranked among the top manufacturing villages in New York
State.[2]

Fulton is 300 miles from Brooklyn, more or less. Today, the trip by car
would take a good five hours—assuming, that is, a steady clip of 60 miles
per hour, with no traffic, no pit stops, and no other delays. By public trans-
portation, the journey would take over seven hours. There is train service
only as far as Syracuse; the final stretch to Fulton would have to be done by
bus.

For Arthur Cummings, the journey from Brooklyn to Fulton involved
at least a full day's travel. He probably made the trip by train; with good
connections, it would have taken him ten hours or more from Brooklyn.

Another possibility was to travel up the Hudson River to Albany, then across to Syracuse and up to Fulton by canal. That trip, however, would have taken much longer; the canal boats were pulled by horses along adjacent towpaths at an average pace of four miles per hour.[3] He could also have gone by stagecoach, had he wished to subject himself to dusty, rickety, bone-jarring discomfort for hours and even days on end; that seems unlikely for the son of a prosperous merchant.

Falley Seminary, established in 1834 by the pastor of the Presbyterian Church in Fulton, began as a small, one-room school for the education of young women. Originally located in a building behind the church, the school constructed its own spacious quarters in 1836; that same year, it was incorporated as the Fulton Female Seminary. Its founders intended the seminary as "in every sense of the word a Christian institution"; its mission was to prepare its students for "polished, refined and Christian society…, their principles formed and their conduct shaped by the precepts of the Bible." In 1842, the seminary opened to young men as well, under a new name: Fulton Academy. Seven years later (1849), under the patronage of the Black River Conference—a Methodist body—it became Falley Seminary. A history of the school published in 1890 described its purpose:

> The Seminary stood an untiring advocate of Christian education in the broadest sense, and for the idea that no young man could be properly fitted for the duties of American citizenship unless he was thoroughly instructed in the Christian idea, as applied, not only to literature and science, but especially to the institutions of our republic, founded, as they are, upon the principles of the Christian religion.[4]

The name of the school honored George F. Falley, a local businessman and political figure who, together with his wife, Mehitable, was the school's biggest benefactor. His great-grandfather, Richard Falley, had commanded a company of militia at the Battle of Bunker Hill and was a great-grandfather of President Grover Cleveland, who visited the seminary on several occasions.[5]

The building that Arthur Cummings knew—a handsome, four-story brick edifice in the Georgian style, fronted by two imposing columns and topped by a cupola—was built in 1849–1850. Its position on a hill a short distance from the village offered commanding views of the Oswego River and Canal and the beautiful, undulating countryside. In 1856, ownership of the seminary passed to Professor John P. Griffin, a Presbyterian minister, who maintained the school's excellent reputation for scholarship and discipline along with its Christian values.[6]

Over the years, Falley graduates distinguished themselves in the worlds of education, finance, and business.[7] The seminary prided itself on providing its pupils a solid foundation for inquisitive and independent thinking, attributes that Arthur Cummings put to use in inventing the curveball and developing his skills as a strategic pitcher. The school's curriculum was well-rounded. Its courses in the natural sciences provided Cummings with knowledge that he would use in developing the curveball. Other courses included mathematics; history; English; ancient and modern languages; theology, ethics, and philosophy; logic and rhetoric; and the "ornamental branches," i.e., the arts. Each teacher concentrated on teaching a particular field of study—a rarity in those days.

Arthur's Falley education was built upon a strong moral and ethical foundation based on Christian principles, with Bible study playing a central role. This no doubt reinforced his New England Congregationalist upbringing and contributed to the development of his strong sense of right and wrong. A portion of each school day was devoted to Bible study, and Sunday mornings and afternoons were spent at church, where attendance was strictly enforced.[8] The cost of a Falley education when Arthur Cummings attended was relatively modest: $8 to $10 per term for tuition, and $55 for room and board.[9] As a live-in student, he would have shared a room on the first floor of the school building with five other students, each room equipped with a stove, buttery (an area for storage of food and provisions), and toilet.[10] He might have enjoyed the following description of the living accommodations—no doubt tongue-in-cheek—by one of Falley's alumni:

> Supreme satisfaction was only found in occupying one of the spacious rooms in the Seminary building, with all its palatial appointments, with spring beds, resting on which you would almost sink out of sight into the great masses of curled hair which composed the mattresses; with pillows so large and downy they never needed pillow shams, with large and easy reclining chairs, floors carpeted in moquette or axminster, steam, electric bells, polished mirrors, rare pictures elegantly mounted, ceiling and walls delicately frescoed or richly papered, janitors to do your bidding—anticipating your every desire, ever ready to perform any service, taking entire charge of your room, making up your bed so it was always soft.[11]

Notwithstanding the seminary's religious underpinnings and its rigorous curriculum, life at Falley was hardly austere. In addition to the serious academic side of the student experience, a published history of the institution describes a range of out-of-classroom intellectual and social activities, as well as all manner of student hijinks and escapades, comparable to those that might be found in many boarding schools today.[12]

And there was baseball.

Arthur Cummings played on the Falley baseball team, called the Hercules club but also known by the less-than-herculean, self-effacing nickname, "Butter Fingers Nine." And he continued to work on developing his curveball, devoting every free minute to his quest.[13]

Meanwhile, Cummings and his Hercules teammates, young as they were, attained a measure of immortality.

It was common in those days for silver balls to be awarded to the victors of significant baseball games, a tradition said to have originated with the National Association of Junior Base Ball Players. When it established a formal championship mechanism in 1861, the association had a silver ball made for presentation to the victorious team as an emblem of superiority.[14] The practice, however, was more likely an embellishment of the rite of awarding the game ball—and in those days but a single ball was used for the entire game—to the winner as a trophy of victory.[15]

In 1865, the Agricultural Society in Oswego County, where Fulton was located, called for a baseball match to be played at the county fair in Fulton from September 26–28, offering to award a silver baseball to the winning team.[16] The National Base Ball Club, from the city of Oswego, issued a challenge to any team based in the county to play for the trophy. When Arthur Cummings and other members of the Falley squad got wind of this, they were eager to accept the challenge, although some feared the prospect of going against the older and far more accomplished National nine. A rival of the Nationals, the Ontario Base Ball Club, also wished to compete for the silver ball, but they felt they were not strong enough to compete against the Nationals. They approached the Falley boys with a proposition: combine the strengths of their respective clubs to form a "picked nine" to take on the Nationals. If the combined squad won, the Butter Fingers and Ontario would play off against each other for the silver ball.

It took some convincing, but the Falley owner and principal, Professor John P. Griffin—a strict disciplinarian who was nevertheless deeply respected by the students—finally agreed to allow the Hercules players to participate.

In preparation for the contest against the Nationals, the Ontarios went up to Fulton on September 23 to play a friendly match against Falley's Butter Fingers Nine. Falley played well, defeating Ontario by 20 runs in a lively matchup. The vaunted Nationals, meanwhile, seemed suddenly to be vulnerable: they had made a poor showing against a team from Rochester on September 15, prompting blistering criticism from their hometown Oswego newspaper. It was a harbinger of what was to come.

The match between the Falley/Ontario picked nine and the Nationals took place on September 27 at the county fairgrounds in Fulton. On the Falley/Ontario team were four Falley players: Cummings, as pitcher, plus the Hercules catcher, second baseman, and shortstop. Ontario contributed the remaining five. The contrast between the Falley boys and their opponents presented quite a sight. The Nationals were men 25-30 years old, in full baseball uniform, while Cummings and his Falley teammates were kids still in their teens, playing in their street clothes. The four Hercules players, daunted by the prospect of contending against the powerful Nationals, entered the ball grounds a bundle of nerves.

The Falley/Ontario squad kept things close in the early going, trailing the Nationals by only two runs after two innings. But three big Falley/Ontario innings put them ahead; by the end of the fifth inning, they were up ten runs over the Nationals. Despite scoring seven runs in the bottom of the sixth, the Nationals would never regain the lead. The final score: Falley/Ontario picked nine 27, Nationals 23. Arthur Cummings helped his own cause by scoring four of his team's runs; only his schoolmate Rush Brown—the Falley/Ontario catcher and captain of the picked nine—scored more. In fact, the four Falley players combined outscored their five teammates from Ontario, 16–11.

In its account of the game the next day, the Oswego paper judged it "probably the best that has been played in this county this season." It had particular praise for the Falley hurler: "Cummings is a good pitcher, and for size and age, a remarkable one."[17]

The playoff game between Falley's Butter Fingers Nine and the Ontarios for the silver ball was to take place on Saturday, October 21. But that weekend, a fierce storm—the worst in quite a long time—roared through the area, the wind lashing Lake Ontario into a fury and dropping a veritable smorgasbord of precipitation: rain, hail, snow and sleet. The Saturday game, like just about every other scheduled event, was a washout; it would not be played until the following spring.[18]

The long-awaited matchup took place at the Falley ball field on May 19, 1866, before a large crowd of enthusiastic spectators. The game got under way at ten in the morning, and it started well for Falley's Hercules team. Batting first, they rang up five runs, and in the Ontario half of the opening frame, Cummings held them scoreless. Good hitting by Falley and sloppy fielding by Ontario enabled the Butter Fingers to retain the lead into the seventh inning, when they posted ten runs. At that point, the Falleyites had a very healthy 15-run lead. But then things got interesting.

In the top of the eighth inning, Falley failed to score, its batters suddenly bewildered by the Ontario pitching. In their half of the frame, 11 Ontario base runners crossed the plate, and just like that, Falley's lead had been whittled down to a mere four runs: 34–30. In the top of the ninth, the first three Falley batsmen went out on foul tips. Then Ontario came to bat. Their first three batters hit safely, scoring two runs and narrowing the gap further. But Arthur Cummings regrouped and retired the next three hitters in succession to seal the Falley victory, 34–32.[19]

Artie Cummings had been working on developing the curveball for some time, and it was still very much a work in progress at the time of the games for the silver ball. It is possible that he gave the pitch a dry run at those games. Buster McKinstry, his roommate at Falley and the right fielder on the victorious Butter Fingers Nine, recalled that Cummings did use a curveball in the contests for the silver ball, with effect. McKinstry's recollection, published over 40 years after the games (1909), was reprinted in a piece written by Cummings for a book by Elwood A. Roff (1912). In the piece, titled "The Story of the Curve Ball," Candy Cummings acknowledged that he had tossed a curve during the games for the silver ball. He made clear, however, that his first real use of the curveball did not occur until 1867, in Cambridge, Massachusetts.[20] That was the seminal moment, the moment when he introduced the curveball into baseball. In his other published writings about his experiences at Falley, he didn't mention his having tried the pitch at the Hercules silver ball games. He didn't consider it to have been consequential.

And so, improbably, the silver ball was won by the underdogs—the Butter Fingers Nine of Falley's Hercules Base Ball Club. To commemorate the event, the team had the silver ball trophy engraved with "BFN of HBBC. Won May 19th, 1866," and the names and hometowns of the nine Falley players who defeated Ontario that Saturday morning. Among the inscriptions is "W.A. Cummings, Brooklyn, pitcher."

Silver ball trophy won by the Falley Seminary baseball team on May 19, 1866. Candy Cummings pitched for the Falley team. In the view on the left, "H.B.B.C." stands for the Hercules Base Ball Club, the name of the Falley team, and "B.F.N" stands for its nickname, the Butter Fingers Nine. The ball is inscribed with the names and hometowns of the team members who won the trophy. "W.A. Cummings, Brooklyn," can be seen in the image on the left, upside down on the left-hand side of the ball (National Baseball Hall of Fame and Museum/Milo Stewart).

The Hercules players presented the ball to Professor Griffin, who for many years kept it on display in his reception room as his most prized trophy.[21] It then had a mysterious and eventful history.[22]

After Falley Seminary closed its doors in 1883, the silver ball came into the possession of Buster S. McKinstry. McKinstry, the proprietor of a clothing store in Fulton, put the ball on display in his shop. Later, the trophy was moved to the Fulton Public Library and placed on exhibit. Then, in May 1921, it went missing. The police investigated the disappearance as a theft, but they turned up nothing. A month later, a high school student showed up at the library bearing the silver ball, telling the dubious story that he had seen a young boy playing with it and persuaded him to hand it over. The library had offered a $10 reward for finding and returning the ball, but the student turned it down. Guilty conscience, perhaps?

Following the completion in 1924 of a new high school in Fulton—on the site that had been occupied by Falley Seminary—the ball was moved there from the public library and exhibited in a case with other trophies. It then vanished once more—stolen one night, it was supposed, by hoodlums who had broken into the school and taken it, together with other mementos. A prominent Fulton businessman, Jesse A. Morrill, enlisted the help of Fulton's police chief in finding it. Morrill, an owner of the busy Morrill Press printing company,[23] had a particular interest in recovering the trophy: he had been a student at Falley and a spectator at the celebrated match at which the silver ball was won. But the ball eluded discovery for several years. Then one day, a police officer approached Morrill and handed him the silver ball, telling him that it had been unearthed by some WPA workers who were digging on a project behind a local cemetery. It was thought that the thieves had buried it there after the heist.

The ball remained in Morrill's possession until 1939. That June, the Baseball Hall of Fame in Cooperstown formally opened its newly constructed building and museum and inducted its first group of immortals into its pantheon of baseball greats. William Arthur Cummings was among them. In conjunction with those events, Morrill donated the silver ball to the Hall of Fame. The Hall showcased the trophy as the centerpiece of an exhibit with historically noteworthy baseballs, including ones used by two luminaries of 19th-century baseball, Albert Goodwill Spalding and Harry Wright, both of whom pitched for the Boston Red Stockings in the 1870s. Today, it rests peacefully but proudly in the Hall of Fame's climate-controlled archive.

From the Stars
to the Excelsiors

Arthur Cummings spent two years at Falley Seminary, graduating in 1866. Meanwhile, his summers in Brooklyn were devoted to baseball.

Almost immediately upon his return home after his first year at Falley, he was approached by boys from several local ball clubs, all wanting him to pitch for them. He decided to join the Star junior club. It was, Cummings later wrote, a team of lads around 17 years old "who were a remarkably smart lot of players and were only weak in the [pitcher's] box. They were sharp, active boys, well up on all the points of the game, good base runners, and worked well together."[1] Affiliated with Brooklyn's first-rate Star Base Ball Club, the Star juniors played at the senior club's grounds opposite Carroll Park and had the use of their clubhouse. This marked the beginning of Cummings' ascent in the world of baseball.

The Stars' grounds had a peculiarity that the players used to their advantage—an oval basin in right field about 80 feet in diameter and a foot deep. When it rained, it filled with water. Games were usually delayed until the field dried out. One exception was a game between the Stars juniors and another Brooklyn team, the Ironsides. It had rained heavily for an hour before game time, flooding streets and cellars, and of course the basin in the Carroll Park grounds' right field. When Stars batsmen hit balls toward the basin, the Ironsides right fielder refused to go after them for fear of getting wet, drawing hoots of mirth and derision from the Stars' bench. He was eventually replaced by an Ironsides teammate. Playing without shoes and socks, the new right fielder chased after a ball and tumbled into the pond. "Well," recalled Cummings in an article he wrote in 1898, "you should have seen that chap as he straightened up after the deluge. He was a sight, yellow mud from head to foot, and one eye closed with a big patch of mud and literally covered and soaked all over. Everyone laughed and screamed, but he was madder than a wet hen and sputtered and wanted to fight everyone for laughing at him." With experiences like that, the Stars developed a knack for hitting to right field.[2]

In the same 1898 article, Cummings recalled that, of the 39 games the Star juniors played with him in the pitcher's box, they won 37, losing only two, and claimed the championship of Brooklyn. Those statements cannot be independently confirmed, although historian David Fleitz has called attention to the 37–2 record in his entries about Candy Cummings in various biographical anthologies.[3] In the Brooklyn and New York papers, there are only three references to Star juniors' games in 1865— they won two and lost one— and none of them was for the championship. As the papers gave no box scores for these games, it cannot be determined whether Cummings pitched in them.[4]

The player on the left is Joe Leggett, captain and catcher of the Excelsior club of Brooklyn, in 1860. The Excelsiors were one of Brooklyn's top teams. In 1865, Leggett recruited Candy Cummings to play for the team (A.G. Spalding Baseball Collection. New York Public Library Digital Collections).

At one of the Star junior games, Arthur Cummings was approached by Joe Leggett, catcher for Brooklyn's renowned Excelsiors, who had come over to observe the youngsters.[5] Leggett was one of the great backstops of his era. He also swung a mean bat: in 1859, he led the National Association of Base Ball Players (NABBP) in runs scored, and the following year led the league in both runs and batting average. Leggett was respected as a man of integrity. It was he who, as the Excelsiors' captain, and with his side in the lead, had pulled his players off the field during the championship game in 1860 versus the Atlantics to protect them from aggressive and threatening fans.

As the players were warming up before the Star juniors' game, Leggett walked over to chat with Cummings and had him toss a few pitches. Leggett knew a promising young hurler when he saw one. He had caught the best in the business: Jim Creighton, one of the era's greatest pitchers until his untimely death in October 1862, and then Asa Brainard.[6]

Leggett was impressed with Cummings and asked him if he would like

to join the Excelsiors' junior squad. Cummings replied with an enthusiastic "yes," that is, as long as his father consented. Leggett hurried to Arthur's
father, obtained his agreement, and the Excelsiors voted Arthur in as a
member. Baseball skills alone weren't enough for membership in clubs such
as the Excelsiors; new members also had to be persons of good comport-
ment and character, and they had to be compatible with the other members
not only temperamentally but also in terms of vocational or economic status.[7] Arthur Cummings apparently fit the bill.

It was as a member of the Excelsior juniors that Cummings began to
be noticed. From time to time, he was called upon by the senior club's first
nine to fill in for its pitcher, Asa Brainard. Originally a fielder, Brainard had
taken over pitching duties for the Excelsiors after the death of its star hurler,
Jim Creighton, and soon developed into a superlative pitcher in his own
right.[8]

Cummings' first opportunity to play with the senior lads came on
August 14, 1866, in a friendly match between the Excelsiors and New York
City's Mutual club. By then, the Excelsiors' home field was the Capitoline
grounds in the Bedford section of Brooklyn, one of only three ballparks in
Brooklyn completely enclosed by fences. It had been raining before game
time, and the grounds were not in good shape. Expecting the game to be
called off, five Excelsiors players, including Brainard, did not show up.
Rather than back out, the Excelsiors assembled a nine, substituting players drawn from its junior squad for the absentees. Among them was Arthur
Cummings, tapped to replace Brainard in the pitcher's box.

As expected, the Mutuals, a strong club, handily defeated the
cobbled-together Excelsiors squad, which was lacking many of its best
players; the score was 32–13. Nevertheless, the *Brooklyn Eagle*'s account of
the game the following day applauded the play and sportsmanship of both
sides, giving Arthur Cummings particular—and prophetic—praise: "if, as
stated, this was his first senior match, he has only to keep on in the way he
has begun, and he will one day (not far distant) be ranked among the best
pitchers of the country." A New York City newspaper, the *Sunday Mirror,*
was equally effusive. Referring to Cummings, it wrote: "He pitched exceedingly well and is undoubtedly a very promising young pitcher." But pitching wasn't his only noteworthy skill. "He is very plucky withal," the paper
added, "as the manner in which he bore with a very severe hit with a ball off
Jewett's [the Mutuals' catcher] bat fully proved."[9]

It was customary in those days for the home club to host the visiting
squad to a convivial post-game dinner, where the teams would exchange
toasts—even several. The Excelsiors–Mutuals match was topped off with
a chowder-and-lager supper, followed by entertaining speeches and jovial
singing, at the Excelsior club's rooms in downtown Brooklyn, opposite City

Hall.[10] Of this tradition, Arthur Cummings later wrote, "there arose such a rivalry between some [clubs] to see who could get up the best suppers, that it was abolished in '68, as it drew too much on the members' pockets."[11] Actually, the 1859 convention of the NABBP had unanimously recommended abolition of the custom, "owing to the spirit of emulation that arose among the clubs"—as Henry Chadwick explained—"each aspiring to excel each other in the expense and splendor of these entertainments." However, the practice continued for a time after that, although, according to Chadwick, within "the bounds of moderation, and therefore [without] all its objectionable features."[12]

Three days after his debut with the senior Excelsiors' first nine, Arthur Cummings was again called up from the junior squad for service with the seniors. A club from Albany, the Nationals, had come down to the metropolitan area for a series of games. On August 17, they were in Brooklyn to take on the Excelsiors. Brainard did the pitching, and Cummings was slotted in as shortstop. After falling behind, 5–0, in the first inning, the Brooklynites roared back and ended up pounding the Nationals, 48–29. Cummings again made a fine showing for himself, this time with the bat and on the base paths, scoring five of Excelsior's runs.[13]

Very quickly, the Excelsiors liked what they saw in Arthur Cummings. On August 20, they had him pitch for their second (backup) nine in a friendly match against the Mutuals in Hoboken, New Jersey. The Mutuals were from New York City, but since space for ball fields was limited there, they played their home games at the Elysian Fields, a popular recreation area in Hoboken. (The Elysian Fields had been the location of the dueling ground where Aaron Burr shot Alexander Hamilton.[14]) For a baseball game in those days, it was quite low-scoring. After nine innings (the game went 13 innings, but the newspapers reported on only nine), the Mutuals had the lead, 8–4. Cummings' pitching held the superior Mutuals team scoreless in four of their frames. At an hour and ten minutes, the game had the distinction of being the quickest nine innings ever (to that point) played in Hoboken.[15] After all, in those days there were no TV ads, no visits with the pitcher by coaches or fielders, no game interruptions to review umpire decisions, and no leisurely adjustments of batting gloves outside the batter's box. And pitching changes were rare.

On August 29, Cummings was back in New Jersey with the first nine, filling in for Asa Brainard in a big game against the Eureka team of Newark. One of the region's top clubs, the Eurekas were basking in the glow of inflicting a humiliating, 36–10 defeat upon the champion Atlantics ten days previously.[16] But they had no eureka moment against the Excelsiors.

Cummings was tapped to pitch for Excelsior at the last minute when Asa Brainard again failed to appear. He was a bit nervous at the prospect of facing the Eureka sluggers. When he took his place in the pitcher's box, his "youthful appearance caused a smile of derision to appear on the faces of the [Eureka] batsmen as they faced his delivery."[17] But the youngster had confidence in himself. He turned in a stellar performance, stymieing the Eurekas with cunning changes of speed and raise balls, and the Eurekas were decisively defeated, 24–12. The New York press took particular note of Cummings' excellent pitching that afternoon.[18]

In that era, baseball games tended to be congenial, indeed gentlemanly, affairs. Certainly, matches were vigorously contested, but in general baseball lacked the sometimes bitter rivalries that exist between clubs in today's game. One factor was that these were amateur squads; players played for the love of the game—a quaint concept, to be sure, from the perspective of today's multi-millionaire owners and multi-million-dollar salaries paid to professional athletes. Good sportsmanship on the part of players was expected, and its display was often commented upon by the press.[19] Reporting on the Excelsior–Eureka game, the *New York Clipper* said, "though the Eurekas were defeated, they expressed themselves as fully satisfied that they had been conquered by gentlemen, and had lost the trophy by being out-played."[20] The *New-York Daily Tribune* observed, "The game was played throughout in the most friendly spirit and gentlemanly style, the contest being solely for the pleasure of the contest and the honor of winning the trophy."[21] The paper concluded its report by publishing a letter written to it by the Excelsior captain, Joe Leggett, that may seem remarkable today:

> Through the medium of your column of Field Sports the Excelsior Club desire to return their sincere thanks to the gentlemen of the Eureka Club for their courteous reception, and to express to them their high appreciation of the compliment paid them by the Eureka Club in selecting the umpire on the occasion from the Excelsior Club. [Umpires in those days were typically chosen by the home team, and were usually players or officials of a different club from the ones involved in the game.]

Growing increasingly confident with their excellent young pitcher, the Excelsiors continued to tap Arthur Cummings to pitch for the senior nine, and he kept garnering praise. Then he went traveling with the big boys.[22]

In the evening of September 15, the Excelsior players boarded an overnight sleeper train in New York City to embark on their southern tour, a series of exhibition games against teams in Washington, Philadelphia, and Baltimore.[23] Asa Brainard, the Excelsior pitcher, was with the group; Arthur Cummings was as well, invited by Joe Leggett in case something happened to Brainard. Also in the entourage were dozens of non-player Excelsior club members, who had chartered a special rail car for the trip, as well as members of the Atlantic club of Jamaica, Long Island (different from Brooklyn's Atlantics[24]), and the Eclectic club of New York City.

When the train arrived in Baltimore the following morning, the Excelsiors were met by their hosts, the National Base Ball Club of Washington, who escorted them for the remainder of the journey to D.C., pointing out sights along the way. The nation's capital pulled out all the stops to welcome the visitors in the grandest style. From the time of their arrival, the Excelsiors were treated like visiting royalty, their four days in the city being a whirl of sightseeing, magnificent banquets—oh yes, and baseball.

The Nationals escorted their guests by stagecoaches and carriages to Willard's Hotel, where they were provided with first-class accommodations. Located a couple of blocks from the White House, Willard's was a center of Washington's political and social life. In the 1860s, Nathaniel Hawthorne wrote that the hotel "may be much more justly called the center of Washington and the Union than either the Capitol, the White House, or the State Department." Ten presidents, including Lincoln, were guests there at one time or another.[25]

The next morning, the visitors woke up early, to be escorted by their hosts on an outing up the Potomac to the scenic Great Falls, where they marveled at the natural beauty and enjoyed an extravagant feast. The itinerary the following day included an excursion to Mount Vernon and the lower Potomac[26]

After two full days of sightseeing and lavish treatment, it was time for baseball. The Excelsiors' first big match of the tour took place on September 18, against the Nationals. This game, and all others played in Washington during the tour, was held at the "President's Grounds," located just south of the White House, where the Ellipse is today.[27] The spectacle was described by the *New York Herald*:

> The President's grounds this afternoon presented one of the most attractive sights in the way of a gathering of people ever before seen in this city on any similar occasion, the Excelsior and National Base Ball clubs being the objects of interest of the day, and the trial of skill between them the attractive point. The entire field was encircled by an assemblage of not less than seven or eight thousand people, all of the reserve seats erected for the tourney being occupied. The assemblage of ladies was the most brilliant ever seen at a ball match either here or elsewhere. The deepest interest was manifested in the proceedings of the afternoon, no one leaving the ground until the conclusion of the contest.[28]

President Andrew Johnson made an appearance, arriving mid-game after his weekly cabinet meeting and remaining, with evident interest in the game, until the last out was recorded.[29]

All of that pomp and circumstance did not overshadow the game itself; those in attendance were treated to one of the most exciting and closely contested baseball matches of the season, marked by hearty and frequent applause by partisans of each team at advantageous plays by their respective sides. Surviving several lead changes, Excelsior, with Brainard pitching, emerged victorious, 33–28.

"But the great feature of the match," wrote the *New York Clipper,* "was the friendly spirit manifested throughout the entire contest, even at its most exciting period, for neither party forgot, for a moment, that they had their reputation as gentlemanly exponents of the game to sustain, as well as that for skillful play, the latter being the most important of the two."[30]

This first day of play ended with a banquet more bountiful than the one the night before, "a princely affair," effused the *New York Clipper,* adding, "a more sumptuous entertainment never having been provided for a ball club than that given on this occasion. All the luxuries of the season in profuse quantity, with delicious wines to wash down the tempting viands, marked this feast, and truly it was a gala affair."[31] Among the dignitaries at the head table was a representative of President Johnson. The dinner was followed by enjoyable toasts and speeches, with the silver ball of victory graciously presented by the president of the Nationals, A.P. Gorman. Accepting the trophy was his counterpart from the Excelsiors, Joseph E. Jones, M.D., with "a little speech of mingled poetry, fun and sentiment that fairly 'brought down the house.'" Dr. Jones paid a courteous tribute to "the magnanimity with which the Nationals had permitted the Excelsiors to embrace victory," and he expressed appreciation for "the kindness showered upon their club by the Nationals and others here."[32]

Arthur Cummings did not appear in that first game against the Nationals; his chance came the following day, September 19. In the morning there was a match between the Nationals' junior squad and a picked nine composed of five Excelsior second nine players, two Excelsior juniors, and players from the Atlantics of Long Island and the Eclectics of New York who had accompanied the Excelsiors on their tour. One of the two Excelsior juniors was Cummings, who served as the team's pitcher. At the end of eight innings, the picked nine were down by four runs, but they rallied in the ninth to score seven runs. In the bottom of the final frame, Cummings saved the game by holding the National juniors to a single run, sealing a close, 19–17 win for his team. "Cummings pitched beautifully," said the *Washington's Evening Star,* "troubling the boys considerably towards the last."[33]

The afternoon saw a match-up between the main Excelsior squad and the other big Washington club, the Unions, who had taken over as hosts of the Excelsiors for the remainder of their Washington visit. Following his successful outing in the morning contest, Arthur Cummings was again in the Excelsior lineup, starting in left field but taking over the pitching duties in the seventh inning. The game entered the ninth with Excelsior having a commanding lead, 40–23. But after they had plated ten more runs, the sky darkened, rain began to fall, and the game had to be called.

That was Arthur Cummings' final appearance during this tour. After the game, there ensued the traditional evening gala, and the next morning the Excelsiors and company boarded the train bound for their next stop, Baltimore. After defeating that city's Pastime club, the Excelsiors moved on to Philadelphia. They secured a tie against Philly's Keystones in a rain-shortened game, and afterwards roundly defeated the Olympic club. They then returned to Brooklyn by overnight train.

Cummings played no more games with the Excelsior top nine in 1866. It had been quite a year for him. He made the most of the opportunities to show the senior club what he could do. Playing with a first-class team and accomplished veterans—Brainard, for example, was around nine years older than Cummings, and Leggett was 20 years his senior—and against strong opponents, was a great learning experience. And what a tour! For a kid who had not yet reached his 18th birthday, it must have been the time of his young life. One can imagine his excitement and awe being in the company of the senior players, watching the game in the presence of the President of the United States, and attending the grand banquets and festivities laid on by the host clubs. Years later, Cummings wrote of 1866, "This was the most enjoyable year I ever had in baseball."[34]

Young Arthur Cummings was making quite a name for himself; he became known in the baseball world as "the boy wonder," or variations on the theme, such as the "Little Wonder," tags that would remain with him for years afterwards.[35] At some point, he acquired the nickname "Candy," in those days a moniker given to someone who was the best at what he did. It is not possible to pinpoint exactly when people began calling him that. It might well have been while he was with the Excelsior juniors; during that period, he was already displaying great skill and promise as a pitcher and attracting praise in the press.[36] Another pitcher of the era, Fred Goldsmith, recalled that Cummings was already known as "Candy" in 1869.[37] Some writers, however, claim that he was first given the nickname much later: during his 1876 season with the Dark Blues of Hartford.[38] The earliest newspaper reference to him as "Candy" that has been found was in 1877, late in his ball-playing career[39]; by January 1879, the *Chicago Tribune* was reporting that Cummings was "best known by the sobriquet of 'Candy.'"[40]

It seems, however, that some of Candy's contemporaries were unfamiliar with the nickname. Will Rankin, a widely read baseball journalist who was certainly knowledgeable about the game and its players, wrote this in 1898: "I have known Arthur Cummings since 1866 and took part in many a scrub game with him and others on the Capitoline Grounds, Brooklyn, N.Y., and never heard him called 'Candy.'"[41] But he appears to be an outlier.

In any case, for the sake of consistency and to avoid confusion, this chronicle of Arthur Cummings' life and career will from this point refer to him as "Candy."

When the 1867 season opened, Candy Cummings was back with the Excelsior junior nine, although in the first few weeks he pitched at least once for the senior club, in an inter-squad game on April 27.[42] The 18-year-old also had a day job; he worked as a clerk at one of New York City's venerable investment banking houses, Vermilye & Co. Located in New York's Financial District, the firm made news with some regularity in the 1860s as the victim of thefts and frauds involving government securities.[43] Candy Cummings, however, was never associated with any of those shenanigans.

Toward the middle of the 1867 season, Asa Brainard left the Excelsiors to play for New York City's Knickerbocker club,[44] and Candy Cummings, though still technically on the junior squad, took over the pitching duties for the first nine. He appeared in nine games from June through September, and his team won seven of them, some by healthy margins.[45] In one, on August 16, the Excelsiors demolished the Charter Oak club of Hartford by the whopping score of 52–4. The visitors posted zeros in each of the first five innings and another in the ninth. The *Brooklyn Eagle* gave credit for Charter Oak's impotence to Candy Cummings' pitching: "Young Cummings bothered them very much," it said, "and on their side no batting was done of any account."[46] Cummings spearheaded other mercilessly lopsided Excelsior victories on August 23 (35–8, against Eagle, a New York club), September 9 (38–7, against Brooklyn's Mohawks), September 13 (39–5, against the Active club of Newark, New Jersey, when Cummings retired the Actives without a run in six of the nine innings played), and September 23 (41–22 in seven innings against Eureka, another Newark club).[47] During that stretch, the Excelsiors racked up a total of 297 runs to their opponents' 106.

Candy Cummings' next game was on October 2, when Excelsior hosted the touring Keystones of Philadelphia. The Brooklynites battled admirably but came up five runs short, 20–15. Despite the loss, Cummings' pitching was "in keeping with [his] reputation."[48]

The Excelsiors then left town for another rail trip of their own, to the Boston area for a series of exhibition matches. Cummings went with them—and made baseball history.

6

Candy Debuts the Curveball

The Excelsiors' New England tour did not begin particularly well. In their first day of action, on October 4, a crowd of 10,000 spectators assembled at Boston Common to watch the Lowell club of Boston take on the famed nine from Brooklyn. Not playing to their usual high standard, and despite creditable pitching by Cummings, the Excelsiors lost the game, 28–21.[1]

The following day, they crossed the Charles River to meet the Harvard University nine at Jarvis Field, the school's new sporting ground, but rain forced the game's postponement.

Although it was a college team, the Harvard Base Ball Club was a member of the National Association of Base Ball Players. It was a strong squad in 1867, having posted four wins and two losses against other NABBP clubs before the match-up with the Excelsiors. That was a big improvement from 1866, when they had an almost perfect losing record: 1–5.[2] On June 1, 1867, Harvard became champion of New England by defeating the Lowells. But the collegians didn't retain the silver ball championship trophy for long. In August, the Lowells challenged them to a re-match. However, under the rules, the games would have had to take place during the university's vacation period, when the Harvard players would be scattered across the country. The Harvards offered to play the games in the fall, but the Lowells refused. So Harvard reluctantly surrendered the championship, silver ball and all, to the Lowells without a game being played.[3] Perhaps this was the Lowells' idea all along in timing the issuance of its challenge.

A star of the Harvard team in the late 1860s was a player named Archibald ("Archie") McClure Bush. Prior to entering Harvard College, Bush, a Civil War veteran, had been a student at Phillips Academy in Andover, Massachusetts, where he and a cousin organized the prep school's first baseball team. He had also distinguished himself on amateur teams in Albany, New York. Bush excelled on the Andover squad, as well as academically and socially, but, in the spring of 1867—his final year—he was expelled by Andover's killjoy principal for cutting geometry class and going into Boston with a classmate to watch a ball game. The action taken against this popular pupil led to a near-riot by the Andover student body, inducing yet further expulsions. (The expelled students were reinstated, *post facto,* in 1903.)

Notwithstanding his expulsion, Bush crammed the entire summer to prepare for Harvard's entrance exam. He passed and enrolled as a freshman in the autumn. One of the great college players of his day, Bush was with the Harvard nine all four of his years there—mainly as its catcher, but also as a substitute pitcher—and captained the squad for three of those years.[4]

The Harvard–Excelsior game was finally played on October 7. It was a crisp, cloudless autumn afternoon that Monday in Cambridge—55 degrees at game time—with a brisk wind out of the north and west. Most of the area's residents were not thinking about baseball; their attention had been captured by the triumphal visit to New England of the celebrated Civil War general, Philip Sheridan.[5] Nevertheless, a large crowd of spectators showed up at Jarvis Field to watch the Harvards vie against the famous Brooklynites.[6]

Excelsior, leading off in the first inning, failed to score. In the bottom of the first, Cummings faced the first four Harvard batters, gaining confidence as they flailed at his pitches with nothing to show for their efforts. Then the number five batsman in Harvard's lineup, Archie Bush, took his turn at the plate. "I feared him for his powerful hitting,"[7] Cummings reflected years later. After years of practice, he decided that this was the time to unleash his secret weapon. Bush swung at the first curveball offered by Cummings, missing badly. The slim righty threw it again, with the same result. "As he struck at [the ball] I saw it curve away from him," Cummings recalled; "it seemed to go about a foot beyond the end of his bat." A Harvard batter said that the pitch "came at us and then went away from us."[8]

It was Candy Cummings' first use of his curveball in an actual game, and he knew that he had at last succeeded.[9] He later described his emotions:

> A surge of joy flooded over me that I shall never forget. I felt like shouting out that I had made a ball curve; I wanted to tell everybody; it was too good to keep to myself.
>
> But I said not a word and saw many a batter at that game throw down his stick in disgust. Every time I was successful, I could scarcely keep from dancing from pure joy. The secret was mine.[10]

Why the secrecy? Candy Cummings, of course, wanted to keep his potent weapon to himself for as long as possible. But there was another reason: the way he delivered the curveball was illegal under the rules at the time. Indeed, he acknowledged this when he admitted that he had to fool the umpire in order to make the ball curve.[11] The New York game was governed by the rules of the National Association of Base Ball Players, of which both Harvard and Excelsior were members. As explained in Chapter 3, pitching under the NABBP rules was underhand, with both feet firmly planted, and the arm straight and at the pitcher's side, swinging perpendicularly. Candy Cummings pitched this way, but with a twist—literally. He had an unusually long and supple arm, long fingers, and a very flexible wrist, and he used them to best advantage. "I could swing my hand out at an angle," he wrote, "and it was as effective as a forearm swing."[12] Here's how he described his delivery of the curveball: "I gave the ball a sharp twist with my fingers and a snap of the wrist, which gave the ball a rotary motion."[13]

A casual reader of the NABBP rules governing pitching might find it difficult to glean from their wording that Candy Cummings' twist-and-snap wrist action was prohibited. But behind the written words was a body of understanding and commonly accepted practice. The restrictions that prevailed in the 1860s had been part of the New York game going back to the first NABBP rules, adopted in 1857, and before then to the rules set forth in 1845 by New York's Knickerbocker Base Ball Club. Prior to the Knickerbocker rules, pitchers were unregulated, and batters "were in danger of life or limb from the recklessness of these throwers or feeders."[14] Seeking to avoid this peril, the Knickerbocker rules regulated the way in which the ball was to be delivered by the pitcher.

Although the NABBP rules were amended and expanded a number of times after their initial adoption, until the 1870s the changes merely codified what had hitherto been the understanding as to what the rules meant and how they were to be applied. With that in mind, let's look at the version adopted by the Association in December 1868, which most clearly expresses the pitching restrictions that prevailed in the 1860s:

> "The pitcher must ... deliver the ball as near as possible over the center of the home base, and fairly for the striker." (section 1);
>
> "The ball must be pitched, not jerked or thrown, to the bat.... The ball shall be considered jerked, in the meaning of the rule, if the pitcher's arm touches the person when the arm is swung forward to deliver the ball; and it shall be regarded as a throw if the arm has been bent at the elbow, at an angle from the body, or horizontally from the shoulder, when it is swung forward to deliver the ball, *or if the ball be delivered in any other way than with a straight arm, swinging perpendicularly from the body.*" (section 3) [emphasis added].

The italicized phrase had been part of the rules since the version adopted in December 1866, and merely codified the practice in the New York game before then.

Henry Chadwick, a member of the NABBP's rules committee, interpreted section 3 this way: "The pitcher must have his arm straight and swing it forward straight, or he commits a balk. If he turns his wrist and lower arm outward, ... he makes a balk."[15] But that was how Candy Cummings pitched his curveball. The *Springfield [MA] Republican,* having interviewed Cummings, said in 1919, "The curve ball wizard did his pitching with his forearm and wrist and also with his fingers."[16] Turning the wrist automatically causes the arm to turn; try it.

In those days, Candy Cummings' wrist snap and forearm movement was considered an "underhand throw," prohibited by the rules. Here's how Chadwick defined an "underhand throw": a "swinging motion, but with the addition of bending the arm and wrist with a motion similar to that made when snapping a whip." Referring specifically to Cummings' curveball, Chadwick added, "The curved line delivery, such as that which marks Cummings' style, is … impossible, except by means of an underhand wrist throw." But as Chadwick pointed out, Cummings wasn't the only pitcher using an underhand throw; others had been doing so for quite some time, but to add speed to their pitches, not curves.[17]

How, then, did Candy Cummings and the others get away with it? "Some men," noted Chadwick, "can disguise an underhand throw so as to make it difficult to tell whether the throwing motion is made or not."[18] Even the annual convention of the NABBP, in December 1869, recognized that there was no way to prevent a disguised underhand throw; "the motion is so quick," said the convention's report, "that it is next to an impossibility for the umpire to see."[19] But there was another reason: speed pitching and curve pitching made baseball, still evolving and growing in popularity, more interesting, more exciting. Up through 1870, the batsman was dominant; the pitcher's job was to feed him balls that he could easily hit.[20] Allowing pitchers to use skill and ingenuity in attempting to outwit batters, even if contrary to the rules, was good for the game. Chadwick explained:

> A question which naturally arises under the circumstances is, if there has been little else than throwing for the past ten years, while such a style of delivery has been year by year prohibited by the rules, why is it that it has not been shown up before this? Because just such experience as this style of delivery admitted of was necessary to a full development of the game, and hence it has been winked at, if not countenanced.[21]

The end of the 1860s marked the beginning of a gradual relaxation of the rules governing pitch delivery, culminating in November 1884, when the National League permitted overhand pitching. The liberalization of the rules removed the need for Cummings' secrecy and led to a rapid expansion in the use of the curveball by pitchers. But pitching like Cummings did was still difficult. As he once wrote, "If anyone thinks he can curve a ball 45 feet from the plate under these restrictions, just try it."[22] (Forty-five feet was the distance between the pitcher and home plate until 1881, when the National League increased it to 50. It was later lengthened in increments to the current distance of 60 feet, six inches.) And Cummings' wrist and finger action took a toll on his pitching hand. "Keeping both feet on the ground was a hard strain," he recalled, "as the wrist and second finger did all the work. I snapped the ball like a whip and this caused me to throw out my wrist bone quite often." For an entire season—1874, when he was playing with the Philadelphia professional club—he had to wear a rubber support on his wrist because of the strain. It did a job on his fingers, too, because of the severe pressure that they exerted on the ball. To protect them, he wore a glove on his pitching hand, but it frequently wore through.[23]

Candy Cummings got the better of Archie Bush in that Excelsior–Harvard game. The Crimson's slugger had probably five at-bats, four of which resulted in outs, and he scored only one run. Nevertheless, the college boys defeated Excelsior, 18–6, thanks to Harvard's excellent fielding and the Brooklynites' weak hitting.[24] The enduring legacy of that game, however, wasn't the Excelsiors' loss; it was the game that marked the introduction of the curveball into baseball, and baseball hasn't been the same since.

After the Excelsiors returned home to Brooklyn, Candy Cummings made what was likely his last appearance for the club. On October 26, they hosted the Nationals of Washington, D.C. Anticipating a close game against the strong Nationals squad, the Excelsiors "put forth the best players they had." In the end, they inflicted a decisive defeat upon their visitors, 26–11, behind Cummings' pitching.[25]

And thus ended Candy Cummings' first year playing with a senior nine. It prepared him for great things that were soon to come. Based on his performance with the Excelsiors, no less an authority than the eminent Henry Chadwick dubbed him "the most promising young junior player in the [pitcher's] position in the metropolitan fraternity."[26] The following season, 1868, after a short stint with the Mohawks,[27] Cummings moved to one of Brooklyn's top clubs, the Stars. But before surveying his time with the Stars, let's examine more closely Candy Cummings' innovation—the curveball.

7

The Ins and Outs
of the Curveball

"Utterly absurd," sneered the editor of a Michigan newspaper, in 1886, at the idea that a baseball could be made to curve.[1] Others pronounced it an "optical illusion."[2] There were even those who said that the curveball "pitcher" was actually the wind.[3]

For well over a half-century following Candy Cummings' introduction of the curve to the baseball world, there were skeptics. But time and again, it was proven to be true: a curveball really does curve. And Candy Cummings knew why.

In 1671, Sir Isaac Newton, cogitating upon light waves, which, he suspected, had a propensity to bend, recalled having often observed that a tennis ball, when struck with an oblique racquet, would travel in a curved line. He offered the earliest analysis of the forces causing the curve.[4] Over the succeeding centuries, scientists have experimented and analyzed the movement, twists, and turns of all sorts of balls and other projectiles, including military ordnance, seeking to explain the whys and wherefores of their bending trajectories. Although the sophistication of the experimentation and scientific analysis has increased exponentially, it all comes down to this: A ball that is spinning as it moves forward through the air encounters greater air resistance, and therefore greater pressure, on the side spinning toward the direction of the ball's flight than on the side turning in the opposite direction. The difference in pressure causes the track of the ball's forward motion to veer toward the side with the lower pressure. This phenomenon is known as the "Magnus force," after a German physicist, Heinrich Gustav Magnus, who, in 1852, was the first to analyze the phenomenon through experimentation.[5]

Cummings' curriculum at Falley Seminary included "natural philosophy," i.e., physics. His textbook, *Popular Physics* (known as *Peck's Ganot*), didn't cover the Magnus force, which had been described by Magnus only a few years previously. It did, however, include subjects such as motion of objects, forces, and the like.[6] In the early days of Cummings' experimentation with the curveball, he claimed in 1912, he "did not know what would make a ball curve when thrown through the air, and there was no one to tell me."[7] However, his schooling in the natural sciences gave him a basic knowledge of physics. Perhaps he instinctively drew on this knowledge to analyze, experiment, and finally perfect the technique to make a ball curve: "In practicing," he wrote, "I soon found that the ball in order to curve had to be thrown so it would revolve rapidly while passing through the air."[8] In his later years, he provided his own explanation as to why a curveball curved: He wrote that the twist that he gave the ball upon delivery "causes it to revolve with a swift rotary motion. The air also, for a limited space around it begins to revolve, making a great swirl, until there is enough pressure to force the ball out of a true line."[9]

That was a pretty good summary of the Magnus force.

Once the curveball had become a feature of baseball, scientists and other experimenters began to focus on whether the pitch really did curve. One of the earliest experiments was done by *Scientific American* in 1877. It set up two parallel picket fences, a few feet apart, on opposite sides of and perpendicular to a straight chalk line. The end post of each fence was on the chalk line. A pitcher standing to the left of one end of the chalk line delivered the ball with a twist toward the other end. Curving to the right of the end post of one fence and to the left of the other, it landed to the left of the opposite end of the chalk line. It wasn't terribly high-tech, but it was proof. The magazine's theoretical explanation for the curve was the difference in pressure on opposite sides of the spinning ball—essentially, the Magnus force, although the article didn't use the term.[10]

That a ball could be made to curve was evident to just about every batsman who faced Candy Cummings and curve pitchers who came after him. But others were skeptical.[11] To satisfy the curious, Cummings is said to have given an exhibition of the curveball in Hartford in 1876 to players, owners, and newspapermen. According to a recollection of the event, "Groups gathered behind Cummings and his catcher and watched with amazement the flight of the ball.... There was no denying the ocular proof offered to the skeptics."[12]

Another demonstration was given in Cincinnati on October 20, 1877, during a game between two clubs in the year-old National League—Boston, nicknamed the Red Stockings, and Cincinnati, which also went by the name of Red Stockings but was often referred to as the Reds. After two innings, fence barriers were set up along the first base line, where the test was to take place, so that a ball pitched along the line would have to curve in order to avoid hitting them. To eliminate the possibility of wind helping the ball to curve, two pitchers were used, a right-hander and a left-hander.

Tommy Bond, a righty with the Boston club, and Bobby Mitchell, a south-paw with the Reds, took turns attempting to swerve pitches around the barriers. They succeeded. "The double test was a perfect one," wrote the *Boston Daily Advertiser,* "and professors of mechanics must hereafter seek for the explanation of what has been done, rather than try to demonstrate that it is impossible."[13]

By the 1880s, explanations of the physics behind the curveball were appearing with some regularity. During that decade, two leading baseball and sports publishers, the Spalding and Reach companies, produced manuals on pitching that elaborated upon the curveball. Spalding's *The Art of Pitching and Fielding,* written by Henry Chadwick, and Reach's *The Art of Curved Pitching* provided detailed and illustrated theory—basically the Magnus force—as to why a ball pitched with a spin would curve, together with instructions as to how to execute the pitch. A magazine of outdoor sports, *Outing,* published a similar theoretical analysis.[14] That a baseball could be made to curve, and why it curved, were well-documented.

But skepticism persisted well into the 20th century. In 1941, *Life* magazine, in an effort to settle the matter, conducted an experiment using high-speed cameras to track the flight of curveballs thrown by two top pitchers of that time, Cy Blanton of the Philadelphia Phillies and Carl Hubbell of the New York Giants. *Life's* verdict? An "optical illusion."[15] But it turned out that *Life's* conclusion resulted from a flawed method of measurement,[16] and it was refuted the following year in two scientific papers published in the *American Journal of Physics.*[17] They showed that the curve was real.

Perhaps Hall of Fame pitcher Dizzy Dean said it best: "Shucks, get behind a tree and I'll hit you with an optical illusion."[18]

In Candy Cummings' time, curve pitches were often categorized by the direction of the curve. There were pitches that broke horizontally and those that fell vertically, depending on the direction of the spin that pitchers put on the ball. The "in-curve" (or "in-shoot") and the "out-curve" ("out-shoot") veered to the left or right from the perspective of the batter. The "drop" fell precipitously as it neared the batter. There was also a pitch called the "raise ball." As delivered by some hurlers, this pitch didn't actually slope up; a pitcher wouldn't have been able to create sufficient upward Magnus force to counteract the effect of gravity.[19] But it fell less than it would without the spin, making it appear to the batter that it was rising—in this case, a true optical illusion. Jim Creighton, perhaps the greatest pitcher of the early 1860s, had a form of raise ball that did travel upward and ended up above the batter's hip, but only because his delivery began a few inches off the ground. Others, such as Dick McBride, a pitcher for the Philadelphia Athletics in the 1870s, had a similar delivery. But their pitches weren't made with a twist (although Creighton is said to have used an imperceptible wrist snap) and were not curveballs in the true sense.[20]

Cummings used all four of these pitches.

The track and sharpness of break of a curveball depends on the direction and amount of spin that the pitcher applies to the ball. Nowadays, many pitchers' curveballs are of the "12 to 6" variety: they drop sharply as they approach the plate, although most also have some degree of horizontal break. This is because today's curveballs are thrown mainly with forward top spin, with the result that the ball is both pushed downward by the Magnus force and simultaneously pulled earthward by gravity. Pitches thrown with more sideways spin have greater lateral break. Today, the movement of a pitch can be tracked with a sophisticated technology called PITCHf/x. Introduced in 2006, this tool tracks the trajectory, speed, amount of break, and location of every pitch thrown in every MLB game.[21] It is the source of pitch data and displays that are seen on the telecasts of MLB games and on the MLB Gameday application. Take as examples two current pitchers, Clayton Kershaw of the Los Angeles Dodgers and José Berrios, formerly of the Minnesota Twins and now with the Toronto Blue Jays. PITCHf/x tells us that, in a game between the Dodgers and the Cincinnati Reds on April 15, 2019, Kershaw's curveballs averaged 9.17 inches of vertical drop—PITCHf/x factors out the effect of gravity, so all that drop is due to spin—and only 2.35 inches of horizontal break. Appropriately, his curve has been referred to as "11 to 6"—mostly vertical but some horizontal break. Berrios's curveballs had much more lateral movement. In a game on June 18, 2019, between the Twins and the Boston Red Sox, his curveball achieved only 1.63 inches of vertical break but nearly nine inches of horizontal deflection.[22]

The curveball wasn't the only trick up Candy Cummings' sleeve. He had a keen mind, and he applied it to his pitching. He would size up conditions of the field and the proclivities of the batsmen that he faced, and pitch to them accordingly. He was also a cunning pitcher—"as plucky and nervy a kid as they make," wrote Sam Crane of the *New York Journal*.[23] Long after his retirement from the game, Candy Cummings revealed another one of his gimmicks: In those days, a single baseball was used for an entire game, and reused in subsequent games, until it was almost literally beaten to a pulp. When a ball got wet, say, from rolling on a damp field, its cover tended to develop a slight bulge, which affected its trajectory when pitched. Cummings used this anomaly to make his curveball even more bewildering to batters. But when his inning in the pitcher's box was over, he would smooth the surface of the ball, thus depriving his opposing hurler of the same advantage.

Another gambit used by the wily Cummings: While pitching, he would assume an air of nonchalance, laziness, and lack of ambition, and make it appear that he wasn't trying, when in fact he was executing a carefully devised strategy. "The result was he caught the other fellows off guard," reported the *Springfield [MA] Republican,* "and those who considered him easy were soon pitched into defeat."[24]

The transformative effect of the curveball on the game of baseball cannot be overstated. The *New York Times* put it succinctly: "The curve delivery in base-ball pitching was the greatest change ever introduced into the game."[25] As Francis C. Richter, one of the premier sports journalists of that time, observed, Cummings' "monumental discovery ... completely changed the method of delivery from straight underhanded pitching to the present side-arm and overhead delivery, made the curve ball an indispensable part of every pitcher's repertoire, and changed the art of pitching from the haphazard go-as-you-please style to scientific basis."[26]

The introduction of the curveball, along with changes in the rules legitimizing its use, led to a fundamental shift in the balance of power between pitcher and batter. Up to the late-1860s, the batter was in full command, and the pitcher was simply his facilitator. The underlying notion was that the pitcher should cater to the needs and proclivities of the batsman and deliver balls that he could hit. The batter could designate where he wanted the pitch and whether it should be fast or slow. The pitcher had to meet those specifications as closely as possible, without bending his arm or wrist. The rules gave the pitcher little leeway for strategy.

As the curveball was just coming into use, there were growing calls for pitchers to be given greater amplitude to use their skills to outwit batsmen. More balance between the pitcher and the batter, it was thought, would make the game more interesting. And in any case, the strict rules were hardly being applied rigorously. The timing seems more than just coincidental. Pitchers were already outfoxing batters with swift and slow balls and using spin to induce pop-ups and weak grounders, but the ability to do what had not been thought possible—cause the baseball to curve as it made its way to the batter—was of a different order of magnitude.

At its convention in December 1869, the NABBP introduced an amendment to the rules that effectively weakened the ability of the batter to dictate the location of the pitch and required only that the pitch be within the legitimate reach of the batsman and as nearly as possible over the center of home plate. The pitcher still, however, had to deliver the ball with his arm straight and swinging perpendicularly to the side of his body. He still was not allowed to bend his arm or twist his wrist. The rule gave examples of pitches that weren't within the fair reach of the batter: those that went over the batter's head, bounced in front of the plate, were too far outside for the batter to reach, or hit the batter.[27]

This change was a baby step, but was nevertheless significant. Before the change, explained Henry Chadwick, the pitcher was obliged "to pitch a ball as near a certain point indicated by the batsman as he could do. Now he is only required to pitch the ball within the fair reach of the batsman. Before, the pitcher was allowed no latitude for strategic play, while the batsman had every facility given him to indulge his propensity for heavy hitting at the cost of the pitcher. Now, however, this partiality in the rule has been put a stop to, and both are now obliged to resort to skillful play alone in their efforts to outwit each other."[28]

The NABBP convention in March 1871, refined the requirements concerning pitch location. Under the changes, pitches had only to be over the plate, rather than as near as possible over its center, and between the batter's shoulder and knees—the first defined strike zone. Within those parameters, the batter could call for a high or low ball.[29]

The rules were further relaxed in 1872. They permitted, for the first time, delivery with wrist or elbow action ("underhand throw"), as long as the ball was not delivered overhand or round-arm. The requirement that the arm swing perpendicularly to the side of the body was loosened; under the amended rule, it had only to swing "nearly" perpendicularly. And gone was the requirement that the pitching arm be straight; it could be bent as it swung forward.[30] These changes greatly facilitated the delivery of the curveball. In 1884, the National League (founded in 1876) abandoned the requirement of underhand pitching altogether. The rules it adopted in December of that year permitted any form of delivery, overhand or otherwise; the ball had to be delivered over the plate, between the batsman's shoulders and knees, and at the height called for by the batsman.[31]

With the advent of the curveball, pitcher and batter were put on a more equal footing. No longer would the primary tension in the on-field drama be between hitters and fielders, with pitchers playing only a supporting role; the pitcher would become a central player in the drama.

Over the ensuing years, whenever the equilibrium between pitcher and batter was seen to have gone off-kilter, tweaks were made to the game to try to restore it: penalizing the pitcher for persistently delivering balls wide of home plate or too high or too low ("balls"); penalizing the striker by calling him out for failing to swing at, or whiffing at, fairly-pitched balls ("strikes"); changing the distance between the pitcher's point and the batter; introducing the pitcher's mound and adjusting its height; and fine-tuning the strike zone. (The number of balls and strikes varied from year to year until 1889, when four balls and three strikes became the rule.)[32]

The liberalization of the rules led to the expansion in the use of the curveball by pitchers. According to Francis C. Richter, the pitch had become quite common by 1872,[33] the first year in which the rules permitted a wrist or elbow action. Four years later, the *New York Clipper* reported, "[t]he feature of the pitching of 1876 was the furor for the curve."[34] In 1878, *Spalding's Official Base Ball Guide,* commenting on pitching in 1876 and 1877, said, "The special point was the perfection of curved pitching to which younger players attained, and which caused them to be known as 'phenomenons.'"[35] In 1879, the *Chicago Tribune* reported that the curve had come into general use.[36] By 1885, it had spread far and wide; as one Ohio newspaper put it, "Arthur Cummins [*sic*], when in the Excelsior Club of Brooklyn, was the first to practically exemplify the curve delivery; ... and now a pitcher without the curve would not be tolerated under any circumstances."[37] The curveball conceived and developed by Candy Cummings, employing a finger-and-wrist-snap action, is the one thrown by pitchers today.

The great success of the curveball motivated pitchers to experiment with different ways to manipulate spin and create other types of breaking balls to deceive batters. They all involve some combination of finger pressure and wrist action. One example was the screwball, also known as the fadeaway. Its origin is unknown but it might go as far back as the 1880s; today, however, it's a relic of history—"the Sasquatch of baseball," baseball journalist Tyler Kepner calls it.[38] Thrown with a twist of the wrist opposite to that used for the curveball, the screwball was an off-speed pitch with a sharp break. Among examples of pitches in current use are the slider and the splitter. The slider is gripped with the index and middle fingers close to each other like a fastball but slightly off-center from the top of the ball, and with some twist of the wrist. It comes at the batter looking like a fastball, but then it breaks with more lateral than downward movement. Dating back to the turn of the century, the pitch came into popular usage in the 1950s; today, it's as common as the curveball, if not more so. The splitter (split-fingered fastball) and its forerunner, the forkball, are thrown with the index and middle fingers split in the shape of a V on top of the ball. It approaches the batter with speed and then drops sharply. There are several other examples.[39]

All of these developments can be traced back to Candy Cummings. His curveball was a game-changer. But others would soon try to take credit for it.

8

Curveball Claimants

"When anything of interest is done or something new is brought out," wrote Candy Cummings in 1898, "there are people who always lay claim to it as their idea."[1] And so it was with Cummings and his curveball.

It didn't take long. Within a couple of decades after the curveball began to spread to other hurlers, pitchers began to emerge contending that they, not Cummings, had invented the pitch. But before examining these claims, a point should be made: the proposition that Candy Cummings developed and was pitching the curveball in the 1860s, and was the first to use the pitch, is supported by people who actually saw him do it.

One was James Gordon Spencer. Spencer was born in Brooklyn in 1847, a year before Cummings, and grew up there.[2] He was a teammate of Cummings on the Carrolls, the junior club where Cummings got his start. In 1900, living in Honolulu, Spencer wrote a letter to the *New York Times*. In it, he said:

> Your recent Sunday article on curve pitching interests me as an old baseball crank. I have always claimed that Arthur Cummings was the original curve pitcher. Some time between 1863 and 1870 I belonged to the Carroll Baseball Club, which played in a field back of Carroll Park, in Brooklyn, and Cummings, just from school, was our pitcher. The Star Baseball Club played on the same grounds, and took Cummings for their pitcher because he pitched a "curve," which it was hard to hit.... I am positive that Cummings pitched with a curve before 1870, and I think as early as 1864. The curve was natural to him, and I do not think was the result of study, but was none the less acknowledged and effective.[3]

Allowing for a bit of fuzziness after the lapse of some 35 years, Spencer's facts check out. Arthur Cummings did pitch for the Carrolls in 1864, his only year with the club. The following year, he was lured to the Star Juniors, and later moved to the Excelsiors. He joined the Star senior club in 1868. Spencer's letter was prompted by correspondence published in the *Times* in June 1900, that called into question the attribution of invention of the curveball to Cummings. There is no evident motivation for Spencer, who had been living in Honolulu since around 1878,[4] to go to bat for Cummings, other than to set the record straight.[5]

Another eyewitness to Cummings' curve was Herbert Jewell. He also had been a teammate on Brooklyn's Excelsiors in 1866–1867. Jewell, who served as the team's catcher in addition to playing other positions, was frequently behind the plate when Cummings pitched. Both Cummings and Jewell left the club in 1868 and, after a brief sojourn with the Mohawk club of Brooklyn, ended up on the Stars. The duo remained battery mates through 1870. Suffice it to say, Jewell knew Cummings' pitching.

Some background explains Jewell's contribution in support of Cummings: In 1918, an anonymous correspondent to the *New York Sun* generated a bit of a stir when he stated that he had known Arthur Cummings and was sure that he was the first to pitch a curveball, adding that Cummings had learned the curve from Jim Creighton.[6] That provoked an almost immediate response from another pitcher from Cummings' era, Phonney Martin. In an article in the *Sun,* Martin disputed that Candy Cummings was the first with the curve. Not only that, he claimed paternity of the curveball for himself, saying that he had developed the pitch back in the early 1860s and that Cummings didn't get it until 1871.[7] We'll meet up with Phonney Martin later in this chapter.

A couple of weeks after Martin's article appeared, Herbert Jewell's rejoinder was published.[8] He didn't state outright that Cummings invented the curveball or even that he was pitching it while they were on the Excelsiors in 1866–1867, but that wasn't the focus of his letter. His point was to refute Martin's assertion that Cummings had learned the curve from Creighton. And he did so convincingly. He pointed out that Creighton died in 1862, when Cummings was only 14 and wasn't keeping company with big-time ballplayers like him; and anyway, Creighton didn't pitch the curveball and didn't even know how to. But it was an underlying, albeit unstated, premise of Jewell's letter that Cummings was pitching curveballs while the two were on the Excelsiors. Jewell didn't attribute the curve to anyone else.

Another ball player who knew Candy Cummings and his pitching well was Joe Start. Born in New York City in 1842, Start and his family moved to Brooklyn around 1851.[9] Like Cummings, he played in Brooklyn's amateur circuit in the 1860s before a major league career that spanned 16 seasons. Start and Cummings were teammates on New York's Mutuals in 1872. A superb first baseman, Start had a solid reputation for honesty, integrity, and gentlemanly behavior, earning him the nickname "Old Reliable."[10]

Start was interviewed by the *Boston Globe*'s Tim Murnane in 1895. Murnane asked him if there was any doubt that Candy Cummings was the inventor of the curveball. "No doubt whatever," replied Start. "I remember all about the circumstance, as I was brought up in Brooklyn, and was playing around the same lots with Cummings from 1866 to '70. Cummings was the first to get the curve."[11]

Then there was Henry Chadwick. Unlike James Spencer, Herbert Jewell, and Joe Start, Chadwick didn't play on teams with Cummings; in fact, he was not a ballplayer at all, apart from a few games as a teenager with friends. But this English-born, cricket-loving immigrant to Brooklyn happened upon a baseball game between two New York City clubs at the Elysian Fields in Hoboken, New Jersey. He was immediately smitten and soon became the 19th century's most passionate and famous fan, advocate, and chronicler of the game of baseball. Chadwick was such an influence on the game and its development that he was called "the father of baseball."

Chadwick actually saw Cummings pitch the curveball in the summer of 1866. He said so in 1898. That year, Fred Goldsmith, a hurler who had come up through the amateur circuit in Connecticut and played for major league clubs from 1879 to 1884, instigated a discussion in *Sporting Life* as to who really invented the curveball. Goldsmith insisted that the honor belonged to a pitcher at Yale in the mid–1870s named Ham Avery, and not to Candy Cummings. Chadwick wrote to *Sporting Life*, dismissing Goldsmith's claim:

> Arthur Cummings was a protégé of General Thomas A. Daker [*sic*], of the Excelsior club, of Brooklyn, in 1866.... General Daker called my attention—in 1866—to Cummings' remarkable feat of producing the horizontal curve to the ball in pitching it.... There is no questioning the fact that Cummings first practically developed the curved ball in pitching long before Goldsmith was known in the base ball world.... I saw Cummings pitch the curved ball in the summer of 1866.[12]

"General Thomas A. Daker" was actually Thomas S. Dakin, a Civil War officer and highly respected businessman and public figure in Brooklyn who had a long association with Brooklyn baseball. He was a member of the Excelsiors, and Cummings' teammate, in 1866 and 1867, playing in some of the games that Cummings pitched and umpiring in at least one.[13]

Chadwick made the same point about Cummings in an article he published in 1901 in the sporting journal *Outing*: "Arthur Cummings of the Excelsior Junior nine of 1866, introduced the novelty of the curved delivery that year."[14] (Chadwick must have been referring to the time in 1866 when he actually saw Cummings toss the curveball; Cummings did not introduce the pitch until 1867.)

Before and after the *Sporting Life* debate, the "father of baseball" was consistent in his assertions that Cummings was the father of the curveball. Among the many publications in which he made this point were his books, *The Art of Pitching and Fielding* (1885) and *How to Play Base Ball* (1889).[15] Fred Goldsmith, on the other hand, changed his tune in later life, abandoning his attribution of the curveball to Ham Avery and claiming that *he* had invented the pitch.

George Wright, one half of baseball's Hall of Fame Wright brothers, played on some amateur ball clubs in the New York City area and Washington, D.C., in the 1860s, teaming up with brother Harry on the Red Stockings of Cincinnati in 1869. After the 1870 season, the Reds disbanded and the siblings relocated to Boston, where they helped organize a new ball club, taking with them the nickname Red Stockings; Harry ran the team, and George played the infield. The best shortstop of his era and a fine hitter, George compiled a .301 batting average and .871 fielding percentage, including four errorless seasons, over his 12-year professional career. John

Thorn, the official historian of Major Legal Baseball, considers him "baseball's first nationwide hero"; to the Hall of Fame, he was "baseball's first superstar player."[16]

Tim Murnane once asked George Wright about the first time he saw a pitcher pitch a curveball. It was in 1869, Wright replied. "I remember it as if it were only yesterday." He recalled the experience:

Early in '69 I was a member of the Cincinnati Red Stockings, and in Brooklyn we met the Amateur Stars. Arthur Cummings was advertised to pitch. I had heard about his curveball and, like the other players, was anxious to see the brand new thing in baseball. I was the first man at the bat and made no attempt to hit the two first balls pitched, as I waited to get a line on the new delivery. The ball came straight for the center of the plate and then took a wide curve. I figured that I could only hit the ball by waiting until it came very close.

Henry Chadwick. Called the "father of baseball," Chadwick was the nineteenth century's most influential authority on the game. He was the baseball writer for several New York City newspapers, author of books on baseball, and editor of baseball guides. Chadwick was elected to the Baseball Hall of Fame in 1938 (A.G. Spalding Baseball Collection. New York Public Library Digital Collections).

I hit the third ball pitched, but not very hard, and I was convinced that a ball could be curved.[17]

Wright added that he had seen Candy Cummings pitch many times after that, before any other hurler had pitched a curveball.

Two Midwesterners who chimed in on behalf of Candy Cummings were Alfred H. Spink and Hugh A. Reid. Spink was another prominent sportswriter in his day. Born in 1854 in Quebec, where he and his brothers grew up playing cricket, Al and the rest of the Spink family moved to Chicago after the Civil War. There, the brothers took up America's game. They founded one of Chicago's numerous amateur ball clubs, the Mutuals. Later, young Al followed older brother William, a sports journalist, to St. Louis, and embarked on a career writing about baseball. After St. Louis's first professional team, the Browns, folded, Al Spink helped establish a new pro club, of the same name, to replace it. In 1886, he founded *The Sporting News,* which became known as "baseball's bible" and is still going strong.

Hughey Reid played for some of Chicago's amateur nines in the late 1860s and 1870s, including the Aetna and Franklin clubs. His moment in the sun came on August 26, 1874, when, as a member of the Franklins, he was called on to play right field for Baltimore's professional club, the Canaries, in a game against the Chicago White Stockings. In four at-bats, he managed zero hits and zero runs; but to his credit, he was errorless in the field.[18] That was the sum total of his big-league record.

Al Spink met up with Reid and other baseball men in 1920 at a meeting of the Old-Timers Baseball Association in Chicago. Spink wrote about it in his syndicated column. Holding forth on the subject of who was the first curve pitcher, Reid was confident: "Without a doubt," he said, "Cummings was the first pitcher to put the curve on the ball.... [He] was using the outcurve as early as 1867." Summing up, Reid pronounced, "Cummings, and Cummings alone, was the originator of the curve. There is no doubt at all about this."[19] It's not clear whether Hughey Reid actually saw Cummings pitch in the 1860s; however, he witnessed Candy's curveball firsthand in 1871 when he pitched for the Aetnas against the Stars.[20]

Spink, however, did see Candy Cummings pitch in the 1860s. In his report on the old-timers meeting, he wrote, "I saw Cummings pitch for the famous Stars of Brooklyn on the old Capitoline grounds at Brooklyn in the '60s and '70s, and then all hands admitted that he was pitching a curved ball." (Candy Cummings was with the Stars from 1868 to 1871.)[21] Spink never wavered from this conviction. As far as he was concerned, "Arthur Cummings [was] the first man in America to use the curve ball and the real inventor of that sort of thing."[22]

All of these statements, based on personal knowledge (although there's uncertainty about Hughey Reid), confirm that Candy Cummings had developed and was using the curveball in 1866 and 1867. Further, they support Cummings' assertion that he conceived of the pitch around 1864: Not only was this Spencer's recollection, but also, if Cummings was using the curve by 1866 or 1867, he had to have been working on it for some time before then.

Albert Goodwill Spalding was another one of 19th-century baseball's most prominent and influential figures. Over the course of his long career, he was a professional baseball player, team owner, and sporting goods magnate. As a player, he was one of the premier pitchers of his era. Francis Richter, a respected chronicler of the game, deemed Spalding and Candy Cummings the two best hurlers of the 1870s.[23]

In 1895, Spalding was asked about the first pitcher to throw a curveball. He replied that he'd actually seen Candy Cummings toss his curve in 1870—before any other pitchers were using the pitch—when his Forest City club of Rockford, Illinois, played Candy's Stars:

> Arthur Cummings of the old Brooklyn Stars was the first pitcher to throw a "curve" ball. I met him in 1870, when I played on the old Rockford (IL) nine. We heard a great deal about them, and it scared us a good deal, but we managed to solve his curves and won the game. Cummings had a beautiful pitch. He secured his curve by a peculiar wrist motion. It was a regular pitch, however, and not a throw [i.e., overhand or with the arm wide of the side] such as pitchers use nowadays. I talked with him about it and tried to get the curve, but I couldn't do it.[24]

There might be some question concerning Spalding's recollection that the Forest City–Stars game took place in 1870. During its tour of the East that year, Forest City was scheduled to play a game against the Stars on May 28, but persistent rain that week made the grounds unplayable. However, they were in the metropolitan area for several days; they played against New York City's Mutuals on May 30 and the Atlantics of Brooklyn on May 31.[25] It's possible that Forest City and the Stars got in a scrub game at some point during the Rockfords' stay, although no record of such a game has been found.

In addition to all of these firsthand observations, *Spalding's Official Base Ball Guide* provided second-hand confirmations that Candy Cummings was the first to pitch a curveball. The *Spalding Guide* was an authoritative and influential baseball publication begun in 1877 by Al Spalding and his brothers. In its 1915 edition, the editor, John C. Foster, claimed to have "received abundant personal testimony" from George Wright, John C. Chapman, A.G. Spalding, Doug Allison, N.E. Young, A.C. "Cap" Anson, Weston Fisler, Thomas Pratt, and James White, all baseball contemporaries of Cummings in the 1870s, attesting that Cummings was the first with the curveball.[26] Without details, however, as to the testimony provided by these men, the confirmations have limited probative value; nevertheless, they were reported by a generally trusted source and thus aren't wholly without worth.

The recollections described above (apart from the "personal testimony" reported second-hand by the *Spalding Guide*) are strong proof. But they were given decades after the events they recalled. What about early contemporary accounts of Cummings pitching the curve? They exist.

In an article in *The Sporting News* on April 13, 1898, renowned baseball writer Will Rankin quoted a passage that he said had been printed in the late summer of 1867; it read: "Cummings is certainly a very promising young pitcher. His great point, however, is his power to send the ball in a curved line to the right or the left of the home plate, thus puzzling the best batsmen." Unfortunately, Rankin didn't give the source of this quotation, so it cannot be verified. But other early accounts of Candy Cummings' curve can be.

One of them appeared in the *New York Tribune* on May 9, 1870. Reporting on a 14–3 victory by Cummings' Star club over the professional Mutuals, the *Tribune* said: "The manner in which the Stars defeated the Mutuals on Saturday is easily recorded. The game resolved itself into one of batting, and the side which hit the hardest was the winner. Young Cummings outwitted the Mutuals by his method of delivery, and all efforts to get the range of the bat failed."

What was it about Candy Cummings' "method of delivery" that so stymied the Mutual batters in that game? The *Brooklyn Union's* report of the game left no doubt; it referred to Cummings' "particular power of giving a curve to the line of the ball to the right or the left."[27]

Another reference to Cummings' curve pitching appeared a few weeks later, on June 25, 1870, in the *New York Clipper's* account of a game between Cincinnati's Red Stockings and the Stars of Brooklyn. The *Clipper* set the scene as George Wright, the Reds' shortstop and leadoff batter, stepped into the box in the opening frame:

> [A]s George Wright took his stand and faced Cummings for the first time, the crowd were on the tip toe of expectation to see whether George could hit the Star pitcher's horizontally curved line balls, for it is in the delivery of a ball which curves in or out to the right or left as it leaves the hand of the pitcher that Cummings' effectiveness as a pitcher lays; combined, of course, with speed, accuracy of delivery and good judgement.

The bewilderment of batters—and the mirth of fans—caused by Cummings' curves was captured the following August by *Wilkes Spirit of the Times* in its report of a game between the Stars and the Forest City club of Cleveland (a different club from one with the same name in Rockford, Illinois) on August 20, 1870:

> The Forest City men have earned the reputation of being first-class batsmen, and deservedly so, too, … and yet twelve times out of the twenty-seven which they went to the bat, they had "three strikes" called against them by the umpire. Whatever was the peculiarity of Cummings' pitching, whether it was its

extraordinary speed or its eccentric twist, it was sufficient to baffle the efforts of the Clevelanders to hit it…. It certainly was most amusing to witness the efforts of the different players as they went up to the bat, "determined to hit him this time," make three fruitless attempt [*sic*] to do so and then retire, amid the laughter alike of his "mates" and the public. In fact, it became quite a feature among the "spectators" on the game to bet upon each man being able to strike or not. It was not a question, as usual, of betting on runs, but simply of whether the batsman would be able to hit the ball.[28]

The above eyewitness accounts of Cummings' curveball are the earliest that have been found. But he didn't just wake up one day in 1870 and start throwing curveballs for the first time. The quotations show that he had the pitch moving and breaking pretty darn well by that time; he had to have been working on and using the curveball for some time before then.

Why, then, apart from Rankin's unsourced quote from 1867, can contemporaneous references to Candy Cummings' curveball before 1870 not be found? Here's a possibility. The curveball was still very new, and some considered it to be a physical impossibility. Cummings was the only one who had it. Plus, pitching the curve with a twist of the wrist, as he did, was still illegal under the NABBP rules (although, as we've seen, violations of the rule were often winked at to make the game more interesting). Maybe it took a while for baseball writers to get used to the idea that a baseball could be made to curve, and to trust what their eyes were seeing.

Although Candy Cummings' use of the curveball in the 1860s was supported by the likes of Chadwick, Spalding, and others, there were deniers. In the files of the Baseball Hall of Fame library in Cooperstown are Phonney Martin's original scrapbooks. They contain a letter from one Oliver Brown, an outfielder who was a teammate of Cummings' on the Stars in Brooklyn in 1868. In his letter, Brown asserted that Cummings never pitched a curve prior to 1870. But this doesn't stack up against the declarations of Spencer, Jewell, "Old Reliable" Joe Start, George Wright, and the estimable Henry Chadwick. Brown further wrote that he "believe[d]" that Martin was the only one to pitch the curve up to that point; he wasn't sure about Martin, it seems. In any case, as we will see, Martin's "curve" was really a slow drop ball, which he pitched without twisting his wrist; it wasn't the curveball that Cummings conceived and developed.

Against that background, let's look at some of the contenders for the curveball crown.

Joseph McElroy Mann. "Mac" Mann was a student at Princeton from 1872 to 1876 and played on the college baseball team. In 1900, he came across a review of Cap Anson's book, *A Ball Player's Career,* in the *New York Times.* Written by a self-declared but otherwise unnamed "old college ball tosser," the review noted, as did Anson himself in his book, that Cummings was the first curve pitcher.[29] It turned out that the "old ball tosser" was W.J. Henderson, Princeton '76, a pitcher, teammate, and classmate of Mann's.[30]

But Mann somehow misread the review, and apparently he did not consult the book itself. He wrote a letter to the *Times* that was published eight days after the review appeared. In it, Mann stated, "I was especially gratified to see that Mr. Anson, who has been identified with baseball for fully thirty years and who knows it from A to Z, should give me credit for practically introducing curve pitching."[31] In fact, neither Anson nor the review did any such thing. Instead, Anson wrote that Cummings was the first to introduce curve pitching, about 1867 or 1868, and that Mann (whom he mistakenly referred to as "Mount") did not get the curve until around 1875.[32]

The *Times* review added that Mann had learned the curve from seeing Cummings pitch at Princeton in 1874. This referred to a game between Cummings' team at the time, the Pearls of Philadelphia, and the Princeton nine, on October 23, 1874. In his letter to the *Times,* Mann said that he'd watched Cummings warm up before the game and between innings by throwing the ball to the second baseman, and the ball curved. However, Mann continued, in his five times at bat, he failed to notice any curve pitched by Cummings, despite having been told by Cummings' catcher that he "sometimes" pitched a ball that curved.

Fine. But here's what the Princeton publication *Athletics at Princeton: A History* had to say about Candy Cummings' pitching at that game; it quoted Philly's catcher as saying that Cummings' pitches "went zigzag." Continuing the story, the publication added, "He probably meant that the ball curved, for the pitcher was *Cummings,* whom the professionals call the 'inventor of curves.' Undoubtedly, *Cummings* did pitch curves in this game, and even earlier."[33] [Emphasis in original.] So how, one might ask, did Mann miss them in his five at-bats?

Be that as it may, Mann also said in his letter that he had learned the curveball "accidentally" toward the end of the 1874 season. Favoring a sore finger, he said, he released the ball with a different delivery and noticed that it curved. He practiced the new pitch all winter and began to use it the following season. Mann added that he had not seen anyone pitch a curve before him, from which he concluded that he was the first. But since Candy Cummings was pitching curveballs from the time Mann was 10 or 11 years old (Mann was born in 1856[34]), Mann obviously wasn't the first.

The final word on Mann's claims, at least in the *Times* letter columns, was given by the veteran baseball journalist, Will Rankin. His letter was published in the *Times* on September 29, 1900. Dismissing Mann's assertions in no uncertain terms, Rankin affirmed that Cummings had been pitching curveballs since 1866, and that a handful of other pitchers had the curve before Mann "accidentally" discovered it in 1874.

Ham Avery. Charles Hammond "Ham" Avery was the Yale pitcher whom Fred Goldsmith, in his controversial *Sporting Life* article in 1898, tapped as the first to pitch a curveball. Born in Cincinnati in 1854, Avery was in the class of 1875 at Yale and pitched for its baseball team in 1873, 1874, and 1875, also serving as its captain during the latter two years.[35] The *Sporting Life* story quoted Goldsmith: "I was a boy in New Haven when I first saw Professor 'Ham' Avery pitch a curve. I watched him with open eyes and mouth, and we could scarcely believe it. He was a professor in philosophy at Yale and was pitcher and captain of the team."

According to Goldsmith, Avery demonstrated the pitch at Hamilton Park, Yale's baseball ground, and afterwards showed it off at the Capitoline grounds in Brooklyn. Goldsmith didn't specify when that was, but since Avery was a Yalie from 1872 to 1875, it had to be after Candy Cummings had developed and introduced the curve.

Incidentally, Avery was never a professor of philosophy. After graduating from Yale in 1875, he went to law school in Cincinnati, and in 1878 began a long and successful career as a practicing attorney.[36] This is one of many problems with Goldsmith's story, which we will encounter again shortly.

"Phonney" Martin. He was also referred to in the press as "Farney," "Farley," "Fraley," and other variations on the theme, but, as his first name was Alphonse, "Phonney" is presumably correct. Three years older than Candy Cummings, Martin got his start in organized baseball in 1863 with junior clubs in the New York City area. From there, he went on to play for some of the region's big senior nines, including Empire of Hoboken, New Jersey; New York's Mutuals; and the Eckford club of the Williamsburg section of Brooklyn.[37]

Martin's nickname was "Old Slow Ball" (although some writers referred to his delivery as medium-paced[38]). His signature pitch was a drop ball—an underhanded toss that traveled in a vertical arc and fell as it approached the batter. Hughey Reid described it as a "slow teaser that reached the plate about shoulder high and dropped while still spinning."[39] The *New York Clipper* of April 3, 1869 stated, "He is an extremely hard pitcher to hit, for the ball never comes in a straight line, but in a tantalizing curve." When batters did manage to hit it, they usually popped it up or sent it for an easy infield grounder. But soon batters caught on to Martin's slow toss, and his success with the pitch didn't last long. By 1877, it was already a thing of the past; in December of that year, the *Clipper* noted, "skillful batsmen can as easily punish the best of 'slows' as they can straight swift balls, and it was not long before the Martin style of pitching became too easily punished to be longer available."[40]

Martin, in an article published under his own byline in the *New York Sun* on March 17, 1918, explained that he delivered his drop pitch with a "particular manipulation of the ball with the first two fingers and thumb of the hand, that caused the ball to turn toward the batter. The ball when delivered," he continued, "started with a slight curve upward and broke down at the plate, as if it had lost its force of motion." Significantly, Martin added that, unlike Cummings, he didn't twist his wrist; that, he wrote, would have constituted an illegal "underhand throw" under the pitching rules in the 1860s and early 1870s, resulting in the removal of the pitcher from the game.

As far as Phonney Martin was concerned, his pitch was a curveball and he was its daddy. In the early 1900s, decades after having retired from the game (in 1873), he waged a campaign to convince everyone. He made his pitch in the newspapers.[41] He typed essays and wrote notes. He amassed clippings, correspondence (some of which he solicited), and other materials purporting to support his contention. Many of these can now be found in his scrapbooks archived at the Baseball Hall of Fame library. In one of his tracts, titled "A.C. Martin Invented the Drop Curve Fifty Years Ago," he pronounced. "I claim and as a matter of fact am entitled to the honor of being the first man to use a curve in baseball." In another, he wrote, "In presenting this to the public it is my aim to acquaint the reader in a brief and comprehensive manner with the inside history of the introduction of the curve in the game [by himself, of course] including the circumstances leading to it." It was a full-court press.

In his *New York Sun* article of March 17, 1918, and in other materials, Martin claimed that he perfected his drop pitch in 1861–1862, while he was a soldier in the Union army, and began using it as early as 1863. However, there is no corroborating proof. The earliest references that have been found were from 1865 and 1866, both commenting upon Martin's "'slow, twisting' pitches."[42] Evidently unaware that Cummings had been delivering curveballs since 1867, Martin argued that Cummings didn't pitch his curve until 1871. That, however, appears to have been an assumption on Martin's part, based on the fact that Cummings' curve, delivered with a snap of the wrist, would have been illegal under the pitching rules.[43] But the assumption was mistaken, as we've seen. For the first few years that Cummings used the pitch, until the pitching rules relaxed, he concealed his wrist action from the umpires, who were prone in any case to turn a blind eye to such infringements.

As "concrete corroboration" that he had the curve before Candy Cummings, Phonney Martin cited in his *New York Sun* piece an article published in 1910 by E.J. Edwards, a well-known journalist with the *Sun* whose column was syndicated in several papers. In the article, Edwards recounted a conversation with Cummings that supposedly took place during a chance encounter between the two in a Hartford street in the "late fall of 1876." At that time, Edwards was an apprentice journalist at the *Hartford Courant*,[44] and Cummings was living in Hartford and playing for that city's famous National League club, called the Dark Blues. According to his article, Edwards asked Cummings, "Mr. Cummings, I have heard that you were the first man ever to pitch a ball with a curve. Is that so?" Cummings replied, "No, I don't think I was the first man to pitch a curve ball. I think Martin of the old Eckfords had a curve. *Not mine, but kind of a curve*" (emphasis added).[45]

Even if the story related by Edwards were true, neither the quotation from Cummings nor the article as a whole supports Martin's claim to have invented the curveball. In fact, Edwards concluded the piece by referring to Cummings as "the discoverer of the curved ball, which has made modern baseball possible."

But Edwards' story has significant problems. First, it contains lengthy quotes from his conversation with Cummings 34 years after it occurred. It is quite unlikely that he would remember verbatim the extensive dialogue so long after it happened. Did the then-apprentice journalist record the conversation in a notebook, which he saved for more than three decades? Possible, but....Edwards' story had Candy Cummings dressed in painters' overalls, carrying a paintbrush and a pot of paint, and looking lost. Sensing Edwards' surprise at seeing him in that garb, Cummings supposedly told him that he was a house painter by trade, and, anticipating that his baseball career was nearing an end, was "getting a hand in" that line of work.

But at that time, Cummings wasn't a housepainter by trade; he did not go into that business until around 1885, several years after his retirement from baseball, when he was living in Athol, Massachusetts. Anyway, would he really have been spending his time in the late fall of 1876 preparing to enter a new vocation? In 1876, the Dark Blues' season ended on October 21; then they played a series of games against the Boston Red Stockings for the New England championship.[46] That was no time for Cummings to be trying his hand at a back-up career as a painter. Could the encounter have taken place in November or even December, still technically late fall? During that period, Cummings was more likely occupied with arrangements for the following season, when he would become manager and pitcher for the Live Oaks of Lynn, Massachusetts, and for his major role in the convention to be held four months hence, in February 1877, for the establishment of baseball's first minor league.

No, Edwards' account was very likely a work of fiction.

Was Phonney Martin's drop pitch a curveball? What he did, according to his own account, was to modify what was essentially a lob by adding a forward spin, without, however, using his wrist.

Martin was not the first hurler to put some spin on the ball. One ball tosser said to have done so before Martin was Bernard Hannegan, a member of the Union club of Morrisania, then a separate municipality in Westchester County but now part of the Bronx. In a game against Brooklyn's Excelsiors on September 7, 1860, the Unions held the Excelsiors to seven runs, the lowest total in the team's history to that point. As reported by the *New York Clipper,* this was due to "the very effective pitching of young Hannegan, … who imparted such a twist to the balls he pitched, that it was almost impossible to hit them squarely and fairly into the field."[47] Others who pitched with a twist were Frank Henry, Princeton College class of '66, who played on one of Princeton's first baseball teams, called the Nassaus; E. Davis, another Nassau; and J. While, a hurler for the Forest Citys of Cleveland. But the spinning action employed by those pitchers did not induce the ball to curve and was not intended to do so; its purpose was to put enough "English" on the ball so that, when it made contact with the bat, the batsman would not hit it squarely, and would instead knock it for a harmless pop fly.[48]

It wasn't the spin that caused Martin's pitch to arc upward and then drop; it was the lob and the slow speed. Gravity would have caused the ball to behave that way even without the spin, although the drop might have been enhanced somewhat by the ball's forward rotation. "Slow balls," noted Henry Chadwick, "are simply tossed to the bat with a line of delivery so curved as to make them almost drop on the home base."[49] According to his own article in the *New York Sun,* Phonney Martin didn't use the spin to create the curve, but—rather like those twisting hurlers before him—to prevent the batter from making clean contact. "The peculiar feature of this style of pitching," he wrote, "was that when the ball was hit, no matter how hard, it would rise high in the air and the fielders had no trouble in catching the batter out." As if to emphasize this point, the *New York Clipper,* on October 21, 1871, noted that "the particular curve" to Martin's pitch was fatal to unskilled batsmen, "provided he has any support in the field."

The key difference between Phonney Martin's drop pitch and Candy Cummings' curveball was that Cummings delivered his curve with a wrist snap; this, along with his particular grip and finger action, is what generated the spin that caused the ball to curve. The arc in Martin's pitch was on one plane: vertical—the ball rose and then fell. While Candy Cummings had a drop ball, he was best known for his pitches that broke horizontally, the inshoot and the outcurve.[50]

Important baseball figures of the 1860s and 1870s didn't consider Martin's pitch a curveball. One of those was George Wright, who was certainly familiar with Candy Cummings and the other pitchers of his era and had been on the receiving end of Cummings' curve in 1869, when his Cincinnati club met Candy's Stars in Brooklyn.[51]

To Wright, Phonney Martin's pitch wasn't a curveball. Quoted in Tim

Murnane's column in *Sporting Life* on March 25, 1911, Wright explained, "the ball Martin tossed up was hard to meet fair, as he sent it in with a spin, but it was a slow ball, usually sent very high, that dropped as it reached the plate without the semblance of a curve."[52]

In his *New York Sun* article of March 17, 1918, Martin himself seemed to acknowledge that his pitch was something different from a true curveball. He gave credit to another hurler, Bobby Mathews, as the first to pitch a curve. Mathews didn't return the favor; he considered the drop ball to be "deceptive work" and not a true curveball.[53]

Bobby Mathews. "Little Bobby" Mathews, at 5'5" and 140 pounds, give or take, was one of the top pitchers of the 1870s and 1880s. Born in Baltimore in 1851, Mathews began his career in 1868 with the junior nine of the Maryland club of Baltimore and was elevated to its senior squad the following year. In late 1870, he was poached from the Marylands by a team from Fort Wayne, Indiana, called the Kekiongas.[54] Then a member of the National Association of Base Ball Players, the Kekiongas were one of ten clubs that broke away from the NABBP in 1871 to form the National Association of Professional Base Ball Players (NAPBBP)—baseball's first professional league and considered the first major league. Opening Day of the new league, May 4, 1871, saw the Kekiongas host the superior Forest City nine of Cleveland. Little Bobby, then age 19, pitched a gem for his Fort Wayne team, shocking Forest City with a five-hit, 2–0 win. The game was touted as "the finest game of base ball ever witnessed in this country." On that one day, Mathews secured the triple honor of tossing the first pitch, winning the first game, and scoring the first shutout in major league history.[55]

Over the next 20 years, 16 as a player, Bobby Mathews's career took him to a number of different clubs on the East Coast, and out to San Francisco. In 1873, he moved from the Baltimore club to the Mutuals of New York, switching teams with Candy Cummings, who went to play for the Baltimores. During all four of his seasons with Mutuals, 1873–1876, Mathews was a teammate of Joe Start, who later vouched for Candy Cummings as the inventor of the curveball.

Mathews himself never claimed to have invented the curveball. According to a report in 1883, he acknowledged that Cummings had been throwing curves before him, and that, in fact, he learned the pitch by standing behind batters and watching Cummings' delivery.[56] Cummings himself maintained that Mathews had learned the curve from him, a claim supported by Henry Chadwick and others.[57] In one account, Cummings pinpointed the event to a game in Brooklyn between the Stars club, for which he played from 1868 through 1871, and a picked nine. Bobby Mathews, he said, had heard about his curve and made a special trip to Brooklyn to see it. The Stars won handily behind Cummings' pitching, and after the game,

Mathews came to the dressing room to congratulate him. "I volunteered to let him into the secret of my curve," said Cummings, "and he became a willing pupil. At the end of the season he mastered the twist of the wrist that I used, and his curve was as effective as mine."[58]

It was Phonney Martin who credited Mathews as the first to pitch the curve ... legally, that is. "Mathews," he said, "was the first pitcher, and the only one, who proved that curved pitching could be used legally in a professional game of baseball." According to Martin's recollection, Mathews pitched an out-curve as early as 1869, when he was with the Marylands. There had been hurlers before then who, Martin said, tried to get away with pitching curveballs, such as Fred McSweeney of New York's Mutuals, but their attempts violated the strict pitching rules of the time, and they were penalized by ejection from the game. Mathews, wrote Martin, "managed to conform to the rules and still impart an outcurve to the ball." As for Candy Cummings, Martin was convinced that the star hurler didn't pitch the curve before 1870 or 1871; he couldn't have, reasoned Martin; it wouldn't have been legal then.[59]

Legal or not, there is strong corroboration of Cummings' curve pitching in 1867, indeed before then, which would make Mathews a later entrant into the curveball fraternity. The commentators agreed. Some, such as Al Spalding and Cap Anson, considered that Mathews was the next after Cummings to put a curve on a baseball, in the early 1870s.[60] Others said that it was a raise ball that Mathews was pitching from 1869—not an outcurve as Martin had stated—and he didn't get the curveball until ten or so years later, after he changed his delivery.[61] Tim Murnane wrote that he'd batted against Mathews in the early 1870s "and never noticed any curve whatever on the ball." Hughey Reid said the same thing.[62] More likely, it was a raise ball that Mathews was pitching then; he could have delivered it without twisting his wrist. A later change in delivery, to introduce a wrist snap, would have enabled him to pitch the curveball.

Fred Goldsmith: The Curious Case of the "Yellowed Clipping." Goldsmith's was perhaps the strangest of the claims to paternity of the curveball.

Born in New Haven in 1856,[63] Fred Goldsmith became another top hurler of the late 1870s and 1880s. He was one of several pitchers who had the curveball in 1875, after restrictions on pitch delivery had been loosened.[64] Goldsmith started out in the amateur circuit in New Haven and Bridgeport, Connecticut; in 1876, he joined his first big-time club, the Tecumsehs of London, Ontario. In 1876, he posted a remarkable record of 41 wins and five losses, and he pitched the Tecumsehs to the Canadian championship that year as well as the next. There followed further highly successful seasons, including a 21–3 record and 1.75 ERA with the Chicago White Stockings in 1880. He led the Chicagos to the National League pennant in 1880 and the two seasons that followed.

In his *Sporting Life* article on July 16, 1898, Goldsmith acknowledged that he did not invent the curveball, but, he said, neither did Candy Cummings; according to him, it was Yale's "Professor 'Ham' Avery" who first used the pitch. Goldsmith disputed the generally accepted notion that the honor belonged to Cummings: "Arthur Cummings ... did not any more invent and make successful the curve ball which became such a power than I did." Goldsmith said that he was a boy in New Haven when he first saw Avery pitch the curve, that he'd learned the pitch from Avery, and that he'd used it in a tournament in Lynn, Massachusetts, in 1874. (There was a tournament in Lynn in 1874, but it was among teams from the Boston area; Goldsmith's team at the time, from Bridgeport, Connecticut, did not participate.[65] Perhaps he meant another tournament the following year in Bridgeport, in which his team did compete.[66]) He added that Avery had demonstrated the pitch, using three posts, in New Haven, and then gave the demonstration at the Capitoline grounds in Brooklyn.

Goldsmith's denial that Candy Cummings originated the curveball was emphatically refuted by Henry Chadwick, Will Rankin, and Cummings himself. Chadwick noted that he had actually seen Cummings pitch the curveball in 1866, well before Goldsmith claimed to have done so. Cummings said that he had taught the pitch to Avery.[67] And Rankin, in a story titled "Goldsmith's Day Dream," launched a scathing criticism of Goldsmith's article. Countering Goldsmith's assertion that Cummings was not the first to pitch the curveball, Rankin cited Cummings' use of the pitch in 1867, before anyone else, as a matter of incontrovertible historical fact. Dripping with scorn, he proceeded to attack numerous factual errors in Goldsmith's article. Rankin topped it off with this: "Now what is more natural or more in keeping with this illustrious gentleman than the undertaking to make history without having one iota of a fact to weave into his yarn, and that he failed so lamentably is not to be wondered at. But that he should be able to work in so many misstatements is simply marvelous."[68]

Decades later, Goldsmith changed course, but not in the direction of Chadwick and Rankin. On the contrary, he became convinced that he was the inventor of the curveball and was tormented by the notion that Candy Cummings was receiving undue credit for the pitch.

Goldsmith's about-face began in 1924—perhaps not coincidentally, the year of Candy Cummings' death—when, at age 68, he was interviewed for a story in the *Detroit Free Press*. He insisted that he had been tossing curves before Cummings' introduction of the pitch at Harvard in 1867, and that Ham Avery, a philosophy professor and ball player at Yale, helped him develop it. When Goldsmith mentioned that he could make a ball curve, people scoffed at the idea and laughed it off as an optical illusion. But, he said, Henry Chadwick believed it, adding that in 1868, Chadwick arranged for Goldsmith to travel to the Capitoline grounds in Brooklyn to give a demonstration of the pitch. Three posts were set up in a straight line, two on the ends and one in the middle. Goldsmith stood at the post at one end and pitched a ball so that it curved around the center post and swerved back to the third post. "The fans of those days were dumbfounded," said Goldsmith, "but they had to accept the evidence of their eyes."[69]

Goldsmith elaborated on those proceedings in an article under his own byline in *The Sporting News* on March 3, 1932. In this version, his demonstration of the curveball took place not in 1868, but in 1870, and it was arranged, not by Chadwick as he'd previously stated, but because of a story that appeared in the *Yale Journal* on the subject of whether a baseball could be made to curve. In his piece, Goldsmith reprinted an article purportedly written by Henry Chadwick and published in the *Brooklyn Eagle* on August 17, 1870, describing the three-pole demonstration. According to that reprint, Chadwick concluded: "that which had up to this point been considered an optical illusion and against all rules of philosophy was now an established fact"; it was signed "Henry Chadwick—Editor." Goldsmith claimed to have a clipping of Chadwick's article in his possession.

Goldsmith's story, together with the text of the purported Chadwick article of 1870, showed up in subsequent issues of the *Brooklyn Eagle,* and elsewhere. On June 9, 1937, *Eagle* sportswriter Ed Hughes wrote that, a few days previously, Goldsmith had appeared at a park in Detroit, where he was living, claiming that he was the first to pitch the curveball and brandishing a yellowed clipping of what he said was Chadwick's article. Hughes noted, however, the general consensus that Candy Cummings had used the curveball in that Excelsior–Harvard game in 1867, making *him* the first curve pitcher. But a couple of months later, on August 18, 1937, the *Eagle* appeared convinced; it pronounced that the alleged Chadwick article "quite definitely proves that Goldsmith invented the curve."

In March 1939, Goldsmith, then critically ill and bedridden, was interviewed by *The Sporting News*. He had been in bad health for some time, but he took a turn for the worse after reading a review of a film that credited Cummings, rather than himself, with invention of the curveball. "It is said he brooded over the disappointment so much," said *TSN*, "that it brought a relapse."[70] (According to the *New York Post*, the movie that caused Goldsmith such anguish was *A Hundred Years of Baseball,* put out by the National League.[71]) In the interview, Goldsmith again claimed that he had the curveball even before Cummings' use of the pitch in 1867 at Harvard. He added, however, a new contention: that he taught the pitch to Ham Avery. His story appeared in *TSN* on March 30, 1939:

One day in New Haven, Goldsmith recounted, he was walking home, tossing a baseball up and down, when a young fellow, wearing a Yale sweater, came along and asked him to play catch. "He was," wrote Goldsmith, "Hamilton [sic] Avery, at that time a pitcher on the Yale team." Standing on opposite sides of the street, Avery and Goldsmith commenced pitching to each other. Goldsmith decided, "I'd let him have a new pitch I'd worked out," and tossed Avery a curveball; Avery made a dive for it but missed, leaving him "mighty puzzled." Goldsmith pitched four or five more curveballs, after which Avery asked him to come to the Yale ballpark to show it to his teammates.

Goldsmith died on March 28, 1939, two days before the article appeared in *The Sporting News,* which was published weekly. In a perhaps over-dramatized account of his final moments, the *New York Post* reported, "he clutched a yellowed newspaper clipping in his trembling hand as the Great Umpire summoned him."[72] It would have come as a bitter irony to Goldsmith that, a bit over a month after his death, Candy Cummings, who, Goldsmith believed, wrested undeserved credit for inventing the curveball, was elected to the Hall of Fame.

Goldsmith's story—stories, really—do not withstand scrutiny. First, there are his evolving claims as to who pitched the first curveball. In 1898, he said that Ham Avery of Yale was the first; in 1924, he told the *Detroit Free Press* that he'd had the curve even before Candy Cummings used it at that Excelsior–Harvard game in 1867, and that Ham Avery helped him develop it; then, in the 1939 iteration, Goldsmith said that *he* showed *Avery* the pitch while the two were playing catch on a street in New Haven. Incidentally, that story of the game of catch had also undergone an evolution. According to Goldsmith's prior version, it was Avery who helped *him* develop the curveball while playing catch in New Haven.[73]

What about Goldsmith's claim that he had pitched curveballs before 1867? This seems highly unlikely. Goldsmith would have been 11 years old in 1867, and 10 or even younger when he supposedly learned the pitch.

Then there are Goldsmith changing accounts of the demonstrations. First was his account in 1898 about Avery's exhibition, using three posts, in New Haven and then Brooklyn. By 1924, this had evolved into a demonstration by Goldsmith in Brooklyn, also using three posts. Ultimately, Goldsmith's three-post demo found its way into Chadwick's purported article in the August 17, 1870, issue of the *Brooklyn Eagle.*

In fact, Goldsmith's varying accounts of demonstrations of the curveball are suspiciously reminiscent of Cummings' demonstration in Hartford in 1876, and one the following year in Cincinnati. The latter involved Tommy Bond of the Boston Red Stockings and Bobby Mitchell of Cincinnati's Reds, and an array of three barriers, rather like Goldsmith's three posts.[74] That wasn't the only element that Goldsmith appears to have borrowed from other sources. There's also his comment in 1924 that people scoffed at him when he told them that he could pitch a curveball; that brings to mind Candy Cummings' description in 1898 of the laughing and "chaffing" he received from his young friends at his efforts to make a ball curve.[75]

Which brings us to the storied yellowed clipping. Goldsmith first claimed the existence of the clipping in his *Sporting News* piece of March 3, 1932, as evidence that he had the curveball before Cummings. By Goldsmith's account, the clipping, containing an article purportedly written by Henry Chadwick, described a demonstration of the curveball by Goldsmith at the Capitoline grounds on August 16, 1870. Goldsmith would then have been 14; would he have been wowing the baseball world, including the likes of Henry Chadwick, with a new and revolutionary pitch at that young age? Also, as *Eagle* sportswriter Ed Hughes rhetorically asked in his column on June 9, 1937, why did Goldsmith wait so long before alleging the existence of the clipping and challenging Cummings' claim to invention of the curveball? It was, wrote Hughes, "something like a fellow beating Edison to all his inventions and just bobbing up to tell us about it."

There's more. The article in Goldsmith's yellowed clipping was purportedly signed "Henry Chadwick—Editor." But Chadwick was not an editor at the *Eagle* when the article was supposedly published. A notice in that paper on August 1, 1870, just 16 days before the article purportedly appeared, reported that Chadwick had resigned his position with a different Brooklyn paper, the *Daily Union,* to take charge of the baseball column of the *New York Tribune.* The notice added that Chadwick had been with the *Union* for the previous six years, and with the *Eagle* for three years before that. If he had been an editor at the *Eagle* when it published the notice, the notice might be expected to have mentioned that fact, but it did not. On August 8, 1870, a week after the *Eagle's* notice, the *Cleveland Leader* reported that Chadwick had been hired as the baseball editor of the *New York Clipper,* a position that he would hold for well over a quarter of a century thereafter.[76] Yes, Chadwick was a writer for the *Eagle* from 1865 to 1894, contributing baseball and cricket reporting to the "Sports and Pastimes" column of that paper.[77] It was one of several papers in the New York area to which he contributed. But he was not an editor at the *Eagle* in August 1870.

With the death of Goldsmith, his "yellowed clipping" disappeared and has never been found. Researchers looking for the article as originally published have come up empty.[78] A search of the *New York Clipper* has produced no such article on August 17, 1870, or on any other day that year.

Could Goldsmith have been mistaken about the paper in which Chadwick's article appeared? It appears nowhere in the *Brooklyn Eagle* of August 17, 1870, or, so far as can be determined, any other date. The *Tribune,* a weekly, did not publish on August 17, but a search of that paper for the year 1870 has not revealed the article.

Finally, the yellowed clipping is inconsistent with Chadwick's own comments in *Sporting Life* on August 6, 1898, where he wrote that he had seen Candy Cummings pitch the curveball in the summer of 1866, adding, "There is no questioning the fact that Cummings first practically developed the curved ball in pitching long before Goldsmith was known in the base ball world."

The yellowed clipping to which Goldsmith clung supposedly to his dying breath was, most likely, not genuine.

So Goldsmith's claim to have been the first with the curveball doesn't hold water. Connecticut baseball historian David Arcidiacono speculates that Goldsmith might have learned the pitch around 1874 or 1875 in New Haven,[79] but this would have been long after Candy Cummings first used the curveball, and by that time the pitch had spread to several other pitchers. Although, by all accounts, Goldsmith became proficient with the curve, he could not have been its inventor.

There were other hurlers prior to Cummings whose pitches were said to have traveled in curved lines.[80] These claims can't be verified, and many are doubtful. For one thing, the "curve" might simply have been a drop pitch, like Phonney Martin's. For another, it isn't known how those pitchers made the ball curve, if indeed they did. Almost anything could have caused it—an unintended variation in delivery, or a surreptitious scuffing of the ball with the pitcher's belt buckle; the wind; or a deformity in the ball, which was common in the days when the same baseball was used for an entire game, and then for subsequent games. At least one of those claimants, it turned out, wasn't trying to throw curves and didn't know how he did it. Even after controversy brewed over whether it was Cummings or someone else who pitched the first curveball, none of them stepped forward to stake their claims.

Can it be said that no one prior to Candy Cummings ever pitched a ball that curved on its way to the batsman, or at least tried to do it? Of course not. Hurlers were always trying to get an edge over batters who, under the rules that prevailed before the 1870s, held the clear advantage. Pitchers were essentially at the batters' service; their job was to deliver balls that batters could hit and put into play. So finding a way to deceive batsmen, and thus even the odds a bit, was the pitchers' holy grail. It is entirely possible that at some time, in some place, during the early history of the game, there was a hurler who experimented with different deliveries and succeeded in making a ball curve. But none did what Cummings did. It was he who had the inspiration for the curveball and the foresight to realize its possibilities. He likely understood the physical principles involved and found the way to use them to make a ball curve at the will of the pitcher, by using wrist and finger action to cause spin. Doggedly devoting his time and energies over a period of years to analyzing, experimenting, and pursuing his idea, he systematically developed the curveball and ripened it into a useful and potent pitcher's weapon. Candy Cummings' curveball served as a model for other hurlers, and the pitch soon spread across baseball. Although he pitched underhand, his technique is the foundation of the curveball thrown by pitchers to this day. In short, Cummings created the pitch; he was "the inventor of the curveball." No one else has been able to establish a superior claim.

Tim Murnane put it this way:

> There may be some doubt as to who discovered the North Pole, but none whatsoever to the boy who discovered and first brought into practical use the curving of a base ball.... Did Shakespeare write Hamlet? Did Edison invent the kinetiscope [*sic*]? They surely did. Well, just as certain did Arthur Cummings not only discover but was the first to make use of curved pitching.[81]

9

Hop-Scotching to the Stars

"The scepter hath departed from Brooklyn," lamented the *Brooklyn Eagle* on October 11, 1867.

Since 1859, when the baseball world began to recognize a team as champion, the "scepter" had resided in Brooklyn. For most of that time, one club, the Atlantics, reigned. So it came as quite a shock, at least to fans in the City of Churches, as Brooklyn was (and still is) called, when a club from Westchester County, the Unions of Morrisania, wrested the title from the Atlantics.

Over five successive seasons, the Atlantics had defeated the Unions in every match the two teams played. The Unions, for their part, had lost every best-of-three series against top clubs through mid–1867. When the two teams met for their championship series that year, the Atlantics were the clear favorites. But the baseball gods had something different in store. In the first game, played on July 31 at Morrisania, the Unions delivered a severe spanking to the overconfident Brooklynites, beating them, 32–19. The second and deciding game, on October 10 in Brooklyn, was a nail-biter. The Unions emerged victorious, 14–13, and became champions of baseball.[1] "It seemed hard to realize the fact," wrote the astonished correspondent for the *New York Clipper*, "so sudden and so unexpected."[2]

It was generally considered that the Unions' victory was an aberration and that they wouldn't be able to retain the title. Other teams, believing that the championship was up for grabs, began beefing up to try to claim it.[3] One was the Mohawks, one of Brooklyn's newer clubs, founded in 1864.[4] Although a good team, the Mohawks had not figured among Brooklyn's best, but in early 1868 the club began to acquire players. It started by plucking two from the Excelsiors' first nine: catcher Bill Lennon and an outfielder named Tracey, who had been with Excelsior for only a few months. Both were solid players and were expected to strengthen the Mohawks considerably.[5] With an anticipated loss of their veteran infielder, George Flanley, the Excelsiors would have to fall back on its junior squad, including Cummings.[6] (Flanley eventually jumped to New York City's Mutual club.)

But on June 22, 1868, the *Eagle* reported that "two splendid players" on the Excelsiors' junior squad, Cummings and rookie first baseman George Hall, had joined the Mohawks; according to the *Eagle,* there were rumors that "two or three others equally as celebrated" would join them. In fact, both the Mohawks and the Stars had been scrambling to grab Cummings, and it was the Mohawks who emerged victorious.[7] Herb Jewell, who caught Cummings on the Excelsiors, also left the team; he joined the Stars, with a layover at the Mutuals. The Excelsiors' infielder/outfielder, John Clyne, went directly to the Stars.[8]

What was causing the Excelsiors to hemorrhage players, and what was the attraction of the Mohawks? The Excelsiors hadn't been the same club since the loss in 1862 of the best pitcher in the game, Jim Creighton. Through the Civil War years, the team's ranks were depleted by players going off to the battlefields; they muddled along, playing few games and achieving records, but were nowhere near as dazzling as their 18–2–1 season in 1860.[9] With the return of their soldier-players at war's end, they improved in 1866 (13–6–1) and 1867 (11–5)—better, but no match for the Atlantics' numbers in those same years (1866: 17–3; 1867: 19–5–1).[10] The Excelsiors' prospects were certainly not boosted when Asa Brainard, who had taken over pitching duties after the death of Creighton, jumped to New York's Knickerbockers in mid–1867. The Mohawks, on the other hand, were an up-and-coming club, "determined to have a first class nine."[11] There were rumored moves afoot to consolidate the Mohawks with the Stars under the name of the latter club, which would field a team combining the best players from each.[12] That never came to pass, but the prospect must have seemed attractive.

A few days after joining the Mohawks, Candy Cummings played his first—and only—game with the club. It was a friendly match organized by the Mohawks and the Mutuals to give practice to their respective new nines. For eight innings, Cummings and his curveball were fairly effective; his pitches "had, when struck, a decided tendency to go up in the air and were very apt to fall into the hands of some of the warriors who were lying in ambush for them."[13] The final score, which was virtually meaningless, was Mutual 32, Mohawk 17.

Candy Cummings did not appear in another Mohawks game for five weeks. Then, buried in the *New York Herald* on August 12, 1868, appeared a brief note: "Jewell is to be catcher for the Stars and Cummings pitcher." Other former Excelsiors players followed them out the Mohawks' door.

So what happened? We don't know for sure, but it seems likely that the ex-Excelsiors had joined the Mohawks believing that it was on its way to becoming a top-notch team and a credible competitor for the championship. But that didn't pan out. For one thing, the rumored merger with the Stars didn't take place. Baseball historian Peter Morris suggests the further possibility that other top players who had been expected to join the Mohawks didn't do so.[14] At any rate, the Mohawks were left a weakened club; the rumor mill even had it folding, or at least unable to put together a decent game. The team survived, but there was something to

Candy Cummings (right) wearing a Stars of Brooklyn uniform. His teammate on the left is not identified. The bib with the team emblem is typical of baseball uniforms of that period. Cummings pitched for the Stars' first nine—its top squad—from 1868, when he was nineteen years old, to 1871. The Stars were champions of amateur baseball in three of those years, 1869–1871 (The Rucker Archive).

the murmurings: after losing their best players, the Mohawks didn't play a match game until October 8, and they finished the 1868 season with an utterly forgettable record of zero wins and six losses.[15]

Candy Cummings' debut as the regular pitcher of the Stars first nine was on August 14, 1868, against the Olympics of Washington, D.C. Also appearing with the Stars for the first time were Cummings' teammates from the Excelsiors, catcher Herb Jewell and infielder/outfielder John Clyne. The game was played at the Stars' new home field at the Capitoline grounds in Brooklyn. Built in a large area of farmland in the city's Bedford section and named after the Capitoline Games of ancient Rome, the Capitoline opened in 1864. It was a sporting mecca for men and ladies, boys and girls. In addition to baseball, it was used year-round for a host of other sporting activities, including cricket, lacrosse, horseback riding and equestrian events, croquet, bicycling, and more. It was the scene of hot air balloon launches, parades by returning Civil War regiments, and P.T. Barnum's circuses. In wintertime, after the baseball season had ended, a pond on the grounds was a popular spot for ice skating.

The Capitoline's baseball fields—initially one which opened in 1865 and later split into two—were enclosed by a high fence and were well-equipped with grandstands and other facilities. In right field of one of the diamonds was said to be a round brick structure, and anyone hitting a home run over it won a bottle of champagne.[16] The venue was originally the home ground of the Atlantics; then other teams moved there, including three clubs that had occupied the baseball fields at Carroll Park in South Brooklyn: the Mohawks, the Excelsiors, and the Stars.[17]

The Stars' match-up with the Olympics on August 14 was the last game of the Washington club's tour of the Northeast. After a stop in Philadelphia, where they defeated that city's Geary club, the Olympics traveled to New York City and boarded an overnight steamer up the Hudson, bound for Troy. It was the beginning of what would turn out to be a brutal tour of the Empire State.

In their first game, they were embarrassed by the Union club of Lansingburgh, New York, near Troy, 44–8. After defeating the Nationals of Albany, 12–10, in a rain-shortened, five-inning affair, the Washingtonians steamed back down the Hudson for a series of games against clubs in New York City and Brooklyn. The metropolis was not kind to them; they were punished by New York's Mutuals (25–14) and Brooklyn's Atlantics (55–22).[18]

It was after this sorry series of games that the bruised Olympics faced the Stars. The result was yet another loss for the Washingtonians, but at least they weren't humiliated. It was a close one: Stars 15, Olympics 13, in a game defined by light batting and excellent fielding. The Olympics' downfall was the ten runs they conceded to Brooklyn in the fifth inning. For their part, the Stars, behind their new battery, played well; the *New York Herald* heralded Cummings' pitching and Jewell's catching as "first class."[19]

A day after their satisfying defeat of the Olympics, Candy Cummings and the Stars demolished the Harlem club of New York City, 57–9. It was the first of two bloodbaths the Stars inflicted on the Harlems; the second came on October 1, when the Stars slashed and burned to a 76–9 victory.[20] Otherwise, the remainder of the 1868 season was spotty. The Stars did well against lesser clubs (Peconic of Brooklyn, Active of New York, Independent of Brooklyn). But they had their troubles against others. They dropped two to the Haymakers of Troy, 23–16 on August 28 and 25–12 on October 12. The first inning of the August 28 game was a debacle for Cummings and the Stars. In that frame alone, the Haymakers scored 12 times, due in part to their success in punishing Cummings' pitching and in part to poor fielding.[21] On September 12, the Stars lost to the Unions of Morrisania, 17–14; on its face, it was not a terrible result, except that the Stars, behind Cummings, were ahead, 12–0, after two innings, and over the next seven frames managed to concede 17 runs to the Unions while scoring only two of their own. To the *Brooklyn Eagle,* it was emblematic of the "misfortune that has pursued the Star club."[22]

Nevertheless, Candy Cummings' first season with the Stars was an overall success. Prior to his first game on August 14, the team had won only two games and lost six. From the time that he took over pitching duties, they won seven and lost four.[23] The Stars were out of the running for the championship in 1868, but they must have been encouraged by their new hurler.

And what of the championship "scepter"? It returned to Brooklyn on October 6, when the Atlantics snagged the title back from the Unions of Morrisania. But the elation and relief of the Brooklynites didn't last much longer than the flutter of a butterfly's wings; 20 days later, the Atlantics lost the championship to the Mutuals of New York City. Defeat must have come particularly hard to Brooklyn, given that the Mutuals had been organized in 1859 specifically to seize the title from the Atlantics and had failed at every prior attempt to do so, and that, for the first time in the history of baseball, a club from New York would wear the crown as champions. Brooklyn was, as the *Eagle* put it, "in sackcloth and ashes."[24]

The year 1869 was a pivotal one for baseball; it marked the formal introduction of professionalism into the sport. Prior to 1869, the rules of the National Association of Base Ball Players expressly precluded it: "No person … who shall at any time receive compensation for his services as a player, shall be competent to play in any match."[25] That rule had been on the books since the beginning of the NABBP. But it didn't stop clubs from making illicit payments to certain players to secure their services or to lure them from other teams. In his encyclopedic history of baseball, Peter Morris maintains that one of the earliest beneficiaries of such pay-to-play schemes may have been Jim Creighton, the Excelsiors' star pitcher. Creighton, says Morris, received under-the-table payments for several years before his untimely death in 1862.[26] Into the 1860s, some clubs devised other means to compensate players. One notorious example was the Mutuals of New York City. Referred to as "Tammany's Club," it was controlled by the leader of the city's Tammany Hall political machine, "Boss" William M. Tweed, and his cohorts. Tweed saw to it that Mutual players were put on the city payroll, most with no-show jobs, and others with, shall we say, flexible working hours. Another was the National club of Washington, D.C. It lured players with promises of jobs in government departments that required little or no work.[27] In fact, baseball was part of the job description for these posts. Displayed in the museum at the Baseball Hall of Fame in Cooperstown is a newspaper ad placed by the Nationals seeking a first baseman. It offered the successful candidate a "first-rate position in the Treasury Department: must work in the Department until three o'clock, and then practice at base ball until dark." John Thorn, in his biographical sketch of George Wright, lists several players with the Nationals in 1866 and their nominal positions at the Treasury and other government departments.[28]

By the late 1860s, what was previously an open secret had become recognized as an established fact. It was well known that several ball clubs were compensating players by paying them directly or in some other form. Even Albert Spalding, in his book *America's National Game,* admitted that in 1867, he'd accepted a $40-a-week job with a Chicago grocery wholesaler, ostensibly as a bill clerk but in reality to play baseball for Chicago's Excelsior club. "Most clubs of prominence, all over the country," he wrote, "had players who were either directly or indirectly receiving financial advantage from the game."[29] Eventually, the NABBP was forced to face that reality. At its annual convention in December 1868, it recognized that "though a prohibitory rule had been on the statute-books for years, it had been merely a dead letter."[30] Noting that it was impossible to frame a rule on the subject that could not be evaded, and even if it could, would be impossible to enforce, the convention gave in and effectively created two classes of players—professionals: those who played for money or other form of compensation, and amateurs: those who (supposedly) didn't.

Not long afterwards, the NABBP club in Cincinnati, "unwilling to be bound by rules which nobody respected or obeyed,"[31] placed all of its players on salary and formally declared itself to be a professional team. It took the name Red Stockings, from the long red hosiery that accented its new uniform.[32] The Mutuals and a number of other clubs also went professional.[33]

Brooklyn's Stars, however, remained an amateur team—nominally, anyway. In January 1872, the *Chicago Tribune* included the Stars among what it termed "the semi-professional class of amateurs"—those clubs

Hurley, Sub. ;   G. Wright, S. S. ;   Allison, C. ;   McVey, R. F ;   Leonard, L. F.
Sweasy, 2d B. ;   Waterman, 3d B. ;   H. Wright, C. F. ;   Brainard, P. ;   Gould, 1st B

Red Stockings of Cincinnati. In 1869, the Red Stockings team was the first to formally declare itself to be a professional club (A.G. Spalding Baseball Collection. New York Public Library Digital Collections).

which, according to the paper, were sharing gate money with some of its players. By early 1872, however, some of its top players, including Cummings, had moved on to fully professional clubs. The Stars, having realized that their semi-pro status "was not a source of profit or credit to the club as an old amateur organization," decided to abandon the custom of sharing gate money and revert to strictly amateur status.[34]

The division of baseball clubs into professional and amateur had implications for the championship. The title, remember, was conferred by consensus, rather than pursuant to a written league rule. Should amateur clubs vie against the professionals for the same crown? Many thought not, and there came to be recognized two championships, one professional and one amateur.

The Stars entered the 1869 season as the strongest among amateur teams in the region, and they were seen as well-placed to become amateur champions.[35] The *New York Clipper's* pre-season series on "Sketches of Noted Players" was sweet on the Stars' hurler: "Arthur Cummings, of the Star club," it said, "is a young, but first-class pitcher. He is the most noted of the juniors the Excelsiors trained up. He is swift in his delivery, and one who is fast attaining the first rank…. He is a good batsman, is perfectly fearless in facing hot liners, and throws a nice ball to the bases."[36]

The Stars began their 1869 season rather late. Early on, some members of the team got some practice playing on "picked nine" squads,[37] but it wasn't until June that the club began to play regular games. Their first match-up was on June 12, against a lesser amateur nine from Flatbush, the Eagles (a different team from an excellent club of the same name from New York). The Stars shellacked the Eagles, 56–16,[38] positioning themselves nicely for their coming encounter with the reigning champions, New York's Mutuals.

The Stars and Mutuals played their first game of a home-and-home series at the Capitoline, the Stars' home grounds, on June 19. Going against a financially well-endowed professional club, the amateur Stars were considered easy pickin's for the Mutes. No one, even the Stars players, gave the Brooklyn club a chance; according to the *Brooklyn Eagle,* "the Stars themselves did not dream of victory before the game. It would have been impudence to have done so."[39] But to the surprise of everyone, the Stars prevailed, handing the Mutuals their worst defeat of the season thus far.[40] The final score was 26–12. The Stars outplayed the New Yorkers in every aspect of the game, "in the field, at the bat and at [the] pitcher's point." As for the Stars' hurler, Cummings "bothered the Mutuals as they have not been bothered this year."[41] He sent his opponents down without conceding a run in five of the nine innings.

In the re-match, on August 14, the Stars came out on the losing end, although by a small margin, 22–18, despite Cummings' effective pitching. The *New York Clipper,* in fact, paid Cummings the ultimate compliment for his performance in that game, putting him in the same class as the man who was undoubtedly the best pitcher in baseball in the early 1860s: "Cummings delivers the ball with the care and precision of a Creighton." In the rubber game on October 2, however, the Mutuals' victory was decisive: 16–6.[42]

Candy Cummings and the Stars took on other professional clubs in 1869: the Olympics of Washington, D.C., whom the Brooklynites embarrassed, 49–11—"Cummings was too much for them," commented the *Eagle*[43]—as well as Brooklyn's Atlantics, who bested the Stars in all three of their meetings, but by relatively narrow scores in each case. Interestingly, though, the amateur Stars outscored the pros in aggregate by 144 runs to 120.

On September 30, the Stars faced the Oriental club of New York in the first game of what was supposed to be a home-and-home series for the amateur championship. The Stars roundly defeated the New Yorkers, 18–9.[44] But that was it for the series; there were no further games between these two clubs.

The Stars' big challenger for the amateur title was the crack Champion club of Jersey City, New Jersey. The first game of the home-and-home between the two clubs, at Jersey City on September 15, resulted in a 16–13 victory for the Stars. The Jerseyites evened the series at the Capitoline grounds on October 9, greatly outplaying the Stars for a 24–9 victory. For the third and deciding game, the two clubs were back at the Capitoline on October 26. The odds-makers slightly favored the Champions to win the laurels, particularly because of the difficulty Stars batters had shown with the slow pitches of the Champions' pitcher, William Willis. But the Stars took a couple of hours before the game to practice hitting "slows," and during the game they succeeded in knocking the ball all over the park. In the chill wind that prevailed, the gloveless Champion fielders—no gloves were worn in those days—were unable to hold onto the Stars' hard-hit balls. The Champion batters, for their part, "could do nothing with Cummings' swift pitching."[45] With a final score of Stars 27, Champions 8, the Stars, behind the pitching of Cummings, were champions of amateur baseball.

10

A Star with the Stars

The year 1870 was a big one for Candy Cummings. It was the year he became a full-fledged ace with a national reputation. And he got married— twice, actually, to the same woman.

His bride was Mary Augusta Roberts, who lived with her family a few doors down from the Cummingses on East Warren Street in Brooklyn. Born in Middletown, New York, a village in rural Orange County, Mary was the daughter of Charles E. Roberts and Susan (Dingee). Candy and Mary were married on February 12, 1870, in the North Presbyterian Church on West 31st Street in Manhattan. For reasons that aren't clear, they had a second marriage ceremony in Brooklyn on June 29. The Cummings and Roberts families were close: in November, just a few months after Candy's marriage to Mary Roberts, his younger sister Gertrude married Mary's brother, Sam.[1]

Early in the year, there was a rumor going around that Chicago's professional club, the White Stockings, had tried to tempt Candy Cummings with an offer of $2,500 to pitch for the club. But his father didn't like the idea, and Candy remained in Brooklyn as a member of the amateur champion Stars.[2] With most of the Stars' other first nine players from the previous year back on board, the success of the club was expected to continue in 1870.[3] "This is, undoubtedly," declared the *New York Clipper,* "a tip-top nine, and if they will only be punctual at their match games and play each man always on his home position, they ought to achieve a more noteworthy success than they did last year."[4] Punctuality was a problem for the Stars. The team members had day jobs, and for some, it was sometimes difficult to make it to the baseball grounds in time for the scheduled first pitch.

The Stars' first match game of the 1870 season was against the Mutuals, at the Union grounds in the Williamsburg section of Brooklyn. Less than a mile and a half away from the Stars' home field, the Capitoline grounds, the Union was a couple of years older; it had opened in 1862. Like the Capitoline complex, it was originally a skating pond. Encircled by a wooden fence to keep out non-paying and indecorous fans, the Union had baseball's first enclosed grounds.[5]

On May 7, a crowd of a couple of thousand flocked to Williamsburg to see the professional Mutuals take on the amateur Stars. The Mutuals were heavy favorites. Stars fans didn't dare to hope that their team might actually win; they came to see how strong an opposition the amateur champs could mount.[6] They were shocked; the Stars pounded the powerful Mutes to defeat by a score of 14–3. "The Stars gave them such a thrashing," said *Wilkes' Spirit of the Times,* "that Mutual stock went down a long way below par."[7]

The engine of the Stars' victory was Candy Cummings. The Stars "displayed some very fine play," wrote the *Spirit of the Times,* "but it was the grand pitching of Cummings which enabled them to make such an example of the Mutuals."[8] The *New York Sunday Mercury* agreed: "The Mutuals found Cummings to be the most difficult pitcher they had ever faced."[9] In a comment that alluded to Cummings' curveball, the *New York Tribune* added, "Young Cummings outwitted the Mutuals by his method of delivery, and all efforts to get the range of the ball failed."[10] This is borne out by the box score: he held the Mutuals scoreless in six of their frames, and allowed only single runs scattered randomly over three innings. The *Brooklyn Daily Eagle* placed the Stars' 21-year-old pitcher at the top of his craft: "[Y]oung as he is, [Cummings] has no superior today in his position."[11]

Next up for the Stars were the indomitable Atlantics. A Stars–Atlantics matchup was always a big draw, but the meeting of these two clubs just a week after the Stars' triumph over the Mutuals brought fans out to the Capitoline grounds in droves. They all wanted to see if Cummings and his Stars could do to the Atlantics what they had done to the Mutuals. But the Stars fans left disappointed. The team came out on the losing end, 8–1, victims to the Atlantics' great fielding as well as effective pitching by their hurler, George Zettlein, and to their own error-laden defensive play. The only run Zettlein allowed came in the first inning; the Stars posted goose-eggs in their remaining eight frames. That the Atlantics' score was not higher was thanks to Cummings; Atlantics batters "found more or less trouble in hitting Cummings."[12]

Candy Cummings notched more successes in May, including a 15–9 win on May 21 against the professional Eckfords, who had flown the championship pennant for a short while in 1869. He toughed through an illness to secure that victory: "[T]he Eckfords, like the other professional nines, found Cummings a difficult pitcher to punish. Sick as he was he kept their score down to a small figure."[13] In the return match a couple of weeks later, on June 4, he and his Stars beat the Eckfords even more decisively, 24–6.

In mid-June, 1870, Cincinnati's Red Stockings came to town as part of their grand tour of the East, playing against teams from Boston down to Washington, D.C. On their card for June 14 was a game against Brooklyn's

Atlantics. The best team in baseball by far, the Reds had not lost a game since October 1, 1868, when they suffered a 31–12 shellacking by the Atlantics. Their 21-month undefeated streak—with one tie, one win by their opponent's forfeit, and one game that they either won or tied (the full score is not available)—ran 104 games, including a few exhibition matches. So they and their fans were stunned when they were beaten by the Brooklynites, 8–7, in an 11-inning nail-biter. The Reds' loss closed the curtain on the longest undefeated streak ever in the history of baseball.

Four days later, on June 18, it was Candy Cummings' turn to face the Red Stockings. Still numb from defeat at the hands of the Atlantics and fatigued by a heavy touring schedule, the Reds seemed vulnerable. The game was a huge draw. Eight thousand fans showed up at the Capitoline on an excessively hot afternoon to witness the contest between the country's best professional ball club and the best amateur nine. Many of those 8,000 had apparently managed to sneak into the enclosed ball field without paying, since only 5,000 tickets had been sold. The Stars, as was their habit, showed up late, and the first pitch wasn't tossed until 3:35, a half-hour after its scheduled time.

This game was the first time that many Cincinnati players had faced Candy Cummings and his curveball. One of those was George Wright, one of the great players of his era and a superb hitter. As Wright settled into the batter's box in the top of the first inning, the expectant crowd was anxious to see whether he could hit Cumming' benders. Wright was patient. "'Arthur,' being a dodgy pitcher in trying to out-manoeuvre his adversaries, George waited for the passage of a few balls to see what the pitching was like."[14] Satisfied that he had sized up the pitching sufficiently to chance a swing, Wright hit a ground ball that found the gap between the shortstop and third baseman. He reached first base safely and began to toy with Cummings, to good effect.

> The moment Wright reached the base and the ball had been passed to Cummings, Wright began jumping a yard to the right and a yard to the left in a laughable yet annoying manner, the whole causing Cummings to watch with the "tail of his eye," and often hurl the ball unexpectedly to [the] first baseman; this monkeyshine business led, as all expected, to a bad throw ultimately, whereupon Wright made second base amid loud laughter. A passed ball gave him third, and another let him home, thus completing his run before his follower at the bat had struck once at the ball.[15]

After a couple more innings, other Cincinnati batters caught on to Cummings' curve pitching. They figured out that they needed to watch the ball from the moment of delivery until it reached the bat, instead of predicting the location, speed, and spin of a pitch at the time the ball left the pitcher's hand, as they would do with other pitchers. Through the top of the fifth inning, the Reds pushed 11 runs across the plate.

A few batters into the Stars' half of the fifth, a new ball was put into play, replacing one that a Stars batter had hit foul over the fence and was stolen by a souvenir seeker. The new ball, harder and therefore livelier than the first, was probably provided by the Stars, since it was the type of ball its players preferred and used when they could. The Stars batters loved it since they could wallop it all over the field; the softer baseball was more difficult to pound. They took full advantage, cranking out hits and punishing the Reds' crack hurler, Asa Brainard. By the end of the sixth inning, the Stars had tied the game at 11–11. But that was the end of their scoring for the afternoon. In the top of the seventh, Cincinnati showed that they, too, could do damage with the new ball, posting five more runs. That put the score at Red Stockings 16, Stars 11, a tally that remained to the final out.

The Stars' preference for a harder and livelier baseball caused the *New York Clipper* to vent lengthy, and at times snide, criticism. "Any club nine," it said, "can lunge out at the ball and hit it hard, and probably make bases on hits, but it does not necessarily follow that therefore they bat skillfully…. A lively rubber ball admits of this style of batting, and hence it is a favorite with all inferior batsmen who are heavy hitters…. But a dead ball obliges the batsmen to use judgment and skill; … of course, inferior batsmen are opposed to a dead ball."[16]

All things considered, the Stars' defeat by the professional Red Stockings was a respectable result for the amateurs, and Candy Cummings and his teammates could hold their heads high. One newspaper's account of the game took particular note of Cummings' performance: "Cummings pitched remarkably well, considering that he has been sick lately. The Reds found him the most troublesome pitcher of all they had met with."[17]

From the distance of decades, however, Cummings remembered that game not with satisfaction, but rather with some bitterness directed at his teammates. "It was a sore disappointment to me, as I worked hard for victory, and to have it thrown away on muffed fly balls and poor throwing was discouraging, to say the least."[18] Sure, there had been some miscues by Stars fielders. But it was Cummings who, right off the bat, set in motion and then contributed to the events that led to Cincinnati's first run. It was he who gave up Wright's lead-off hit; and it was he who became so rattled by Wright's antics that he threw wildly to first, sending Wright to second, and followed up by delivering to the next batter two off-track pitches that his catcher couldn't handle, allowing Wright to complete the circuit to home. Twelve of Cincinnati's 16 runs were earned, and thus attributable to Cummings rather than to fielding errors. These 12 runs alone were enough to give the Red Stockings the win. But Cummings didn't recall that, or at least didn't record it in his written reminiscence. He set very high standards for himself which, more often than not, he met. He was not loath to praise opposing teams or his teammates when he thought credit was due. Unfortunate instances like this one, in which he blamed others for defeat without acknowledging his own shortcomings that contributed to it, were not typical; they didn't define his character.

On June 25, a week after the Red Stockings game, Cummings demolished the Eagle club of Flatbush, shutting them out by the ridiculous tally of 96–0. "The villagers from Flatbush," reported the *New York Clipper,* "[found] Cummings a pitcher difficult to punish, and run getting an impossibility." Given the score, that was an understatement. It could hardly have been a consolation to the Eagles that only 20 of their opponent's runs were earned; the Stars' other 76 were handed to them by absolutely dreadful fielding by the Eagles.[19] It took only seven innings for the Stars to rack up their 96 runs. At that point, recalled Cummings, the Stars asked the Eagles if they'd had enough. "Yes, and more too," was their reply. And with that, the shell-shocked boys from Flatbush threw in the towel.[20]

After that game, Candy Cummings took a few days off for his and Mary's second marriage ceremony, followed by their wedding trip. The Stars didn't suffer from his absence; even without him, they blew away a couple of teams from Connecticut, defeating the Mansfield club, 44–9 (in five innings) and the Wesleyan college nine, 54–10 (in seven innings).[21]

In his first game after his return, against the Osceolas, an amateur club from Brooklyn, Cummings was rusty. "He was very wild in his delivery," said the *Brooklyn Daily Eagle,* "trying more for speed than for some time heretofore." The contest, on July 12 at the Capitoline grounds, started late because Stars were again tardy in showing up, and only six innings could be played before waning light and a falling rain caused the umpire to end it. This was a mercy to the Osceolas, who at the finish trailed the Stars badly, 39–7, despite Cummings bout of wildness.[22]

Catching for Cummings was no picnic. As the *New York Clipper* observed, to be most effective, Cummings needed a catcher who could handle his "peculiar delivery." The paper explained: "Cummings imparts to the ball such a rotary motion as it leaves his hand, and gives it such a bias to the right or the left, that the catcher is obliged to be on the alert to watch the eccentric rebound in order to avoid passed balls." This delivery, added the *Clipper,* makes "the rebound of the 'twisted' ball exceedingly difficult for the catcher to judge accurately." The risk of passed balls, reckoned the *Clipper,* was two and three times greater than when the ball was delivered without a twist.[23]

But it wasn't only the twist. As shown during the game against the Osceolas, Candy Cummings had begun to use a faster delivery than he had in the past. This made the tough job of being his catcher even more difficult. Catchers in those early days played without mitts, masks, or padding;

wearing such protection was considered unmanly and was thought to be a hindrance to catching a ball. Catchers didn't start using masks until well into the 1870s, and even then, masks were used by only a few.[24] So catchers were prone to injury. Here's one description of what it was like:

> It is no joke to catch for Cummings, or for any of these fast pitchers. There is not a professional catcher in the country with his proper complement of his fingers and thumbs. The ball cannot be handled save with the bare hands. If it be true that a cat in gloves catches no mice, it is no less true that a man in gloves catches no balls. Hence it happens that a regular catcher is constantly enjoying the bliss of having his thumbs forced out of joint, his fingers broken, his nails torn out, the palm of his hand split down double to the bone.[25]

Candy Cummings' regular battery mate on the Stars, Herb Jewell, had caught for him since their days together on the Excelsiors. Cummings liked him and once described him as "the pluckiest man I ever saw behind the bat." That was a reference to Jewell's custom of standing right behind the batsman—unlike most other catchers, who stood well back of the plate for protection—and catching without protective gear.[26]

But there was a feeling among some baseball observers that Candy Cummings might perform even better if he were paired with a catcher more suited to his form of delivery. A hint of this came in an exhibition game played on August 6 to raise funds to benefit the family of a well-known and respected sportswriter for the *New York Tribune,* William J. Piccott, who had died suddenly three weeks previously. The game was a matchup between two picked nines, one composed of the best players from New York clubs, and the other the cream of teams from Brooklyn. Cummings pitched for the Brooklyn side; his catcher was Bob Ferguson, of the Atlantics. In a preview of the game, the *Brooklyn Daily Eagle* said:

> The great novelty of the affair will be the catching of Ferguson, to Cummings' pitching. It has been a common saying, that had Arthur a catcher on whom he might rely, so he could let himself out when he chose, he would be far more effective than now, and would cast into the shade all the pitchers of the period; for that reason, Fergy, with his characteristic good nature, kindly volunteered his services, if Arthur preferred. The "boy" was willing, and will do his best, knowing if Rob [sic] cannot catch for him, no one can; so look out for squalls, for Arthur has let all the reefs out, and will enter the match under full sails, with colors flying.[27]

The Cummings-Ferguson battery was, in the words of the *Eagle,* "invincible," and Brooklyn's nine defeated the New Yorkers, 14–5. "Arthur pitched with rare skill and judgment," said the paper, "while Fergy backed him in a style to bring forth comment of applause from all; indeed, neither Arthur nor Rob ever did better."[28]

In early July, Nat Hicks, the excellent catcher for the Nationals of Washington, D.C., left the club and ended up coming to the Stars.[29] Cummings was well aware of Hicks, not least from having opposed him in games between the Stars and Nationals.

Hicks was just what Cummings needed. Not only was he a skilled backstop, he was also fearless behind the plate. Like Herb Jewell, Hicks didn't shy away from standing right up close behind the batter, thereby risking—and incurring—injury from catching fast and spinning pitches with his bare hands, as well as from rebounds and foul tips. He was one of the very few who could handle Candy Cummings' curve pitching. Peter Morris goes so far as to credit Hicks with being instrumental in enabling Cummings to perfect his curveball.[30]

On August 20, 1870, the Stars took on the Forest City team of Cleveland, a professional club, and played Hicks to catch Cummings; Jewell manned right field. The Stars lost narrowly, 9–7, but Hicks did, indeed, enable Cummings to pull out all the stops. He pitched "swifter than ever before and with more of that dangerous curve he imparts to the line of the ball in delivery," making "fearful work" for his catcher.[31] *Wilkes' Spirit of the Times* reported on the game: "Cummings, 'the seductive pitcher' of the Stars being able to let out his full strength, which he has been unable to do hitherto, in consequence of not being backed up with a thoroughly efficient and practiced catcher. The result was a success, this being, perhaps, the most extraordinary game ever played on a base ball field." The journal went on to describe Cummings' effective pitching: "Whatever was the peculiarity of Cummings' pitching, whether it was the extraordinary speed or the eccentric twist, it was sufficient to baffle the efforts of the Clevelanders to hit it."[32] The same paper, in a year's end review of the 1870 season, adjudged Cummings' pitching in that game to be "one of the finest exhibitions we witnessed throughout the season, and unquestionably proved him to be the finest pitcher in the country."[33]

The Cummings-Hicks combination again proved effective in a game against the Mutuals on September 10. The New York club had suffered a stunning defeat by the Stars back in May, and they came over to the Capitoline grounds for the return match. This time, the result was different. Despite Cummings' pitches, which were coming in "hotter and hotter," the Brooklynites, playing one of their worst games in memory, were soundly beaten, 16–7.[34]

The Stars ended their 1870 season with a game against the Harvard college squad for the amateur championship. The Harvards, one of the top amateur clubs and the champions of the college teams, were already one game up in their home-and-home series with the Stars. On August 13, at the Capitoline grounds, they had handed the Brooklyn men a hefty defeat by a score of 12–6. The second game was played on November 2 at Harvard's Jarvis field—where Cummings had introduced the curveball three years earlier. But he did not make the trip up to Cambridge with his team, due to sickness in his family. The Stars feared defeat without Cummings in the pitcher's spot, but they emerged victorious, 11–7.[35] That tied the series one game apiece. For reasons that aren't clear, no third game was played, so the championship pennant remained with the Stars in Brooklyn.

In November, the *Brooklyn Daily Eagle* ran its wrap-up of the just-ended 1870 baseball season. It was full of praise for Candy Cummings' performance over the year: "Cummings ranks as one of the most effective pitchers in the country, and each season's experience will improve his play."[36]

The 1870 season was Cummings' third with the Stars, and speculation was growing that he might be itching to move on to greener and more lucrative pastures. As early as September, there were rumors circulating that he would be going pro the following year. One had him pitching for the Atlantics; according to another, the Chicago White Stockings had "offered him heaps of stamps to go with them."[37] A few weeks later, there was a report about a new professional club being formed in Indianapolis. Aiming to build a team that would be second to none, its organizers were, according to the report, in communication with "some of the best players in the country for the purpose of enlisting their services." One of their targets was Candy Cummings.[38]

The rumor mill continued to churn into 1871. On March 13, before the baseball season opened, the *Brooklyn Daily Eagle* confidently stated that the Atlantics would be fielding a team with Cummings as its "central star." Eleven days later, however, the paper had to reverse itself. It reported that there was a division in the ranks of the Atlantics: with all of the team's professional players having gone to other organizations, some of the remaining club members wanted the Atlantics to play strictly as an amateur team, while others wanted to remain professional. Continuing with the story, the *Eagle* said: "The Club, in their efforts to secure a first-class pitcher as the nucleus of a strong professional nine, offered Cummings $1,800 a year for his services, but he declined it, or rather did not accept. The Stars say that if he plays at all he will play with them. If he does they should be grateful to him for his liberality in giving up a good salary to play with them for nothing."[39]

All of the gossip came to an end on April 22, when Candy Cummings took to the pitcher's box for the Stars in a pre-season practice game against a "field nine" composed of players from other clubs. To their chagrin, the Stars were defeated by a run, 13–12, prompting the *Eagle* to observe that the game demonstrated the Stars' need of players, particularly a catcher, who could support Cummings properly.[40]

Although Candy Cummings stayed with the Stars, four of the players on the team's 1870 championship nine didn't. One who left was Nat Hicks, the catcher who had paired so well with Cummings toward the end of the 1870 season. He went pro, signing on with the Eckfords. To replace him, the Stars took a backstop named Price. The *New York Sunday Mercury* liked the Cummings-Price battery; "Arthur Cummings," it said, "is still the club pitcher, and has no superior in that position. Price is to catch for him, and as he has plenty of pluck to stand punishment, he will no doubt succeed in that position as well as his predecessors."[41]

Price's tenure with the Stars was short. He caught Cummings in three pre-season practice games against junior clubs and was able to handle his swift curves. But he appeared in only one game after that. The Stars' first big contest of the season was against the professional Olympics of Washington, D.C., on May 26 at the Capitoline grounds. The Brooklynites were without Price, whose father had died the day before, and had to make do by co-opting a platoon of players from the field to submit to catching Cummings' fast, twisting deliveries. Fraley Rogers (normally an outfielder) and Hy Dollard (outfielder and shortstop) were successive occupants of that dangerous place behind the plate, but their hands split, and a third player, the second baseman Breen, was called in to take over. In the end, the Olympics nipped the Stars, 21–20, but neither side made a good showing for itself; of the 41 runs scored, only three were earned, two by the Stars and one by the Olympics, due to "some deplorable muffing in the field by both nines." Some of those were passed balls due the inability of the Stars catchers to handle Cummings' "hot ones."[42] The *Brooklyn Daily Eagle* took the club severely to task. "[T]he moment they found they had no one to support the swift pitching of Cummings," it said, "they should have either tried the slows or changed the pitcher. They could not have done worse in either case than they did by keeping on with the swift pitching with a disabled man in the catcher's position."[43]

Four days later (May 30, 1871) at the Capitoline, Candy Cummings and the Stars hosted Chicago's powerful White Stockings, who were on a tour of Eastern cities. The grounds were sporting a new covered stand, called the "Grand Duchess," with places for around 400 fans. To sit there cost a 15-cent supplement beyond the usual 25-cent price of admission (ladies were admitted to the grounds free), but it was worth it. Located right behind home plate, it offered a full, unobstructed view of the entire grounds; it also provided welcome shade from the hot sun and protection from rain.[44] The *New York Herald's* baseball reporter seemed particularly captivated by the "large number of beautiful young ladies" that the new accommodation had attracted. Spending fully half of his game commentary on this feature, he wrote, "The ladies lent an additional charm to the fine appearance and still finer display of skill on the part of the players."[45]

But back to the game. With Price still absent, the Stars again slotted in Rogers behind the plate. This time, as if in response to the *Eagle's* scolding a few days previously, Cummings slowed down his delivery, tossing "slow twisters" which bothered the Chicago batters considerably.[46] The Stars, however, muffed their way to a 7–1 loss, giving away all but one of Chicago's runs. One bright spot was Cummings' performance: "we never saw him pitch with more judgment and effect than in this game," the *Eagle* said, "for he had practiced batsmen against him, and he outwitted them from the start."[47]

Price was back in the lineup for the Stars' matchup on June 3 against the Forest City club of Rockford, Illinois, another professional organization. But he was sick and could man the catcher's position for only seven innings before he had to be replaced. Fraley Rogers, who had caught Cummings before, had a sore hand; so, in apparent desperation, Cummings took over as catcher in the eighth and Rogers moved to the pitcher's spot. It was another bad showing from the Stars. With the fielders committing 28 errors, the amateur champions ended up losing, 23–10.[48] Sure, the fielders weren't wearing gloves, but 28 errors were excessive even by the standards of the time. The team's malaise seemed to have affected Candy Cummings as well: he was "less effective in his pitching than usual."[49] Overall, it was "about as poor a game as the Stars ever played," said New York's *Sunday Mercury*. "The fact is," warned the paper, "the Stars are not in the condition to play up to their standard, and they had better stop playing professional clubs until they are."[50]

That was Price's last game for the Stars. Badly in need of someone to catch Cummings, they resorted to shifting around their fielders. They picked Tommy Barlow, their shortstop, to serve behind the plate; his position was taken over by Hy Dollard, who moved in from left field. Barlow remained Cummings' catcher for the rest of the season.

The change seemed to reinvigorate the squad. On June 10, sporting new baseball caps, they met the Athletics of Brooklyn, who were challenging the Stars for the amateur championship. In the second inning, after being hit by Athletics batsmen "in a way he despised," Cummings got his curveball working and gave up only three earned runs from that point. The Stars narrowly lost the game, 14–13, but it was "the most closely contested and exciting contest between amateur clubs of the season, in this vicinity."[51]

Ten days later, the Stars, facing a strong professional team, the Forest Citys of Cleveland, played their best game of the season to that point. Both teams, in fact, excelled, prompting the *Clipper* to declare the contest "one of the finest displays of ball playing ever witnessed" at the Capitoline.[52] Forest City "Chicagoed" the Stars, i.e., shut them out, 6–0, but all of their runs were unearned. Five of the six were scored in the fourth and fifth innings, thanks to passed balls by Barlow. Candy Cummings was changing speed frequently, and Barlow was unable to handle his offerings.[53] In its commentary on the game, the *Brooklyn Daily Eagle* counseled, "Cummings should arrange a code of signals with the catcher not only for throwing to first base but for a change of pace in pitching, otherwise the catcher is very apt to pass a ball when the pace is suddenly changed unawares."[54] Seemingly reading the mind of the *Eagle* reporter, the Stars battery restored order from the sixth inning onward, with Cleveland scoring but one additional (unearned) run in the ninth. Overall, the *Eagle* was satisfied with Barlow as Cummings' backstop: "[H]e is, beyond doubt, the most effective man they have had there since Jewell left." The term "Chicagoed," incidentally, had its origin in the humiliating defeat of Chicago's professional club, called the White Stockings, by New York's Mutuals on June 23, 1870, by the "extraordinary score" of 9–0, "a score almost without parallel in the record of matches between first class clubs."[55] The expression rapidly gained popularity and was widely used in baseball reports in the years following.

In July 1871, the *New York Clipper,* then the nation's foremost source of in-depth baseball reporting and commentary, cemented Candy Cummings' reputation as a full-fledged star. Its issue on July 8 commenced a series highlighting notable contemporary baseball players. In a format that ran for more than three decades and covered over 800 baseball personalities, the paper printed on page 1 of each issue a woodcut portrait of an individual player, and a biographical sketch on an internal page. As the first player to be featured, the paper chose William Arthur Cummings. Now, he wasn't the first player to have his picture on page 1. Previously, in 1869, the *Clipper* had run a group portrait of members of Cincinnati's Red Stockings and a few lines about each player; and three issues in 1870 had on their front pages a pair of "Base Ball Celebrities," but without accompanying bios.[56] Candy Cummings was the first to receive individual treatment. The *Clipper* was flattering in its description of him:

> He pitches with great speed for his size and weight, has full command of the ball, and exhibits great skill and judgment in a strategic point of view. His great point, however, is his power to send the ball in a curved line to the right or the left, thus puzzling the best batsmen. He is playing with great effect this season, and in his position now has no superior. He is a gentlemanly young player, plucky and fearless in facing hot balls, and has plenty of endurance.

After dropping a couple of games to the Atlantics, Candy Cummings and the Stars boarded a river boat and sailed up the Hudson to Troy for a game against that city's professional club, the Haymakers. The game had been scheduled for July 31 but was rained out, so it was played the following day, August 1. The Stars lost that game, too, but narrowly, by a score of 9–8. Cummings was again impressive. He gave up only two runs in the first six innings, during which his team scored six. But Troy pulled ahead in the eighth inning and added the winning run in the ninth, which the Stars couldn't answer.

"Cummings surpassed himself," said the *New York World*, "and his manner of delivering the ball troubled the Haymakers more than any other pitcher they have faced this season."[57] But it was a different story in Troy two weeks later.

Back in 1870, the Stars had been contacted by several clubs in the West and Canada, inviting the Brooklynites to arrange a tour to their cities the following year. The Stars, amateurs with day jobs, mainly as clerks, arranged with their employers to take their 1871 summer vacations in mid-August. The first stop of that 1871 tour was back in Troy. In their game with the Haymakers on August 15, Candy Cummings was sailing along through three innings, but in the fourth, he collapsed. The home team "seemed to have got the hang of Cummings' pitching and punished him badly." He gave up a single, two doubles, two triples, and a homer, yielding seven Haymakers runs. The final result was a decisive defeat for the Stars, 11–6.[58]

Following that inglorious start to their tour, the Star nine feasted on clubs in Syracuse (Stars 25, Alerts of Syracuse 5; Cummings only pitched one inning as the ground was so rough and uneven that Barlow couldn't catch him); Hamilton, Ontario (Stars 66, Maple Leafs of Hamilton 6); and Guelph, Ontario, where the Stars defeated the Canadian champions, the Maple Leafs, 28–11. Bigger challenges loomed on the horizon, so Cummings skipped the Stars' next game, in Detroit, and went on to Chicago to rest. He was about to take the Windy City by storm.[59]

There was great anticipation in Chicago for Candy Cummings' appearances. When the city's amateur club, the Aetnas, champions of the West, hosted the amateur champion Stars, Cummings was, reported the *Chicago Tribune*, "the principal point of attraction and interest." He and his club gave the spectators their money's worth. The *Tribune* adjudged the game on August 22 to be "one of the prettiest, most perfect, and thoroughly enjoyable games of the season."[60] Cummings dazzled the assembled fans. "[H]is delivery," gushed the *Tribune's* reporter, "is the handsomest, most accurate, and completely puzzling to the batsman ever seen in Chicago. The number of balls hit and missed, the number of fouls, as well as the number of balls on which strikes were called, was remarkable." Cummings' curveball completely baffled Aetna batters; he was "the most difficult pitcher to punish they had ever faced."[61] He was also a star with the bat. He came up at the top of the ninth inning, with two out, the score tied 3–3, and a man on second. "I thought I would try for the right field fence," he recalled years later. "So I commenced to laugh at and guy the pitcher, and got him a little rattled. He finally … gave me a good ball, which I sent against the fence on a line."[62] The runner on second scored, and the Stars emerged victorious, 4–3.

That evening, wrote Cummings, after a bath and a good supper, he was approached by some of the directors of the Aetnas. They offered him a five-year contract to play for their club at $3,500 per year, plus expenses of moving to Chicago. It was a huge salary by 1871 standards, but Cummings didn't like the city, so he declined. It was a decision he later regretted. "I was foolish," he wrote. "I should have signed. I was told two years after that, that, had I said five thousand, they would have signed me at once."[63]

The biggest game of the Stars' tour was against Chicago's White Stockings on August 23. Again, Cummings "completely outwitted" the opposing batsmen. But the Stars' error-laden play gave that one away, 7–2; only one of the Stars' runs was earned.[64] The Brooklynites weren't happy. The *New York Sunday Mercury* said, matter-of-factly, "[t]he Stars were dissatisfied with some of the decisions of the umpire." They were particularly incensed, wrote Candy Cummings, at a ruling on a play with bases loaded and two out, when a Chicago batter hit a fly ball to the Stars' left fielder. Believing that he had caught the ball for the third out, the Stars began to return to their bench, upon which they were informed that the ump had ruled that the ball hadn't been caught. "We kicked," wrote Cummings, "but it did no good, so we went back to the field, but had no heart to play." As far as the Stars were concerned, they'd been "robbed in Chicago."[65]

After that game, the amateur champion Stars headed to Cleveland for the next opponent of their tour, the Forest Citys.

That was the first time the Stars had visited Cleveland, and the city's press was beside itself with excitement, especially at the prospect of seeing Cummings pitch. Three days before the game, on August 21, the *Cleveland Daily Leader* mentioned that Forest City would be taking on the Stars on the 24th, and noted, "The Stars have with them their celebrated pitcher, Cummings, who is conceded to be one of the best in the business." On game day (August 24), the *Cleveland Plain Dealer* posted the following item: "This afternoon the Brooklyn Stars play with the Forest Citys on the club grounds. The pitching of Cummings, of the Stars, is represented to be something wonderful. All in all he is probably the most celebrated, and not a few regard him as the most effective pitcher in the country." The *Leader,* for its part, couldn't contain its enthusiasm. It mentioned the Stars and Cummings in no less than four places in its August 24 issue. One was on page one: "Lovers of the national game should not fail to be present this afternoon to witness the contest between the amateur Stars, of Brooklyn, and the Forest Citys, as one of the finest and most interesting games of the season can confidently be expected…. Cummings, the celebrated Star pitcher, is with the club, and, of course, is one of the great attractions." On page four of the same issue, the *Leader,* seemingly breathless with anticipation, printed three separate reminders in different locations on the page. There was this: "Go and see the Stars play the Forest City nine this afternoon. It is worth going out to the grounds merely to watch Cummings' pitching"; and this: "Cummings, the marvelous pitcher of the Star club, will toss the sphere in the great game this afternoon. Go and see him"; and this: "Remember the great game of base ball at the Forest City grounds this afternoon."

With such a buildup, the fans expected a great game. In that respect, they weren't disappointed; "the game was very finely played, and interesting first to last," said the *Leader* on August 25. Although Candy Cummings was laboring under a "serious inconvenience, a badly used up finger," the paper assured its readers that his pitching was "nearly as effective as usual. His ease in delivery, grace and effectiveness are truly wonderful, and well fit him to take the front rank among pitchers." In the end, the Stars narrowly lost the game, 9–6, due—again—to errors.[66]

The Stars ended their tour on a positive note, delivering a soaking to Cincinnati's Live Oaks—or, as fed-up Cincinnati baseball fans called them, the "Dead Oaks"—on a rain-dampened field on August 26, by a score of 28–5. The Stars played well and Cummings "maintained his enviable reputation," while Cincinnati's persistently hapless bunch "played a wretched game throughout."[67]

The final big order of business for Candy Cummings and the Stars in 1871 was to wrap up the amateur championship. They played the second

"Arthur Cummings, Pitcher of the Star Club, Brooklyn, N.Y." Cummings, shown here in formal attire, pitched for the Stars from 1868 to 1871 (National Baseball Hall of Fame and Museum).

game of their series with the Athletics of Brooklyn on September 16, and prevailed decisively, 16–5. "The 'Ath's,'" reported the *New York Herald,* "seemed unable to bat the inimitable Cummings, who put the ball in in his very best style."[68] In the rubber match, on September 27, Cummings put an emphatic, indeed embarrassing, end to the Athletics' dreams of the championship. The Athletics' sole run was scored right in the first inning. Their 31 errors certainly didn't help their cause. Cummings and his team nearly shut them out, 25–1.[69]

But the championship crown was not yet fully secure on the heads of the Stars. The reigning champs still had to take on the Aetnas of Chicago, the champions of the West. To that point in the season, the Aetnas had beaten every amateur nine they had faced, including the Stars, whom they narrowly defeated back in August, 4–3, in a well-played game. But the rematch between the two clubs, on October 7, was different. "Cummings not only pitched with more than his accustomed effect," reported the *New York Clipper,* "but he was finely supported, especially by his catcher, Barlow, who bore off the palm in fielding on the Star side."[70] The Stars had their way with the Aetnas, defeating them by the surprisingly lopsided score of 22–4, and retained the amateur championship.

The 1871 season would be Candy Cummings' last with the Stars, and his last in Brooklyn. In his four years with the club, he had grown to become the best pitcher in baseball. He was in great demand. But where would he go next? Professional baseball had formally come into being in 1869, when the Cincinnati Red Stockings became the first avowedly professional club, and the ranks of pro clubs grew quickly in the years following. During his time with the amateur Stars, Cummings received enticing offers from several professional organizations, but, as he later recalled, he "held off a good while, as I did not care much about playing with them."[71] But in 1871, he could resist no longer.

11

Candy Goes Professional

The NABBP's reluctant decision in December 1868 to divide its member clubs into two camps, amateur and professional, didn't work out so well. That was to be expected. Having different interests and different needs, the two categories of clubs cohabited uneasily within the same organization. Amateur teams played only for recreation and enjoyment, and they needed a structure and rules adapted to such play; professional teams had to make money to pay their players, and they sought a framework that advanced their pecuniary interests. One problem for the amateur teams was that the professional clubs, dangling attractive salaries, were able to lure away many of the best amateur players. A big issue for the professional clubs was how to establish a better method for determining the champion, the need for which was brought to light most clearly by a big dispute over which club had won the crown in 1870. Amateur clubs, on the other hand, were not interested in this question. Another problem faced by professional clubs was that some, whether through mismanagement or otherwise, were unable to generate enough revenue to stay afloat. One example is the Union club of Morrisania: in early 1869 it gave up professional ball, which it found too expensive, and resorted to amateur status.[1]

It didn't take long for the rift between amateur and professional clubs to manifest itself. At the NABBP's annual convention in December 1869, one was pitted against the other, each trying to gain control of the proceedings. Henry Chadwick was a staunch opponent of professional baseball. Noting that, of the nearly 1,000 ball clubs in the country, only a handful were professional, he was dismayed at the ambition of the very small minority of professional clubs to take control of the Association "to serve their special interests and to further their personal ends, at the expense of the great majority of the playing fraternity."[2] His influence was felt at the convention. The National club of Albany, New York, an amateur team, moved a resolution "that this Association regard the custom of hiring men to play the game of baseball as reprehensible and injurious to the best interest of the game."[3] It was narrowly defeated, but only after a lengthy and acrimonious debate. The Association did, however, decide to abolish the rule dividing teams into two classes, amateur and professional, and it voted down a proposed rule that would have fixed the status of professional clubs. The delegates, writes baseball historian Bill Ryczek, left the convention "in an ill mood, each with the feeling that things would be different in 1871."[4]

And indeed they were.

At the invitation of the Excelsiors, the amateur clubs convened in Brooklyn on March 16, 1871, and by the end of the evening, they had formed a new organization solely for themselves, the National Association of Amateur Base Ball Players. It was felt that only a clean break from the professionals would enable the amateurs to govern their own affairs, isolate them from "the odium attached to those abuses which have emanated solely from the professional class of the fraternity," and "return to the old social and recreative status of the game."[5]

The following evening, March 17, ten professional clubs assembled in lower Manhattan. The meeting had been proposed and its date agreed to the preceding month, so it was not prompted by the amateurs' actions the previous day. In fact, its original purpose was to deal with administrative matters such as the dates for club tours and the selection of umpires, as well as the establishment of rules for the championship. But following the formation by the amateurs of their own organization, the main order of business became the establishment of a separate organization solely for professional clubs. Thus the National Association of Professional Base Ball Players was born.[6] It is considered by many to be baseball's first major league.

At its inaugural meeting, the National Association also formalized the institution of a championship and adopted a Code of Championship Rules, filling a need for certainty in determining how baseball's champion was to be chosen. To that point, there had been no written rules on the subject; the champion was determined by common understanding within the baseball community, and this led to disputes over the right to fly the championship pennant. The issue had come to a head in 1870, when the Mutuals and Chicago's White Stockings each laid claim to the crown, based on their respective interpretations of convention. Under the new Code, clubs intending to vie for the championship would have to notify the National Association before the beginning of the season and pay a $10 entry fee. Each contesting club would play a five-game championship series with every other club. At the end of the season, the club winning the greatest number of games in these series would be declared "champions of the United States." The NA even decided to purchase a "championship streamer" which the victorious club could fly until the close of the following season.[7]

One of the clubs that founded the NAPBBP was the Mutual Base Ball Club of New York City. Cummings signed with the Mutuals in late 1871, after the baseball season had ended. The moment of his leap from the amateur ranks to the professionals should have been a high point in his advancing, praiseworthy career. But it wasn't.

Candy Cummings was a man of solid character. Newspaper accounts were pretty uniform in describing him as having a quiet, gentlemanly, and courteous demeanor.[8] The *New York Journal* called him "as honest a player as ever lived," adding, "He was thoroughly appreciated and admired by the better element of players and lovers of the game."[9] He also had a strong sense of right and wrong and didn't shy from standing up for what he considered matters of principle, sometimes to the extent of being downright bullheaded. But even as a young adult, he was prone to manifestations of immaturity, especially in business matters.

It would have been a shame if this immaturity were to sully Candy Cummings' otherwise fine reputation. But it almost did, more than once. An early example occurred in late 1871, when he signed contracts to pitch the following season for three different professional clubs: the Haymakers of Troy, New York; the Athletics of Philadelphia; and New York City's Mutuals.

Here are the basic facts of this unfortunate matter, as gleaned mainly from dueling letters written by Cummings and the Haymakers to the *New York Clipper*.[10] On September 26, 1871, the Haymakers dispatched one of their players, Lipman Pike, to meet with Cummings in Brooklyn and try to secure his services for the following season. At their meeting, Cummings said he was willing to sign with the Haymakers provided that they paid him a $300 advance. (It later became clear that the amount of the advance was to be $400.) Pike wired the proposal to the club's directors back in Troy, who responded that they would send the check upon their receipt of Cummings' signed contract. Relying on this assurance, Cummings signed.

Under the terms of the contract document, he was to receive a $2,000 salary, payable in 12 equal installments; however, it said nothing about an advance payment. Not being included within the four corners of the written contract, the Haymakers' undertaking to pay the advance was not legally binding. So why did Candy Cummings sign? Because, he said, he was "green in signing contracts," and he supposed that he was "dealing with men of honor."

Shortly afterward, Cummings signed with the Athletics of Philadelphia.[11] He did so, he claimed, after waiting a while for the advance from the Haymakers, which was not forthcoming.

The Haymakers' version sheds a different light on the matter. They claimed that Cummings had asked for the original and copy of the contract so that he could compare them. The Haymakers became suspicious of this request and withheld paying the advance until they could meet with him.

At the meeting, the Haymakers tendered a check, but Cummings demurred, saying he wanted to be able to assure his wife that the two contract documents were identical. The two sides compared the contracts on the spot, Cummings confirmed they were identical, and they agreed to meet the following day. At that meeting, Pike again tendered Cummings the advance, but he refused it, declaring simply that he would not pitch for the Troy club. On October 9, 1871, he put it in writing: "I hereby give you notice that you will have to get another pitcher for the season of 1872, as you cannot expect me to keep my contract after you broke yours." He added, for good measure, that he felt he had no hope of receiving his agreed salary because the club was $4,000 in debt, an allegation denied by the Haymakers.

Incensed, the Haymakers made it known that they were holding Cummings to his signed contract and would prevent him from pitching for anyone else. The Athletics wanted none of this headache and withdrew from the fray; according to Cummings, the contract with the Philadelphia club was "mutually annulled."

Not long afterward, Cummings signed with the Mutuals for a salary of $1,700.[12] The Mutes appealed to the Haymakers to release him, but the Troy club declined to do so unless Cummings apologized. He did so in a letter to the Haymakers dated February 5, 1872, published by the *Clipper* on February 24. "I had no personal objection against playing with the Haymaker Club," he wrote. "My family were very much opposed to my leaving Brooklyn." This was, of course, different from the excuses that he'd given the Haymakers on October 9, but it was perhaps closer to the truth. In any case, he offered "most cheerfully ... my sincere apology for any of my actions that have been construed by you, gentlemen, as an insult to the Haymaker Club. I assure you, gentlemen, I thought I was right. I wish to deal honorably and trust you may so construe my motives." That cleared the way for the Haymakers to give their release, and for Cummings to join the Mutuals.

It's not clear what Candy Cummings thought he was "right" about. Perhaps, not realizing that the Haymakers' verbal offer of an advance was unenforceable, he felt that he was entitled to break his contract because the Haymakers had broken their verbal undertaking. But in the Haymakers' telling of the story, they had tendered the advance twice and Cummings had refused it.

Neither side emerged from this mess smelling like a rose. Clearly in the wrong, Cummings made matters worse with his shifting stories and his accusation that the Haymakers had acted dishonorably in failing to keep their part of the bargain. That, if the Haymakers are to be believed, was not true. The *New York Clipper* was highly critical of Cummings. In its January 20, 1872, issue, it said, "a player's reputation for skill in any department of the game is a matter of secondary importance to that of being known for his honorable adherence to regularly made engagements…. Cummings' conduct … is anything but creditable to him, and he has lessened his value as a player materially…." Even Cummings' hometown paper, the *Brooklyn Daily Eagle,* had harsh words. Addressing him directly, it advised, "Do not sign any more papers unless you are resolved to honorably adhere to your agreement; and when you feel like writing to the papers and venting your boyish pettiness, take pains to avoid a display of a lack of a knowledge many supposed you possessed, and, above all, avoid kicking down the ladder that helped you attain the creditable position you held before you left the Star club."[13]

But the Haymakers did not distinguish themselves either by hurling public invectives against Cummings, even after he apologized. In their letter to the *Clipper* of February 12, 1872, after childishly suggesting that Cummings had no brains, the club director called him a "fickle-minded youth," "weak and imbecile," and treacherous. Mercifully, once the 1872 season began, the affair passed into obscurity.

In January 1872, the *New York Clipper* reported that the Mutuals had designated three players to pitch for them in 1872. The regular starters would be Cummings and John McMullin, a pitcher and outfielder salvaged from the Troy Haymakers. George Bechtel, an outfielder and occasional hurler taken from the Philadelphia Athletics, would serve as the "change pitcher," that is, a reliever.

Typically, teams in that era carried one regular pitcher, who was expected to pitch the entire game. If he was injured during play or couldn't continue for some other reason, one of the fielders was tapped to relieve him. The *Clipper* had for some time been advocating that clubs carry two regular pitchers. Its point was that one hurler may have success against some opponents but be punished by others; a second pitcher could pick up that slack.[14] Starting in the 1870s, rosters would also carry a change pitcher to take over when needed; when he wasn't, he would play in the field. Still, starting pitchers usually weren't replaced; they just soldiered on to the end. On at least one occasion in 1872, Candy Cummings pitched while sick. It was on August 8, an excessively hot day in Brooklyn, when the Mutuals hosted the Baltimore club. Cummings felt so ill that it was thought he might not be able to take the ball that day. But he showed up at the last moment and slogged through 12 stifling innings. For 11 of them, he was somehow able to hold the Baltimores to an 8–8 tie. But in the top of the 12th, he had nothing left in his tank, and he gave up four more runs for a 12–8 Baltimore victory.[15]

The *Clipper* wasn't terribly enthusiastic about the Mutuals' slotting Cummings as one of their starters. The upcoming season, noted the paper, would be his first in the professional arena. With the Stars, he had been "'monarch of all he surveyed,' and acted as he chose," but he would find things quite different with a pro club.[16]

One might wonder whether the *Clipper's* view of Candy Cummings might have been soured by his signing-with-three-clubs escapade, of which the journal had been strongly critical. On paper, the choice of Cummings to be one of the Mutes' starters seemed compelling. Although he had been an amateur, by 1871 he had become known as the best hurler in the business. McMullin did have more experience against professional batsmen; but pro hitters weren't completely unfamiliar to Cummings, who had pitched against professional clubs on several occasions with the Stars. McMullin, moreover, had a troubled 13–15 record with Troy in 1871, a performance notable only for his having led the pros in hits allowed, walks, runs, and earned runs.[17] As it turned out, Cummings pitched nearly all the Mutuals' professional games in 1872. McMullin pitched in one of the club's contests and relieved Cummings after seven innings in another, and Bechtel pitched two innings of an exhibition game, after which he was relieved by Cummings. Otherwise, McMullin and Bechtel occupied their usual positions in the outfield.

As foreseen by the *Clipper,* Cummings encountered more challenges pitching in the professional arena than he did in the amateur circuit, where he was king. The youngest of all professional pitchers, he faced better hitters and competed against better opposing pitchers than he did as an amateur, and he also had a more punishing schedule. No longer the top of the heap, he was now in the company of a few hurlers who excelled in their craft. This was reflected in the fact that he received less frequent, and with some exceptions, less fawning press coverage than he had during his time with the Stars. An example of his new baseball environment was a contest between the Mutuals and the Boston Red Stockings on May 8. Described by the *Clipper* as "a test match in the trial of strength in the pitching departments of the two clubs,"[18] the game featured Cummings against Al Spalding, who dominated the National Association and led the league in wins all five years of its existence.[19] Spalding was in top form in this game and outpitched Cummings for a 9–2 victory over the Mutes. In its report on the game the following day, the *Brooklyn Daily Eagle* commented, "The weak point of the Mutuals in this game was the pitcher's position, where, too, their opponents were the strongest, and yet Cummings pitched just as he usually does when effective with other nines; but he had no novices to face him in this game." Nevertheless, Candy Cummings did himself credit in 1872.

Over the course of the season, Cummings and the Mutuals thoroughly dominated two professional clubs, the Eckfords of Brooklyn and the Mansfields of Middletown, Connecticut. The Mutes won all of the games they played against each of those teams, some by embarrassingly large margins. Early in the season, on April 29, they Chicagoed the Mansfields, 12–0, on the strength of Cummings' pitching. He held the Mansfield batters, utterly unable to hit his offerings, to only three scattered hits. In commenting on that game, the *New York Herald* wrote, "without doubt Cummings is the most difficult man to bat that ever pitched a ball."[20] Later in the season, the Mutuals posted football-score margins against the Mansfields of 26–9 (on July 27) and 14–3 (on August 5). They overwhelmed the Eckfords, 24–6 (on May 18) and 27–8 (on June 29).

Another team that Candy Cummings and the Mutes handled with relative ease was the Forest Citys of Cleveland. In the three games they played in 1872, the New Yorkers rolled over the Cleveland team twice, 15–6 on May 21, and 20–1 on July 4, when Cummings' pitching was "never more effective or better supported."[21] In between was an 11–4 loss to Cleveland on June 15.[22]

Albert Goodwill Spalding, one of the top pitchers of his time. Manager and then president of the Chicago White Stockings, he also founded, with his brothers, a widely successful sporting goods empire, and published baseball guides and other books on the sport. Spalding was elected to the Baseball Hall of Fame in 1939 (A.G. Spalding Baseball Collection. New York Public Library Digital Collections).

The Mutuals were more evenly matched against the top-tier clubs in the National Association: Baltimore's Canaries, the Boston Red Stockings, and the Philadelphia Athletics. Of the 11 championship games between the Mutes and Baltimore during the season, four went into extra innings, and two ended in ties (including one of the extra-innings games). Baltimore won five of the games that ended in a decision, and the Mutuals four. In composite runs, Mutual scored 89 to Baltimore's 94. The only blowouts were the season opener between the two clubs on April 22, 1872, won by Baltimore, 14–8, and a bigger one on October 4, in which the Mutuals returned the favor, 18–8, thanks largely to 35 errors committed by the Canaries.[23]

Against the Boston Red Stockings, the Mutuals won only two of the nine championship games played. Six of their seven losses came in their first six contests with the Red Stockings; they didn't win one until September 7. But the two teams were more evenly matched than these raw numbers indicate. Several of the games were exciting contests, and most were close, with only a run or two being the difference between victory and defeat. Coincidentally, three of the games ended with the same score, 4–2, the Mutuals losing on each occasion. The final match game between the two clubs, on September 21 in Boston, was "one of the most exciting contests which ever took place in the ball field in this city."[24] The Mutuals had a three-run lead after eight innings, but in the ninth they allowed Boston to score four times for an 11–10 win.

Candy Cummings performed reasonably well against the Red Stockings; most of the time, Boston's batters found it difficult to handle his pitching. An exception was a 9–2 Mutuals loss on May 8, in which Boston batsmen pummeled Cummings' "deceptive" horizontal curves for 17 base hits and eight earned runs.[25]

As the *Clipper* saw it, both teams were relatively evenly matched in terms of ability. The Mutuals' losing record against the Red Stockings, it posited, was due not to inferior play, but to "a lack of discipline, good generalship, and harmony in working together," areas in which the Boston club was superior.[26] Not only that: many games ended up as tests of strength between two top pitchers, Cummings and Boston's Al Spalding, and Spalding usually won out.

Candy Cummings had a heavy workload in his first season as a professional. Between April 22 and November 1, 1872, the Mutuals played 69 games against professional clubs (56 for the championship and 13 exhibition games)[27]; Cummings pitched in at least 65 of them (54 championship contests and 11 exhibition games), possibly 68. Box scores for three of the Mutes' games (one for the championship and two exhibition games) have not been found, but it's probable that Cummings pitched in most or all of them. In addition, the Mutuals played seven games against amateur clubs, of which Cummings pitched at least six. (A box score for the "possible" seventh game has not been found.) That makes a total of 71–75 games that he pitched over the season, far more than the 40 or so he'd worked the previous year with the Stars. According to retrosheet.org, he led the league in games pitched in 1872.

Typically, Candy Cummings pitched three times a week and sometimes four. In all but two of his appearances, he tossed complete games, including the 12-inning feat of endurance on August 8 when he pitched while sick. Considering that seven games went extra innings, one was called after eight, in one Cummings went seven innings, and in another he replaced the starter after two, the total number of innings that Candy Cummings worked in 1872 was somewhere between 652 and 688.

When compared with starting pitchers today, Candy Cummings' pitching load was extraordinary. Modern major league clubs typically carry four or five starting pitchers and numerous relievers. Over a 162-game regular season, the average maximum number of games begun by each starter, assuming he is healthy and available the entire season, would be 32–40 (depending on a four-man or five-man rotation); the actual number of starts would be less, taking into account absences due to injury or other reasons. In 2018, the average number of innings pitched by each MLB team's starters was 868. In a four-man rotation, each starter would have worked 217 innings on average; in a five-man rotation, each one would have tossed 174 frames. Further, the typical starter lasted roughly 5.4 innings per game.[28] Complete games are rare today; in 2018, the 30 MLB teams played a total of 4,860 games; in only 42 did one of the pitchers toss the entire game—an average of less than one in 100 games. Compare all that to Candy Cummings' 652-plus innings pitched over more than 70 games in 1872, *all but one a complete game,* working three or four times a week. True, moundsmen today, pitching overhand, are throwing much faster and putting greater strain on their arms than did Cummings and other pitchers of the 1870s—they weren't throwing 90–100 mph heat in those days; and even in games in which Cummings was being punished by opposing batters, he completed the game, whereas today, a pitcher encountering trouble would be lifted for a reliever. But still, the workload difference is remarkable.

Candy Cummings' rookie year as a professional ball player was a success. In his era, pitchers weren't credited with wins or charged with losses, as they are today.[29] That was a legacy of the fact that, up to the late 1860s, the pitcher played only a supporting role on the field; his job was to deliver the ball so that the batter could put it into play. It also reflected the fact that many games were lost by virtue of "muffs"—fielding errors—of which there were many in the typical game, rather than by the lack of skill of the pitcher. Fielders, remember, were handling batted balls in flight and on the ground without gloves. But of the 54 professional championship games in which Candy Cummings is known to have pitched, the Mutuals won 32 and lost 20—some due to poor fielding rather than ineffective pitching—and two ended in ties. If those wins and losses were credited to Cummings, as they would be today, he would have a winning percentage of at least .615; if the additional game for which a box score hasn't been found—a win—is taken into account, his record would jump to .623. That placed him among the top four National Association pitchers of 1872 in the win percentage category.

What those raw figures don't show is that, over the course of the 1872 season, Cummings demonstrated that he'd mastered the art of "strategic pitching." According to Henry Chadwick, it was what distinguished an excellent hurler from all the rest. A pitcher may have a good fast ball or curve-ball, wrote Chadwick, "and yet, from his ignorance of strategic play or 'head-work,' as it is technically termed, he will rank only as second-rate in the position." Chadwick defined strategic play as "a resort to legitimate artifice to blind the judgment" of the batter, and summarized its elements this way:

> First, to deceive the eye of the batsman in regard to the character of the deliv-ery, as to its being fast or slow. Secondly, to deceive his judgment in reference to the direction of the ball when pitched to him, as to its being high or low, or put where he wants it. Thirdly, to watch the batsman closely so as to know just when he is temporarily "out of form" for making a good hit; and fourthly, to tempt him with a ball which will be likely to go high from his bat to the outfield and be caught.[30]

An effective pitcher, added Chadwick, will have at his command a "well disguised change of pace," as well as a curveball of which he has such control that he can deliver it just where he wants it to go.

Cummings was well aware of the need for a pitcher to use his head. "If a pitcher uses judgement and remembers his batters," he wrote, "he will soon find their weak point, and should then take advantage of it. You will find there is a certain height where a batsman is weak, and that is the spot to put every ball.... Whenever a batter made a long safe hit off me I remem-bered where I pitched that ball, and he did not get any more near that spot if I could help it."

Few pitchers met the demanding requirements of strategic pitching in 1872. The best, according to Chadwick, was Al Spalding of Boston's Red Stockings.[31] Cummings was another.

One example of his cunning occurred in a game between the Mutu-als and the Athletics of Philadelphia on June 1, the first meeting of the two clubs in the season. The game was played in Brooklyn, before a large crowd of about 5,000. Most of them came expecting to see the hard-hitting Athlet-ics emerge victorious. So did the bookies, whose money was put heavily on the Philadelphians.

The two opposing pitchers performed equally well, the deciding fac-tor in the game being better fielding on the part of the Mutes. On the whole, Candy Cummings had good command of his pitches, and the Athletics found him difficult to punish. The Mutuals eked out a narrow victory, 3–2, both Athletics runs being scored in the sixth; otherwise, Philadelphia's box score was filled with zeroes.

Candy Cummings' real mettle, however, was demonstrated in the eighth inning. With the bases loaded with Athletics, two out, and the Mutu-als ahead by a run, Ned Cuthbert came to the plate. "This was a trying moment for Cummings," said the *Clipper*, "but he proved equal to the emer-gency." With the count two balls and two strikes, Cuthbert was potentially one pitch away from either striking out or walking and forcing in the tying run—only three balls were required for a walk at that time. Cummings, who watched his opposing batters carefully, noticed something, suggesting to him that Cuthbert had lost his nerve. "Cummings, seeing him hesitate, sent in a ball over the plate and just where he wanted it, and 'three strikes, striker out,' was the just call of the umpire."[32] That one pitch saved the game for the Mutuals.

After badly losing the return match, a 19–0 Chicagoing on June 8 in Philadelphia,[33] Candy Cummings and the Mutuals got their revenge at the next meeting of the two clubs, on July 13. They shut out Philadelphia, 8–0, in a masterly display of strategic pitching by Cummings. It was, according to the *Brooklyn Daily Eagle,* "not only the most signal defeat ever sustained by the Athletic club, but the first time in their history they were ever 'Chicagoed.'" Cummings, said the *Eagle,* "seems to have got the measure of the Athletic batsmen, if we may judge from the way he outwitted them in this game…. The way Cummings varied his pace and watched his batsmen was decidedly the best display he has yet made this season."[34] The baseball writer for the *Clipper,* presumably Henry Chadwick, agreed; "We never saw a pitcher outwit his opponents so thoroughly as he did the Athletic batsmen on that occasion," he wrote.[35]

Strategic pitching and headwork are certainly among the attributes of a successful pitcher. Also needed, however, is the support of a skilled catcher who can also handle the hurler's particular style of delivery.[36] Among the professional pitchers, Cummings, with his curveball, "pacer" (fastball) and change of pace, was the hardest to catch.

Before the 1872 season formally opened, it had been expected that the Mutuals' catcher would be Charlie Mills.[37] But then the club enticed Nat Hicks, who had been with the Eckfords the previous year, to join them as well. It was a great get for the Mutes, and for Candy Cummings; Hicks had superbly backed up Cummings in 1870 when they were both with the Stars.

Early in the 1872 season, Mills caught three games for the Mutes and Hicks was used as their right fielder. But a loss to Baltimore on April 22 (14–8) in which Mills caught Cummings, and a wipeout of the Olympics of Washington, D.C., on April 23 (Mutuals 25, Olympics 5), with a Cummings–Hicks battery, convinced the Mutes to make Hicks their man behind the bat for the rest of the season.[38]

At year's end, Chadwick, writing in the *Clipper,* placed Hicks "among the most effective catchers of the season."[39] He was just what Cummings needed. Curveball, change of pace, fastball—Hicks could handle it all. That, his skill in fielding foul balls and foul tips, and his quick and accurate throwing to nab baserunners, ranked him among the best catchers on record.

The focus of the National Association's 1872 season had been the quest for baseball's crown. When the season opened, 10 clubs were in the competition, but by August, three of them had ceased operations. Topping the remaining seven, and emerging as champion, were Boston's Red Stockings, who won 39 games against the other contenders; their closest rivals were second-place Baltimore with 35 wins, and the Mutuals with 34.[40]

At the end of 1872, Henry Chadwick rendered his assessment of pitchers in the professional league. He gave top honors to Al Spalding of the Boston Red Stockings, whom he termed "the most effective pitcher of the past season." The only other two of the same caliber were Dick McBride, "the most experienced pitcher now in the professional fraternity," and Candy Cummings. Cummings, according to Chadwick, was "one of the most effective" of the season, especially when he had a good catcher to give him the necessary support. "Cummings is plucky, endures well, keeps his temper, and is gentlemanly in deportment. His great fault has been a boyish fickleness of disposition. As a pitchist of the period, viz: a swift underhand thrower of skill and judgment, Cummings undoubtedly ranks A No. 1."[41]

With his first years as a professional ballplayer behind him, it was time for Candy Cummings to move on.

Candy Becomes a Lord

In late October 1872 came the news that Candy Cummings had signed with the professional club in Baltimore to play for the following year. He would trade places with Bobby Mathews, who had pitched for the Baltimores in 1872 and would take Cummings' spot as pitcher for the Mutuals.

Candy Cummings in 1873, when he was twenty-four years old. That year, he played for the Baltimore club in the National Association of Professional Base Ball Players (National Baseball Hall of Fame and Museum).

According to the *New York Herald,* Cummings had been enticed to the "Monumental City" by a $2,000 salary "and a well stocked gentlemen's furnishing store."[1] Actually, his salary in 1873 was only $1,800, but that was still considerably higher than the average for pitchers at that time, and he was the highest-paid member of his team.[2]

The club called itself the Lord Baltimores, in homage to the second Lord Baltimore—Cecil Calvert—the British peer who established the Maryland colony; its uniform shirt bore Lord Baltimore's escutcheon.[3] But sporting yellow pants and yellow and black argyle socks—yellow and black being the Calvert family colors—the team was popularly known as the "Canaries."[4]

One of Candy Cummings' teammates on the Lord Baltimores was Lip Pike. In 1871, Pike had played a role in Cummings signing with three different teams to play in 1872. Pike was the one who negotiated with Cummings on behalf of one of the three, the Haymakers of Troy, New York.

Initially, the Baltimores intended to rely exclusively on Cummings to do the pitching; the team roster did not include a change pitcher. To the *New York Clipper,* this was a mistake: "no pitcher can be depended upon to go through with a season's work scatheless of injury or insured against disability from sickness. Besides, there is not a pitcher in the fraternity that cannot be successfully punished by one or more of the existing nines."[5]

As for Cummings' battery mate, Nat Hicks, who backed up Cummings so well the previous season, was remaining with the Mutuals, so the Lord Baltimores planned to use Scott Hastings as their primary catcher. Hastings had been with the Canaries in 1872, having moved over from the Forest Citys of Cleveland in August of that year. The *Clipper* thought highly of him. "We have seen some splendid catching by Hastings," it said, "and some of the very best of throwing to second base." "[I]n facing accurate pitching, [he] has no superior." But the question was, how would he do at catching Cummings? Hastings, noted the *Clipper,* "has yet to be tried against Cummings' delivery, the most trying and difficult to attend to properly that a catcher ever had to deal with."[6]

The Canaries' change catcher would be Bill Craver, another holdover from the 1872 Baltimore nine, who also played infield and outfield. (In 1877, Craver would have the distinction of being banned from baseball by the National League for his alleged involvement in a game-fixing scandal.[7])

As the Canaries' 1873 campaign for the championship unfolded, the Hastings/Craver idea didn't go exactly as planned. Baltimore began the season with Hastings behind the plate, and the combination of Cummings and Hastings proved effective in the first two games. The Canaries dominated Washington's Nationals, 7–1 (Washington barely avoiding being Chicagoed by scoring a single run in the ninth) and 18–2.[8] In the third game, however, on April 26, Baltimore was handed its first loss of the season by the Athletics of Philadelphia, 11–4. Although Cummings "pitched pluckily," Hastings, according to the *Clipper,* "was scarcely active enough to catch behind Cummings, and would show better advantage at second [base]."[9]

That might have been enough for the Lord Baltimores' player-manager, Cal McVey. Hastings was out of the lineup for the next three games, April 30, May 1, and May 5, and McVey, who had been manning second base for the Canaries, slotted himself in as Hastings' replacement. McVey could catch; he had been the Boston club's backstop in 1871 and 1872. In fact, his versatility enabled him to play every position on the diamond (he would add pitcher to his repertoire in 1875).[10] But in the *Clipper's* view, "McVey is a catcher who is not at *home* in the position. He plays finely there as he would any where in the field, but he does not excel in that special position as others do."[11] In any case, Hastings joined Craver on the bench as a substitute catcher,[12] and McVey served as the Canaries' primary backstop. Over the season, McVey logged 25 game appearances behind the plate; Craver caught in 22 games, and Hastings, initially foreseen to be the club's principal catcher, only 19.[13]

In his time wearing yellow pantaloons and Lord Baltimore's crest, Candy Cummings pitched all but one of the Canaries' regular games—42 in total—all from start to finish. His team won 28 of those games and lost 14. If wins and losses were attributed to the pitcher, that would give him a .667 winning percentage. His ERA came in at 2.80, a slight improvement on his 3.01 average with the Mutuals the previous year. These stats placed him third among pitchers in the National Association in 1873. Cummings also showed some flair with the bat; his .250 batting average was the highest in his professional career.

Behind Candy Cummings' pitching, the Lord Baltimores completely dominated three opposing clubs: the Nationals of Washington, D.C.; the Resolutes of Elizabeth, New Jersey; and the Marylands, another NA team from Baltimore. The Canaries won every game that Cummings pitched against these three. True, they weren't very good teams; they finished as the bottom three in the 1873 standings. But Cummings, with excellent support from Canaries batters, defeated each of them by decisive, if not ridiculous, margins.

The biggest thrashings came in the three games that Cummings pitched against the Marylands: 26–5 on May 14, a 20–0 Chicagoing on June 27, and a 35–1 near-shutout on June 30. In the 12 games Cummings pitched against these three teams, the Canaries scored in the aggregate 208 runs—17.33 runs per game—to their opponents' 55.

Just escaping inclusion in that group were the Atlantics of Brooklyn. The Canaries lost only one of Cummings' six games against that club, on May 7—but just barely. In the ninth inning, Baltimore, needing a run to tie the game and two to win, had two men on base, but they were left stranded.[14]

More troublesome to Cummings were the two top clubs of 1873, Boston's Red Stockings and the White Stockings of Philadelphia. Against the Boston nine, which won the championship, Cummings' team won two and lost three, and its record against Philadelphia, which finished number two in the standings, was 2–5. Both clubs seemed to have caught on to Cummings' pitching, with some exceptions. In both victories against Philadelphia, on May 10 (7–4; "one of the most exciting [games] ever witnessed in Baltimore") and August 7 (5–4; "The game was in every respect one of the best played of the season"),[15] Cummings limited his opponents to two

Cal McVey in 1874, when he was with the Red Stockings of Boston. An excellent hitter, McVey was Candy Cummings' sometime catcher on the Baltimore club in 1873 (A.G. Spalding Baseball Collection. New York Public Library Digital Collections).

earned runs in the first game and one in the second. And on June 9, the Canaries thoroughly outpitched and outfielded Boston, 14–6, Cummings allowing only three earned runs.[16]

Then, in late August or early September, Candy Cummings managed to incite another furor that almost ended his career.

The Lord Baltimores had been having financial troubles for some time. Operating at a loss, the club was unable to meet its payroll, and several unhappy players demanded an explanation.[17] But Cummings, claiming that the Canaries owed him $82.73 in salary which it refused to pay, went farther. Not long after his game on August 26, a 17–9 victory over Brooklyn's Atlantics, he quit the club and left town. In mid–September, the club discharged him and imposed a penalty for absenting himself without sufficient explanation.[18] Cummings thereupon signed with the Philadelphia White Stockings to play the following season.[19]

At first, Cummings gained sympathy for his position—until the Lord Baltimores counter-punched by pointing out that Cummings had actually overdrawn his salary account. In fact, said the Canaries, he had always kept ahead by taking pay from his account, so that the club never had a chance to fall in arrears.[20]

When the matter was brought before the National Association's Judiciary Committee in January 1874, it showed little tolerance for Candy Cummings' actions. It censured him for leaving the club in the manner in which he did, but decided to release him from the penalty that the Baltimore club had imposed. Should he engage in such conduct again, warned the committee, he could be expelled from the National Association.[21] The committee's decision did not affect his discharge by the Baltimores, which remained in effect.

But there was possibly more to the story. According to the *New York Clipper*, there were rumors afoot that the Philadelphia club had induced Cummings to act in this "indefensible manner," in order to lessen the chances of the Canaries winning the 1873 championship.[22]

No doubt, the White Stockings would like to have seen Cummings out of the picture for the rest of 1873. By September 1, the Lord Baltimores comfortably occupied the top spot in the NA standings with 29 wins, 28 of them with Candy Cummings in the pitcher's spot. After the Canaries, the Boston Red Stockings, with 20 wins, and Philadelphia, with 19, were neck-and-neck. And Baltimore had no one of Cummings' quality to replace him. They did have on their roster Asa Brainard, who had been a star hurler in the years before professional baseball; in fact, it has been said that the term "ace," referring to a superlative pitcher, was derived from his first name.[23] By 1873, however, at age 34, his career was in definite decline, and Baltimore used him mainly at second base and in the outfield. So the

White Stockings could potentially gain from a Baltimore squad weakened by Cummings' absence.

But did the White Stockings really consider Candy Cummings that much of an obstacle to their pennant ambitions as to resort to shenanigans to remove him from the scene? In 1873, they defeated Baltimore in five of the seven games in which they faced Cummings. Although a couple of those games were decided by a single run—a Philadelphia 13–12 loss on July 4, and a 5–4 win by Philly on August 7—the White Stockings otherwise seemed to have been able to handle his pitching.

In the end, Cummings' absence from the Lord Baltimores did improve Philadelphia's fortunes, but it didn't win them the championship pennant. Boston's Red Stockings went on a 23–4–1 tear in September and October. They ended the season with 43 wins, more than any other National Association club, and thus the NAPBBP's Championship Committee awarded them the pennant. A protest was lodged by the Philadelphia club, which claimed that Boston had used an ineligible player during the season. The NA's Judiciary Committee, however, rejected the protest, and the award stood.[24] Philadelphia came in second, with 36 wins.

Baltimore ended up in third place with 34 wins, only two fewer than Philly and nine behind Boston. After Candy Cummings' departure from the Canaries, all but one of their remaining games were pitched by Asa Brainard. In those games, Brainard recorded only five wins against eight losses and one tie. So Cummings' absence could very possibly have cost the Baltimores the number two spot.

For his regrettable, even juvenile, actions in this affair, Cummings incurred a severe lashing from the pen of Henry Chadwick, a strict moralist, writing in the *New York Clipper*:

> No pitcher had better opportunities to rise, or to earn a good reputation in the professional arena, than Arthur Cummings, and no one has thrown away his chances so boyishly. We do not think Cummings would "sell" a game or prove dishonest to a club, but he has certainly not acted judiciously in his dealings with the club managers who have engaged him, and hence he has incurred the odium of tricky actions to an extent which has largely offset his marked ability as a swift and able pitcher. He has plainly illustrated the truth of the remark that the professional ball-player's reputation for fair dealing is more valuable as capital than all the skill he may possess as a player. At one time Cummings could have commanded $3,000 salary for a season's play. Now he obtains but a third of that amount; and yet, as far as his pitching goes, he is even a better player than before. Straightforward, manly dealing is the only rule that pays in the long run.[25]

Actually, Chadwick understated Candy Cummings' 1874 salary with Philadelphia; it was $1,500. Although a come-down from the $1,800 under his

1873 contract with Baltimore, it again made him the highest-paid player on his new team.[26]

So Cummings' career survived, and even thrived.

The Philadelphia club was the new kid on the National Association block in 1873. In its first season as a NA team, it did remarkably well, and it and its fans were hoping for big things in 1874.

Before closing out 1873, however, Cummings still had some work to do. But it had nothing to do with baseball. For some time, Cummings, an educated man with a keen mind and a scientist's curiosity, had been working on a design for an improved railroad car coupling device. What caused him to get involved in that, one can only guess. Throughout his amateur and now professional baseball career, he'd done a lot of train travel. So he would have been well aware of how dangerous were the car couplers then in use.

Up through the early 1870s, the standard coupling mechanism was based on a link-and-pin design. To link two cars, a crewman had to stand between them, line up the U-shaped ends of the coupler on each car, and insert a pin so that its opposite ends were secured by the jaws of each coupler. This was very dangerous for the crewman, and injuries and even deaths were common. Cummings was one of a number of people who were trying to come up with coupler designs to eliminate the risk.[27]

By the end of 1873, Candy Cummings had perfected his own design, and he sought to patent it. His objective, as he stated in his patent application, was "to provide a safe, simple and efficient device for coupling cars, whereby the risk of life is obviated." In his design, the coupling and de-coupling occurred mechanically, without the need for a crewman to place himself between the two cars and manipulate the pin. Steam or air pressure would be released from a cylinder under the car and operate on an array of pistons that forced the jaws of the coupler to open, grab the linking pin, and close. Cummings filed for a patent for his device on December 6, 1873, and received it four months later, on April 7, 1874.[28]

His invention didn't go anywhere. In 1873, someone else patented a design for a "knuckle coupler." It had the coupling mechanism close by the force of the two cars coming together.[29] The industry was slow to adopt that concept, and Cummings, ever persistent, kept working on his own design. He eventually came up with a new one, which he patented in 1877.

13

Candy's a Pearl

For the 1874 season, the Philadelphia club cast aside its "white stock-ings" and donned new pearl-colored hose. It thus became popularly known as the "Pearls."[1] Why the change? A team from Chicago was entering the NA with the nickname "White Stockings"[2]; and Boston had its "Red Stock-ings." Perhaps the Philadelphians thought there was too much hosiery in the National Association's cupboard. The *New York Clipper* liked the club's new look and wished it well; "We hope," it said, "they will become pearls of priceless value in the baseball market."[3]

"Pearls" wasn't the only nickname for the Philadelphia nine. Others were the Quakers, which had been used since it joined the NA in 1873,[4] and the Philadelphias or variants thereof, such as the "Fillies" (with an "F"). All of these names were used interchangeably in press reports of the team's games. The 1874 club is the White Stockings in Baseball-reference and Ret-rosheet databases.

Cummings' signing on with Philadelphia reunited him with Nat Hicks, the catcher who had backed him up so well on the Stars in 1870 and again on the Mutuals in 1872. Along with Cummings, Hicks was among several new imports to the Pearls' restructured team of 1874. He had been a member of the Mutuals in 1873, but he became disabled in July and could not play for the rest of that year.[5] Then the Fillies picked him up. The *Spirit of the Times* was downright exuberant at the reunion. "[I]n the whirligig of time," it said, "Hicks and Cummings get together again, and as Cummings will pitch with old time confidence with Hicks behind the bat, and as Hicks is just the boy who ain't afraid of Cummings' balls, they will prove a tremendous acquisi-tion to the White Stockings [the Philadelphia club's nickname in 1873, when the article was written]."[6] The *New York Clipper* agreed: "[Hicks] is unques-tionably one of the most effective catchers there are, and certainly no man can equal him in catching for Cumming's [*sic*] difficult bias delivery."[7]

Philadelphia's new battery showed its mettle right off the bat. The Pearls' regular season opened on April 16, when they visited the grounds of their cross-town rivals, the Athletics. The Pearls lost by the unenviable score of 14–5, but through no fault of Cummings and Hicks. To the contrary, the *Clipper* found their pitching and catching to be effective and worthy of special note. The team's downfall was its fielding; of the Athletics' 14 runs, only one was earned.[8]

The Fillies licked their wounds and came galloping back. Six days later, on April 22, Candy Cummings overwhelmed his old club, silencing Baltimore's Canaries, 13–0. He continued to dominate the Canaries on May 4, when he inflicted an even greater drubbing, 23–8.

And so the season went for Baltimore when they faced Candy Cummings and the Pearls. In the five meetings between the two teams, Philadelphia won four. Baltimore's only victory, 5–1, came on July 29, when the Pearls barely escaped the humiliation of being Chicagoed by scoring a run in the ninth inning. Their loss was even more frustrating in that it was inflicted by a pitcher who was not really a pitcher. He was Jack Manning, normally an infielder, whose body of work pitching professional games, up to July 29, had totaled a mere 8⅔ innings, all in relief. Baltimore's usual hurler was Asa Brainard, the onetime ace who was playing in what would be the final year of his professional career. To that point in the season, Brainard had pitched the Canaries to 22 losses and only five wins, so the club tried out Manning as a possible substitute. Manning started the game and was doing so well that Baltimore left him in for the entire nine innings.[9] He went on to become the Canaries' hurler for the remainder of 1874, and Brainard moved to second base.

After his fine start against the Athletics and Baltimore, Cummings went on to have a highly successful 1874 season. He pitched in every game for Philadelphia through October 26, for a total of 54 contests; the Pearls won 28 and lost 26. In three of them, Cummings tossed shutouts: against Baltimore on April 22 (13–0), the Atlantics on June 1 (10–0), and the Mutuals three days later (2–0); and he nearly did it again against the Atlantics on August 26 (23–1). During one stretch, August 11 through September 22, he won 11 straight games.

With Cummings in the pitcher's spot, the Pearls had a winning record against five of the other seven NAPBBP clubs. Their greatest success was against the Chicago White Stockings. The Philadelphians took seven of the ten games the two teams played. Cummings set the tone at the first meeting of the clubs, on June 15. In an exciting contest, he struck out ten White Stockings—an exceptional number in those days—and the Fillies emerged victorious, 8–6,[10] all of Chicago's runs unearned. "The wonderful pitching of Cummings alone won the match," reported the *Clipper*.[11] Two days later, Philadelphia's margin of victory was considerably larger, 15–6, again thanks to Cummings' effective delivery.[12]

Those were but two of several praiseworthy performances that

Cummings turned in that season. Another was against the Dark Blues of Hartford, Connecticut, on May 21 in Philadelphia. It was a game that the *Clipper* dubbed "one of the most exciting and best-contested games this season." At the end of nine innings, the two teams were knotted at four runs apiece. The Fillies pulled ahead by two runs in the top of the tenth, and in the bottom of the frame, Cummings quickly disposed of Hartford's batsmen to seal a 6–4 victory. (In those days, the visiting squad didn't automatically bat first in an inning; the opposing teams flipped a coin before the first pitch, and the winner decided which one was to lead off.) The *Clipper* was full of compliments for Cummings' contribution. "Cummings … fielded brilliantly in his position," it said, "and pitched with all the effectiveness for which he was so noted a few seasons ago."[13]

Cummings was getting great press even when his team lost. In a game against Brooklyn's Atlantics on July 1, the Pearls came out on the losing end, 5–3. For eight innings, they posted zeros in the runs column, and they just escaped being shut out by plating three runs in the ninth. Despite the loss, the *Clipper* was particularly effusive about Philadelphia's hurler. "Cummings' pitching in this game was a model display," raved its reporter. "His action in delivery was apparently so careless that the batsmen were deceived, and even the best men could not properly measure the pace of the ball, so skillfully was it changed from fast to slow, and from medium to swift."[14]

The Pearls' home-town rivals, the Athletics, against whom they opened the 1874 season, turned out to be their most formidable adversary. Of the ten games Candy Cummings pitched against the Athletics, the Pearls lost nine, although three were decided by a single run. One of those losses came on May 7, when the Athletics easily punished Cummings' pitching and nearly Chicagoed the Pearls, 7–1.[15]

Perhaps his mind was elsewhere. While he was at work at that May 7 game, his wife, Mary, was giving birth. The new arrival was a son, whom Candy and Mary named Arthur Roberts Cummings; the "Roberts" was Mary's maiden name. Mary was in Brooklyn at the time. Her widowed mother, who had been living in Brooklyn with her son Charles, was no longer there, so she was probably staying with Candy's family. But it must have been pretty crowded. There were 11 people in the Cummings household: Candy's parents, William B. and Mary P.; five of his unmarried brothers and sisters; and another sister, Gertrude, and her husband Sam, plus their two children.[16]

Philadelphia's sole win against the Athletics didn't come until the final game of the season series on October 21. The Athletics were held scoreless through seven innings, "so effective was the pitching of Cummings, and so faultlessly was he backed up in the field." Philadelphia's batters, meanwhile, were blasting the offerings of Athletics pitcher Dick McBride. The final score: Pearls 11, Athletics 3.[17]

The Red Stockings of Boston was the other team that gave Cummings and the Pearls trouble. Of the nine games that he pitched against the Reds, Philadelphia won only two and lost seven, including an 8–0 shutout on May 29.

During his time with Philadelphia, Candy Cummings yet again encountered rough waters that threatened to sink his career. He was accused of participating in a scheme to fix a game against the Chicago White Stockings on July 15.

Betting on baseball games was not new, but it had become a big problem by 1874. Noting that charges of throwing games had been made against several clubs, the *New York Herald* lamented, "Professional base ball, in fact, seems to be surrounded by a corrupt and vulgar atmosphere, and the disgust of the public has been plainly shown by the comparatively small attendance at the matches…. Another season like that of 1874 will probably make professional base ball as unprofitable as it is discreditable."[18]

Much of the betting was done by means of pool-selling. The organizer of a pool would sell chances on the outcome of a game, for example, that a team would win or lose, or that it would win or lose in a certain number of innings, and the proceeds would go into the pot. Bettors who guessed correctly would share in the payout.[19] In the pool system, the amount of money put on a result was known; if the betting largely favored one team to win, a small number of punters could be tempted to wager on the team to lose and induce players to play the game so as to ensure that result. And if the betting was on a team to win in, say, one or two innings, corrupted players would have to blow only those innings to produce a loss. Henry Chadwick, an ardent crusader against gambling in baseball, wrote in the *Beadle's* guide for 1875, "this pool-selling innovation has proved more damaging in its results than anyone dreamed of."[20] The evil of pool-selling, admonished Chadwick, cast the game into disrepute by creating suspicion whenever a player performed unusually badly, or whenever the outcome of a game was significantly contrary to what had been expected.

Which brings us to July 15, 1874. That day, the White Stockings of Chicago hosted the Pearls for the first game of a three-game set. Philadelphia and Chicago were only a win apart in the NA championship standings: The Pearls were in fourth place with 13 victories, and Chicago was fifth, with 12. So the encounter had significance for both clubs, especially for the Whites, who were trying to draw even with and then surpass the Pearls. Recent history, however, favored Philadelphia, which had won the clubs' two prior meetings on the strength of effective pitching by Cummings.

The game started well for Philadelphia. They held Chicago scoreless for two innings while scoring two runs of their own. But things turned sour for the Pearls. Their fate was sealed in the third inning, when the White Stockings scored five runs, due largely to "indescribably bad" fielding by the Fillies.[21] Chicago scored three more runs in the fifth inning and two in the sixth; for their part, the Pearls managed only one more run. When the final out was made, the White Stockings had defeated Philadelphia by a substantial margin, 10–3, and had moved to a tie with the Pearls for fourth place in the standings.

Officiating that contest was English-born William McLean, a respected professional umpire for the NAPBBP. (Two years later, he would have the distinction of presiding over the first game of the newly formed National League.[22]) In a sworn affidavit, McLean reported that, before the game, he had been taken aside by John Radcliff, Philadelphia's right fielder, at the hotel where the Pearls were staying in downtown Chicago. According to McLean, Radcliff told him that he had given his—Radcliff's—brother $350 to bet on the White Stockings to win, and he offered McLean half of the winnings if McLean made umpiring decisions favoring the Chicago club. Radcliff implicated four other Philadelphia players: Cummings, Hicks (catcher), Craver (second baseman), and Denny Mack (first baseman).

McLean, according to his submission, told Radcliff that he would have nothing to do with the nefarious business, and he insisted that he would umpire the contest fairly. As evidence of the plot, McLean claimed that Cummings had delivered easy-to-hit softballs to Chicago's batters and that the other alleged plotters had also played suspiciously badly. Radcliff filed a counter-affidavit, denying everything that McLean had alleged.[23]

John Radcliff, who had also been a teammate of Candy Cummings with Baltimore in 1873, was no stranger to controversy. In 1868, he was the focus of a convoluted affair involving his signing with the Red Stockings of Cincinnati while still a member of Philadelphia's Athletics. Meanwhile, he received a $500 payment from the Athletics, allegedly in return for his undertaking to remain with the club. All this took place while he was engaging in secret negotiations to play for the Mutuals, from whom he received $100. For his actions, Radcliff ended up being expelled by both the Red Stockings and the Athletics, but he was reinstated to the latter club the following June.[24]

So what about that third inning in Chicago on July 15, the frame that gave the win to Chicago?[25] Was it part of the plot by Radcliff and those whom he implicated to throw the game? It did look suspicious; the Fillies played as if they were in a Laurel and Hardy movie. With one out, Cummings gave up two singles, putting men on first and second. The next ball was hit to the Pearls' shortstop, Chick Fulmer (not one of the alleged co-conspirators named by Radcliff), who tried for a force-out at third, but his throw sailed four feet over the third baseman's head and the runner scored. There were now men on second and third. The next batter popped up to Craver at second, who fielded it cleanly for an out. Cummings then gave up two more hits, producing two additional Chicago runs. After that, Craver muffed a soft grounder. He fielded the next one, however, and threw to Mack covering first, but Mack missed the throw. At that point, wrote a dumbfounded *Chicago Tribune* reporter, "[T]he Philadelphias now went to pieces, and began throwing about wildly to head off the Whites, who were running the bases with great freedom. When they finished, two more runs had been scored." None of the five runs plated by Chicago that inning was earned.

As Chicago's *Inter-Ocean* newspaper observed, it was not only sloppy fielding by the Pearls that allowed the White Stockings to prevail, but also the unexpected ability of the Chicago batsmen to punish Cummings' pitching. "The principal feature of the game," said the paper, "was the remarkably heavy batting of the Whites, which surprised everybody on account of the prevailing opinion that the Whites would find it almost impossible to bat Cummings."[26]

McLean's allegations concerning Radcliff and the other Pearls players were investigated by the Philadelphia club. After considering evidence and testimony of witnesses, it found the charges as to Radcliff to be fully substantiated and voted to discharge him; but it exonerated Cummings, Craver, and Mack. Radcliff appealed to the National Association's Judiciary Committee, which decided to reinstate him as eligible to play in the NA in 1875. He was picked up by a new club in Philadelphia, the Centennials.[27]

Candy Cummings' poor pitching on July 15 could be chalked up simply to his having a bad day. It happens, particularly when a hurler pitches a grueling 54 games in a season, 52 of them complete games. The July 15 contest was not the only time he was off his stride that year. The Athletics punished him on May 7, resulting in the Pearls' defeat by a score of 7–1. On June 25, the Mutuals' batters got to him, although his team eked out a 13–12 win. And on July 24, Hartford hammered him for five runs in the seventh inning, took the lead, and went on to win, 8–4.[28] But those were exceptions.

None of Cummings' writings mention the game-fixing scandal and the ultimately rejected accusation of his involvement in it, and he didn't bring it up in the many interviews he gave about his career. But it must have weighed heavily on him. Being wrongfully accused of cheating doesn't sit well with someone who prides himself as being upright and honest, and that's how people who knew Cummings regarded him. Nevertheless, the episode seemed not to unduly affect his performance. July 15 marked the end of the first half of the Pearls' season. To that point, Cummings' win-loss record was 13–16. During the second half, he was a winner: 15–10, including that 11-game winning streak in August.

Candy Cummings' final game of the 1874 season was against the Red Stockings, on October 26 at Boston. In the first few innings, it was clear that he wasn't himself. "He acted as if he was either sick or sulky," observed a Boston reporter.[29] By the fifth frame, he had given up 12 runs, and he couldn't continue. He left the game, and Philadelphia's right fielder, George Bechtel, came in to replace him. Bechtel had little pitching experience. He had tossed three games for the Athletics in 1871 and another three for Philadelphia in 1873, but that was it. Bechtel finished the game that Cummings started, and in the final four innings was able to hold the Reds to only three additional runs. Boston won, 15–3.

What ailed Cummings that day? It isn't clear. The *Hartford Courant* claimed he was lame, although other papers maintained he was sick.[30] Whatever it was, it prevented him from finishing the season. Bechtel pitched the Pearls' remaining four games of 1874, winning one. For the season, Philadelphia ended up with an even 29–29 win-loss record, and placed fourth in the NA standings, behind the third-place Athletics, the runner-up Mutuals, and the Bostons, who became the National Association's champions for the third straight year.

The 1874 season was Candy Cummings' best yet as a professional ballplayer. His excellent 1.96 earned run average placed him among the top four of National Association pitchers. Only hundredths of percentage points separated him from Al Spalding of the Boston Red Stockings (1.92) and Bobby Mathews of the Mutuals (1.90); the league leader was Dick McBride, with a 1.64 ERA.

In its post-season review of pitchers of 1874, the *New York Clipper* judged Cummings "one of the most effective players" in that position. "He has speed, endurance, and thorough command of the ball, and delivers with that dangerous curve which is so fatal to most batsmen." The paper again, however, cautioned, as it had in previous years, that to pitch with full effect, Cummings needed a good catcher, one who could provide the necessary support for his strategic style of delivery.[31] After his season in Philadelphia, Candy Cummings was on the move again. But to where?

14

Hose of a Different Color

In 1872, the state of Connecticut was represented in the National Association by a team called the Mansfields. Its home was in Middletown, a municipality about 15 miles as the crow flies down the Connecticut River from Hartford. The Mansfields did not thrive, either on the field or financially. Struggling to compete with baseball's best teams and players, it won only five games that year and lost 14. With sparse attendance and other woes adding to its difficulties, the club disbanded on August 13, 1872.[1]

Connecticut did not remain without a pro team for long. Ben Douglas, a former Mansfield player and loyal booster of his home state, saw to that. Itching for the return of professional baseball to Connecticut, 24-year-old Douglas got together a bunch of Hartford businessmen and persuaded them to provide financial backing for a new team in that city. The club was founded in 1874. Its official name was the "Hartford Base Ball Club," but after its uniform was revealed, with dark blue trim on its jersey and a broad, dark blue band on its stockings, it soon came to be known as the "Dark Blues."[2]

In their first season, the Hartfords won 16 games and lost 37, placing the team just above the cellar-dwelling Baltimore Canaries in the NA standings. The club was determined that things would be different in 1875. It set about completely revamping the squad with the ambitious objective of wresting the title away from Boston's champion Red Stockings. It replaced nearly its entire 1874 team with accomplished players and installed a new manager who would rid the club of the lack of discipline and other ills that had afflicted it in the 1874 season. Quipped the *New York Clipper,* "Harry Wright [manager of the Boston club] has looked pale since he heard of the new team."[3]

For their new skipper, the Hartfords hired Bob Ferguson. He would also play third base. Plucked from Brooklyn's Atlantics, Ferguson was a Brooklynite who had come up through amateur squads in that city. He played for the Atlantics for several seasons both before and after the club went professional, and also served as the team's manager. When the

NAPBBP was formed in 1872, Ferguson was elected its first president, thus simultaneously performing the roles of player, manager, and league official.

Ferguson was a no-nonsense guy, strict in his personal habits and expecting the same of others. He didn't drink—he did own a saloon for a while, until he decided "this life is too unclean for me"—and abhorred gambling. In managing his team, he was quick-tempered, dictatorial, and often crude. As a result, he alienated many of his players. But his iron-fisted rule succeeded in maintaining discipline and obedience in his squad, and for that he was respected by other managers and club officials. Eventually, however, his gruff and intemperate ways, including vigorously dressing down his players right on the playing field, led to griping and dissent among members of the team, and it affected their performance on the field.[4]

To pitch for his exciting new club, Ferguson tapped Tommy Bond, whom he had played with and managed on the Atlantics in 1874. Ireland-born Bond was a 17-year-old phenom when he burst upon the professional baseball scene. Like Cummings more than a decade before him, Bond started playing ball on the sandlots in Brooklyn, where his family settled after emigrating in 1862. After a year or so in the semi-pro circuit, he entered the professional ranks in 1874 when he was signed by the Atlantics. Bond showed flashes of brilliance that year; he carried one game to two outs in the bottom of the ninth without allowing a hit, failing by just a single out to become the first major league pitcher ever to achieve a no-hitter.[5]

Before the last out of the 1874 season was recorded, the baseball press began speculating about where Candy Cummings would play in 1875. They couldn't agree. On October 25, 1874, the *Chicago Tribune* reported that he was demanding a salary of $3,000, double what he'd earned with Philadelphia, and that the Brown Stockings of St. Louis, a new club in the National Association, were willing to meet it. But there was a hitch: Candy Cummings would have to "cut loose" from catcher Nat Hicks, whom the club didn't want.[6]

Just a few days later, a Connecticut newspaper, the *Hartford Courant,* got its two cents in, when it cogitated upon who might make up its hometown team. After cautioning that "nothing trustworthy" had been issued in that regard, it predicted with complete confidence the entire Hartford lineup. It would include, said the paper, Tommy Bond as pitcher and Candy Cummings as right fielder and change pitcher.[7] But wait—according to another paper from the Nutmeg state, the *Daily Constitution* of Middletown, Hartford had chosen George Bradley to back up Bond as change pitcher. To that point, Bradley had played only amateur ball, as a right fielder and change pitcher. Meanwhile, the *New York Herald* announced that Candy Cummings was to remain with the Philadelphia nine.[8] The confusion was mercifully resolved the following day, when the *Waterbury [CT]*

Bob Ferguson in 1878, with the Chicago White Stockings. When Candy Cummings was pitching for the Hartford Dark Blues, in 1875 and 1876, Ferguson was the team's strict and volatile manager and also a player (A.G. Spalding Baseball Collection. New York Public Library Digital Collections).

Daily American announced the Hartfords' "official" roster for 1875: it would include both Cummings and Bond.[9] So that was that—until the *Chicago Tribune* again muddied the waters by affirming, on December 6, that Cummings would, indeed, stay in Philadelphia as the Pearls' pitcher.[10]

It was like the old three-shell con game. Under which shell—St. Louis,

Philadelphia, or Hartford—was Candy Cummings? Anyone who bet on St. Louis or Philadelphia would have lost. In 1875, Cummings would play for the Hartford nine. But in what capacity? More confusion. As already noted, the Hartford paper had him playing right field and backing up Bond as change pitcher; for their part, the *New York Clipper* and the *St. Louis Republican* placed him only in the outfield, without mentioning any pitching duties at all, although it was probably implied that he could be called upon from time to time to relieve Bond.[11] But could that be? Would Hartford relegate a first-class and experienced hurler like Cummings to playing second fiddle to young Tommy Bond, who had only a year as a professional pitcher under his belt?

When he was hired, Bond was not yet of Candy Cummings' caliber. Pitching with speed and control, he showed promise. But he didn't have the curveball, and skipper Ferguson wanted him to learn it. Ferguson's plan was to have Cummings pitch for the first part of the season and put Bond in the outfield, during which time Bond would observe and learn the curve from

its master, Cummings.[12] So from opening day on April 24 through the end of June, Cummings pitched 32 of Hartford's 34 games; Bond pitched twice, but otherwise played in the outfield with a few stints at first base. And he studied Cummings' technique.

By June, Bond had developed an excellent curve of his own—the *Hartford Courant* considered it "much more effective than that of Cummings"[13]—and Ferguson decided that Bond was ready to play his part in the pitcher's box. From that point through mid–October, Bond pitched 37 games to Cummings' 15. Cummings sat on the bench during that period, except for a handful of games when he played in the outfield. To finish out the season, Cummings took

Tommy Bond. Bond, a pitcher, learned the curveball while watching Candy Cummings on the Hartford Dark Blues in 1876. He and Cummings shared pitching duties for the club in 1875 and 1876 (A.G. Spalding Baseball Collection. New York Public Library Digital Collections).

over again, pitching seven of the final eight games, with Bond working the finale.

So both Bond and Cummings served as Hartford's principal hurlers. This was an innovation. Many clubs had a pitcher and a change pitcher, normally a fielder who could fill in if the main hurler became indisposed or was unavailable. The Hartfords were the first to carry two regular pitchers sharing the load. It was an arrangement that had been advocated for some time by Henry Chadwick in the columns of the *New York Clipper*. "It is an established fact," he wrote, "that a club nine can bat one pitcher with better effect than they can another, and it is found advisable, therefore, to have two first-class pitchers in a nine, not merely for use in case of an emergency, but to be able to present the pitcher who is most effective against the opposing nine."[14] That's how Hartford used their two ball-tossers; their differing deliveries produced generally positive results.[15] Over the 1875 season, Cummings' pitching load was a bit more than Bond's; he hurled 46 complete games to Bond's 37, and they shared pitching responsibilities in one.

Candy Cummings' regular catcher on the Hartfords was Doug Allison. Two years older than Cummings, Allison was born in Philadelphia to immigrant parents; his mother was Scots and his father English. Unlike other backstops of the time, who would position themselves 20-25 feet behind the plate, hoping to avoid injury, Allison stood right up close to the batter so he could gun down baserunners, which he did with great effect. Nat Hicks, who had paired superbly with Cummings on the Mutuals and the Philadelphia White Stockings, was another pioneer of that practice. Allison and Hicks were also the earliest catchers to use gloves to protect their hands, although each claimed to have actually been the first.[16] Candy Cummings had full confidence in Allison, whom the *Hartford Courant* placed "in the front ranks as a catcher,"[17] and the duo worked extremely well together.

The Insurance City was atwitter in anticipation of the start of the 1875 season. "Hartford is all alive with baseball this season," wrote a correspondent to the *Clipper*. "Everyone you meet is talking about 'our new nine' and its prospects."[18] Featuring top-notch players, the Dark Blues were seen as the chief rival of Boston's formidable Red Stockings for the NA championship; the club's vice-president even offered to pitch in a $500 bonus to the players if they won it.[19] Adding to the excitement, the club's grounds had been upgraded and sported a spanking new pavilion. A visitor wrote that it was "the finest ball ground we have ever seen."[20]

All was set for opening day, April 24, at Hartford. It was an ideal afternoon for baseball. By game time, 2,500 eager spectators had taken their seats to watch their revamped nine take on Brooklyn's Atlantics. Cummings was in the pitcher's box for the home team. The contest started off well enough for the Dark Blues, who scored three runs in the top half of the first inning.

But Atlantic countered with three, and they scored two more in the third inning to take the lead, 5–3. Both sides drew blanks in the next four innings, resulting in many glum faces among the Hartford faithful, who began to sense defeat. But all was not yet lost. The Blues went into the eighth and, amid enthusiastic cheering by the rejuvenated Hartford partisans in the crowd, plated three runs to retake the lead. With his effective pitching and fielding, Cummings retired the final six Atlantics batters in order, sealing the Hartfords' nail-biting 6–5 victory. The two teams met again three days later. This time, the Dark Blues would have shut out the Atlantics if it weren't for a run-scoring wild pitch by Cummings in the fourth inning. The final tally: Hartford 10, Atlantic 1.[21]

Doug Allison. Allison was Candy Cummings' regular catcher on the Hartford Dark Blues in 1875. In 1879, he was on the Capital Citys of Albany, New York; Cummings was the team's manager (A.G. Spalding Baseball Collection. New York Public Library Digital Collections).

It was the start of something big. Cummings and his team would go on to win the next ten games, making it a 12-game winning streak from April 24 through May 17. It included a 13–4 drubbing of the new Philadelphia club, the Centennials, on May 3; a 16–0 Chicagoing of Washington, D.C.'s Nationals five days later, followed by a 9–1 beatdown of the same team; and another shutout, against the Atlantics, 5–0, on May 17.

Cummings' most memorable game during that streak was against the Athletics of Philadelphia. On May 13, fully 3,000 fans from all over Connecticut crowded into the stands at Hartford. Over the first six innings, both sides posted zeros. In the top of the seventh, the Dark Blues scored the first run of the contest. With men on first and second, Hartford's first baseman, Ev Mills, connected for a hit, and the man on second "ran home like a deer, crossing the plate in safety amidst immense enthusiasm and deafening

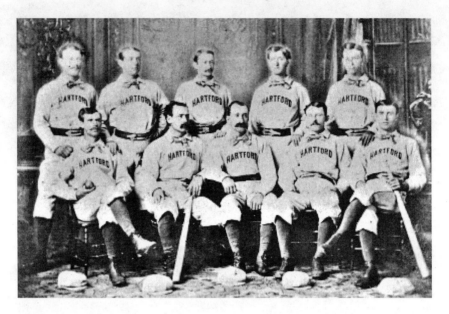

Hartford Dark Blues, 1875. Candy Cummings is in top row, center. The 1875 season was Cummings' best of his career. He was also with the Dark Blues in 1876 (Connecticut Historical Society, photograph, accession no. 1964.19.2., gift of Austin Kilbourne).

cheers from the assembled thousands." Both sides were retired in order in the eighth. In the top of the ninth, the Athletics came to bat, determined to at least even the score. They did one better, driving in two runs. Apprehension, gloom, and dread spread among the chronically insecure Dark Blues fans. But in the Blues' final frame, Mills again came through. With men on first and third, he hit a hard single to right field, sending home the two baserunners to win the game. "The crowd rose as one man," said the *Hartford Courant* on May 14; "such a cheer as poured from the throats of the spectators was never heard on the ground." But that wasn't the end of Hartford's scoring. Even though they had won, under the rules at the time the final inning continued to be played until the third out was recorded. This gave the Dark Blues an opportunity to score three more runs, including two on a hard liner by Cummings. The game ended with a glorious comeback victory by Hartford, 6–2. It was Cummings' finest performance of the still-young season. He "pitched magnificently," cheered the *Courant,* "and added to his laurels and his reputation as the best pitcher in the country."

The Hartfords' season-opening winning streak came to an end on May 18. Having shut out the Atlantics the previous day, Cummings and the Dark Blues faced the Red Stockings. As the first meeting of the season for these two teams, it was the most anticipated and most talked-about matchup of the season to that point. Managed by Harry Wright, the formidable Bostons included Harry's brother, George, a terrific hitter, superb shortstop, and one of the legendary players of his era. Elected to the Hall of Fame in 1937, Wright "may fairly be called the Babe Ruth of his time," writes John Thorn, Major League Baseball's official historian.[22] Boston's pitcher was the great Al Spalding, who led the National Association in wins in each year of the league's existence.

The Red Stockings lineup included other stars of the day, such as Cal McVey. McVey, who managed the Baltimores in 1873 when Cummings was with the team, had previously been with Harry and George Wright in Cincinnati with that city's Red Stockings, and moved with them to Boston when Harry formed the Boston club in 1871. He hit .360 with the Bostons in 1874. In fact, five of the club's regular nine in 1875 were well over .300 hitters. They were an exciting team. But so were the Dark Blues. Under the leadership of the respected—albeit tough to deal with—Bob Ferguson, and with their pitching star Candy Cummings, the Hartfords were expected to give the three-straight-NA-champion Bostonians a run for the pennant. When they met on May 18, both were defending unbroken winning streaks; Boston had won 16 straight, Hartford 12. And each had been on the winning side of a shutout the day before. Both teams came to the grounds brimming with confidence.

It was like the World Series, Super Bowl, and Stanley Cup final rolled into one, so great was the excitement about this game between New England rivals.[23] In Hartford, many factories and businesses closed for the day to allow their employees to attend the match—although not that much work would have gotten done anyway. Extra trains were laid on to bring fans to the city from all over Connecticut, and contingents arrived from New York, Boston, and other parts of New England. Attendance at the game was huge. The crowds started filing in at noon for a 3:30 first pitch, and by game time between 8,000 and 10,000 fans had filled the grounds. It was, declared the *Hartford Courant,* "the largest audience ever assembled in New England to witness a contest for superiority between two rival base ball nines."

Boston led off the scoring with three runs in the first inning, adding two more in the third. The Dark Blues didn't begin to respond until the top of the fourth. On the strength of four base hits, and capitalizing on misplays by Boston fielders, they came back with five runs to tie the game and bring hope to their supporters. But that ended Hartford's scoring for the afternoon. Boston, meanwhile, pushed five more runs across the plate, and the game ended with the Red Stockings victorious, 10–5. It was a game well-played by both sides; the pitching of both Spalding and Cummings was praised as "very effective." Hartford's loss was attributed to Boston's superior batting and base-running.

One of the several thousand Hartford supporters at that game was the great American author and humorist Samuel Clemens, known by his pen name of Mark Twain. In 1871, Clemens had moved his young family to Hartford, a city that was home to numerous writers and publishers.[24] A big baseball fan, he could frequently be found at the Hartfords' baseball grounds, cheering on the Dark Blues. He attended the Hartford–Boston game with his close friend, the pastor Joseph H. Twichell.[25] While they were seated, Clemens's umbrella slipped through the seats and was carried off by a young lad who crept under the stands to retrieve it. Two days later, an agitated Clemens placed this ad in the *Hartford Courant*[26]:

> TWO HUNDRED AND FIVE DOLLARS REWARD—At the great base ball match on Tuesday, while I was engaged in hurrahing, a small boy walked off with an English-made brown silk UMBRELLA belonging to me, and forgot to bring it back. I will pay $5 for the return of that umbrella in good condition to my house on Farmington avenue. I do not want the boy (in an active state), but will pay two hundred dollars for his remains.
> SAMUEL L. CLEMENS.

The *New York World* apparently didn't appreciate the humor. It solemnly cautioned that Clemens' offer of a monetary inducement for the commission of homicide could turn out very unpleasant for its author. But the *Evening Star* of Schenectady, New York, did savor the joke and carried it further. In a completely deadpan, hour-by-hour, fictitious account, it reported as follows: The corpse of a young boy was delivered to Clemens' home in Hartford by a delivery service from Cambridge, Massachusetts. Caught while opening the box containing the body, Clemens was arrested for murder. But he was cleared when it emerged that the corpse had been stolen from the dissecting room of a medical faculty in Cambridge and delivered to Clemens as a joke. It was later retrieved from his home by a janitor from the college.[27]

In the early evening following their May 18 game, the two teams boarded a train bound for Boston, where they would play again the following afternoon.

Back in Beantown, the city was jubilant at the news of its team's triumph. Awaiting the players at the station when their train arrived around midnight were a thousand excited fans, "nearly frantic with delight," accompanied by a brass band. The throng gave their squad a hero's welcome, then escorted the teams to the Red Stockings' club rooms, where the Reds hosted a splendid meal for their rivals.

The day after these festivities, the two teams suited up again and made their way over to Boston's South End Grounds to play another game. The Bostonians again defeated the Dark Blues, 13–2. However, only two of the Red Stockings' 13 runs were earned off Cummings' effective pitching; the 12 errors committed by Hartford's fielders contributed to the rest.[28]

Hartford had signed Tommy Bond in part because he had some

success against the champion Red Stockings the previous year, and the Bostons were Hartford's target in 1875. In fact, Bond's record against the Red Stockings in 1874—four wins, six losses, one tie—was only somewhat better than Cummings': two wins against seven losses. But Cummings' losses were nothing like the 14–0 or 29–0 (that's not a typo) thrashings that Boston inflicted on Bond and his former team, the Atlantics, on July 9 and October 1, 1874, respectively. In any case, Hartford's idea was that Bond would bear the main pitching load against the Red Stockings. And he did; but it didn't produce wins for Hartford.

Following their two losses to Boston behind Cummings, the Hartfords would next meet the Red Stockings on June 17. Ferguson decided that Bond was ready to take them on. From that point onward, he was Hartford's man against the Boston club, with the exception of a game that Cummings pitched on October 29. In his seven encounters with the Bostons, Bond failed to record a victory. The Red Stockings Chicagoed the Hartfords three times, 4–0, 7–0, and 6–0; Bond was the Dark Blues' pitcher on each occasion. To be fair, however, those losses were not the fault of his pitching; he surrendered only one earned run in two of those contests and two in the third game. They were due more to sloppy fielding by the Hartfords and the inability of their batters to hit Boston's ace, Al Spalding.[29]

Candy Cummings did not pitch against the Red Stockings again until the penultimate game of the season, at Hartford on October 29. It was an exciting affair. Boston had the lead, 8–5, in the middle of the seventh inning, but the Dark Blues came back and scored four runs in the bottom of the frame. A couple of outs into the eighth, the game was called due to darkness, leaving Hartford the winner, 9–8. It was their one and only victory against the Bostons that year.[30]

Cummings delivered several standout performances over the 1875 season. Against the New York Mutuals on May 21, just a few days after the opening series against Boston, he hurled what the *Clipper* called "the model game of the season." (Henry Chadwick coined the term "model game" to refer to one in which the winning side's score was in single digits.[31]) After both sides posted zeroes for six innings, the Dark Blues broke through and scored a run in the top of the seventh. In the bottom half of that inning, the Mutuals staged a comeback. Thanks to two base hits and a sacrifice grounder, they had men on second and third with nobody out, and they were almost certain to score. But Cummings saved the lead and the game. After securing the first out on a foul tip taken by the catcher, he induced the next batter to fly out to Bond in right field. Bond fired the ball home in time to nab the runner racing for the plate. That double play ended the threat, and Cummings and the Dark Blues fielders held the Mutes scoreless for the final two innings for a 1–0 victory. The *Clipper* called Cummings' performance in the seventh inning "the finest display of pitching ever seen on the field."[32]

That game had historic significance. It was the second time ever—at least in professional baseball—that the winning team scored but a single run in a game; the first had been only ten days earlier, when the Chicago White Stockings shut out the Red Stockings of St. Louis, 1–0. (In August 1874, two amateur teams played to a 1–0 score, thus beating the professionals to that honor.[33])

There would be five 1–0 games in the National Association that year, and four 1–1 ties, a remarkable leap from zero in all of previous professional baseball history.[34] These scores were part of an emerging trend, reflecting the changing relationship between pitcher and batter.

Scoring had been in steady decline since the NA was formed, dropping sharply from 10.47 runs per game in 1871, to 6.14 in 1875. The table gives the details[35]:

Year	Total Games	Total Runs	Average Runs/Game
1871	254	2659	10.47
1872	330	3390	10.27
1873	398	3099	7.79
1874	464	3470	7.48
1875	690	4234	6.14

The decreasing numbers of runs scored reflected the changing nature of the game. Up through the 1860s, the balance of power decidedly favored the batter. But as shown in Chapter 7, the balance was shifting in the 1870s. Strict restrictions on pitch delivery were loosening, enabling hurlers to deliver the ball in ways that were previously prohibited. These changes facilitated pitching the curveball, which was beginning to make its mark in the baseball world, and more and more pitchers were learning it and using it to deceive the batter. In addition, as the decade progressed, umpires began to apply with greater consistency rules on called strikes and balls, which, although on the books of both the National Association of Base Ball Players and the NAPBBP, had been rarely enforced, in part because of their ambiguous wording. Batters could no longer play a waiting game, requiring pitchers to deliver pitch after pitch until the batter got one just to his liking and decided to take a cut.[36] As a result of developments such as these, the balance of power between hitters and pitchers was finding a new equilibrium, one in which hitting and scoring were more of a challenge.

Not long after Candy Cummings' 1–0 victory on May 21, he twirled another game with the smallest possible score, on June 19 at Chicago against the White Stockings, although in this one, he came out on the losing end. There wasn't a huge crowd at Chicago's Twenty-Third Street Grounds that afternoon—only 3,000 or so. The *Chicago Tribune* speculated that the White Stockings' two previous games, both losses to Boston by large margins, had dampened the enthusiasm of Chicago fans for their team. But those who were there were treated to a corker of a contest. It was also historic: For the first time in recorded baseball history, neither team had scored a run after nine full innings. Nor after ten innings. The winning run did not come until the bottom of the 11th. "The game is wholly unprecedented in the history of base-ball," said the *Tribune*; "such playing and such a result, after so long a struggle, have never before been heard of."[37]

The Dark Blues had a fright in the bottom of the ninth inning, when, thanks to a hit and a couple of errors, Chicago had men on all three bases. But Cummings was able to induce harmless smacks to his infielders to end the threat. His other innings were pretty much smooth sailing—until the 11th. After Hartford failed to score, Chicago's leadoff man, Scott Hastings, got a base hit. The next batter, Jim Devlin, grounded to third-baseman Ferguson, who tossed to Jack Burdock at second to force Hastings. Burdock, in his haste to get the ball over to first for the double play on Devlin, threw wildly, and it sailed into the stands, allowing Devlin to scoot to third. Next up was Paul Hines, who flied out to the left fielder, Tom York. As Devlin tagged up and raced for home, York threw valiantly to the catcher, but the ball went wide of its mark, and Devlin crossed the plate, scoring the winning run.[38] The White Stockings fans went wild. "[E]very pair of lungs exerted themselves to the utmost," said the *Chicago Tribune,* "and stamping and clapping of hands were added to the vocal uproar."

The *Tribune,* seemingly at a loss to find the appropriate words, pronounced it "the most wonderful, and in every respect remarkable, game ever played."[39] The *New York Clipper,* not a paper given to unwarranted hyperbole, agreed: the match was "the finest display of baseball playing, and the most exciting contest yet recorded in the annals of the national game."[40]

This was a game that neither side deserved to lose. Both teams played superbly, and only Hartford's final error, one of only six it committed in the contest, gave victory to the White Stockings. The *Tribune* had high praise for the pitchers: "The pitching was undoubtedly the finest ever seen here, and to it more than to anything else, perhaps, is to be attributed the wonderful game." Chicago's hurler was George Zettlein, who had come up through Brooklyn's amateur circuit around the same time as Cummings; they had often opposed each other. About Candy Cummings, the paper observed, "his pitching was too puzzling to get the hang of, and the Whites

could hit him for but seven base hits and eight total bases." It also had this
to say:

> Cummings was simply remarkable. Small in stature though he is, and of a phy-
> sique apparently incapable of such tremendous work, he pitched through the
> eleven innings with a wonderful effectiveness and with unflagging powers
> of endurance. When the game was extended beyond the usual length, it was
> thought that the little fellow would weaken. But to the last he held his strength,
> and sustained to the end the rapidity and force of his delivery.[41]

Years later, Candy Cummings himself called that game the best he had ever
pitched.[42]

The *Tribune's* expression of wonderment over Cummings' endurance
was a bit overblown. It wasn't the first time he'd gone 11 innings or even
more. In 1872, with the Mutuals, he pitched two 11-inning games (April 25,
against Baltimore, won 13–11; June 10, against Boston, lost 3–2), and one of
12 innings (August 8, against Baltimore, lost 12–8); in 1873, with Baltimore,
he went 13 innings on July 21 in a 12–11 win against the Athletics; and on
August 11, 1874, with Philadelphia, he worked 12 innings, winning 6–5 over
Hartford. For numbers of innings pitched in a season, Cummings ranked
number one among all National Association pitchers in 1872, and number
six in 1873, 1874, and 1875. The "little fellow" could handle it.

The Boston Red Stockings, with a phenomenal record of 71 wins and
only eight losses, ran away with the championship in 1875. In fact, they
pretty much locked it up by mid–September.[43] The real contest was between
Hartford and Philadelphia's Athletics for second and third place. The standings were determined by the numbers of wins recorded by the clubs, not
by their win percentages. On October 1, the Dark Blues trailed the Athletics by just three wins, 46–43. Three weeks later, Candy Cummings began a
six-game winning streak, and by October 27, the Dark Blues had overtaken
the Philadelphians by one win, 53–52. The Athletics equalized by defeating the St. Louis Brown Stockings the following day; but that was their
last game of the season. Hartford, meanwhile, had two more to play, both
against their—and every other team's—nemesis, the Boston Red Stockings.
Cummings pitched the Blues to victory in the first of those two games, giving his team 54 wins for the season, one more than the Athletics.

That should have settled second place conclusively, but it didn't. Three
National Association clubs disbanded during the season, and others failed
to play their quotas of games. Consequently, under the NA championship
rules, their records had to be discarded when figuring the standings. In
addition, the rules stipulated that the championship had to be determined
on the basis of the official records sent to the Championship Committee by
the clubs, and some organizations failed to submit theirs. So, in the end,
only five clubs were in the championship mix. In the final standings, Boston

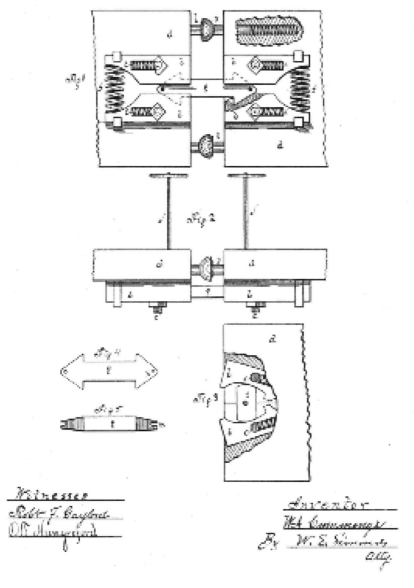

W.A. Cummings' second patented design for a railway car coupling device, on file at United States Patent Office. This design, patented in 1876, was an improvement on his first, patented in 1874.

came out on top, although with only 34 valid wins; Hartford placed second, with 18, just edging out the Athletics who, with 17 victories, came in third.[44]

The 1875 season was the best of Candy Cummings' professional career. He started 47 games and completed all but one of them, winning 35 and losing only 12. He hurled seven shutouts, leading the National Association in that category. His final one, 5–0 against St. Louis on October 18, was the last shutout pitched in a National Association game.[45]

If wins and losses were credited to the pitcher as they are today, Cummings' win-loss record would be .745, his all-time best. His 1.60 ERA— slightly higher than Bond's 1.41—was the best of his career. In other measures of performance, he not only achieved personal bests, but also led all National Association pitchers: shutouts (seven); strikeouts (82); fewest walks per nine innings (.087), and a whopping 20.5 strikeouts for each walk. The latter two stats were achieved by giving up only four walks the entire season. So Candy Cummings seemed to be sitting pretty for 1876.

During the off-season, Cummings spent time improving his design for a railroad car coupling device. The one he'd patented in 1874, which functioned by means of steam or air pressure, was largely ignored. Not willing to countenance failure or defeat, he kept at it. By March 1876, he'd come up with a new, improved concept: a crew member would turn a wheel on the platform of each car, causing the coupling jaws to open. The force of the two cars coming together would cause the jaws of the two couplers to close and engage the opposite end of a linking pin. Candy Cummings registered this design on March 4, 1876, and was issued letters patent on September 11, 1877.[46]

Cummings assigned a one-half interest in his invention to Frederick A. Hart, a vice president of the Aetna Insurance Company. The president of Aetna was Morgan G. Bulkeley, who had taken over the presidency of Hartford's Dark Blues in 1875, the year Cummings joined the club. He occupied that position in 1876 and 1877 and also served as the president of the National League in its inaugural year, 1876.[47] So Cummings and Bulkeley clearly knew each other, and Bulkeley might well have put Cummings in contact with Hart. What exactly was behind Cummings' assigning a half-interest to Hart is unknown. One possibility is that it was in return for financing provided by Hart to help underwrite Cummings' development of his new design.

It has been written that Candy Cummings received a small royalty for his invention,[48] but that hasn't been verified. If he did, it was possibly because elements of his design were incorporated into someone else's invention, and that person paid for the privilege. At any rate, it appears that his concept was little used by railroads, if at all. In 1873, a colonel in the Confederate army, Eli Hamilton Janney, patented a design for an automatic

"Morgan G. Bulkeley, Joel L. English and F. A. Hart, at Aetna Life Outing, Fenwick Hall, Old Saybrook, 1900." Bulkeley was president of the Aetna Insurance Company of Hartford, Connecticut; English and Hart were senior officers of the company. Bulkeley was president of the Hartford Dark Blues from 1875 to 1877, and of the National League in 1876. He was elected to the Baseball Hall of Fame in 1937. He also held several elected offices in Hartford and Connecticut, including governor of the state. Candy Cummings assigned to Hart a half-interest in his second patent of a railroad coupling device (Connecticut Historical Society, photograph, accession no. 1965.31.20, gift of Houghton Bulkeley).

coupling device. First used by the Pennsylvania Railroad in 1877, it went on to become the industry standard.[49]

But tinkering as an inventor was merely an avocation for Candy Cummings; he was a "baseballist" by trade, and a new baseball season was on the horizon.

15

In a Whole New League

All was not well with the National Association of Professional Base Ball Players. Its member clubs were divided along geographical and, more importantly, financial lines. In 1874, eight teams were members of the NA, all but one—the Chicago White Stockings—located in big-market Eastern cities. By the following year, one club, the Baltimores, had folded, and six new teams had joined. Three of the newcomers joined Chicago in what was then known as the "West": two in St. Louis (the Brown Stockings and the Reds) and one, called the Westerns, in Keokuk, Iowa (population 12,766 in 1870[1]). Other new entrants popped up in New Haven (the Elm Cities), Philadelphia (the Centennials) and Washington, D.C. (the Nationals). As the season got going, the baseball press began referring to teams of the East and those of the West as if there were two distinct divisions.

It didn't take much to become a member of the National Association. One just had to get together a bunch of players, find a local baseball ground, and pay the NA's $10 entry fee; no vetting or approval was required. And therein lay a problem. Some National Association clubs were organized as stock companies, with an effective management structure and sound financial backing. Others, including many of the newcomers, were co-operative associations which lacked adequate organizational and financial underpinnings. Encouraged by the NA's token entrance fee, they were formed and joined the Association, hoping to secure games with big member teams that would attract crowds and produce lucrative gate revenues. But for most of them, that was a pipe dream. For one thing, the co-operatives tended to be located in small-market areas. This limited their ability to attract visits from the first-class clubs, some of which were reluctant to incur the expense of traveling to a baseball backwater for little financial gain. Financially struggling co-operatives were unable to travel for games against distant big stock clubs. Adding to the co-ops' lack of drawing power was the fact that their players were compensated by sharing in the gate receipts instead of being paid salaries, so they couldn't secure top talent and thus weren't competitive against the big, established stock clubs. Several teams didn't complete the required number of NA games; three co-operatives folded during the season, and resentment on the part of the stock clubs grew.

There were other ills that afflicted the National Association. A big one was corruption. Gambling had long been a feature at ball games, but dishonest play and "hippodroming"—the throwing of games—had gotten so bad in 1875 that it was affecting attendance and severely tarnishing the reputation of professional baseball. Another problem was "revolving": players jumping from club to club, producing instability. The NA, with a weak central authority, did little to combat these menaces.

Enter William A. Hulbert. A prominent Chicago businessman, Hulbert was a shareholder and officer of the city's White Stockings. After the Chicagos' disappointing seasons in 1874 and 1875, Hulbert became determined to produce a championship team. He lured away four stars from Boston's champion Red Stockings—Al Spalding, Deacon White, Cal McVey, and Ross Barnes—and signed other top players, making the White Stockings a formidable force and leaving the Bostons a shadow of their previously dominant selves.[2]

Hulbert wasn't finished. He proposed radical reforms to rid the NA of what ailed it and restore integrity to the game. After attempting to effect reform within the Association, he concluded that that wasn't possible and that a whole new organization of professional clubs was needed. His first step was to convene a meeting of four Western stock clubs: Chicago's White Stockings, Cincinnati Red Stockings, the Brown Stockings of St. Louis, and a newly-formed professional club in Louisville, Kentucky, nicknamed the Grays.

The next move was to present the plan to a select group of additional clubs. On February 2, 1876, representatives of the initial four plus the Boston Red Stockings, Hartford Dark Blues, Philadelphia Athletics, and New York Mutuals gathered at the Grand Central Hotel in New York. They adopted the constitution and bylaws of the National League of Professional Base Ball Clubs—today's National League—and formally withdrew from the National Association. The formation of the National League, an association of clubs rather than players as was the National Association, marked the shift in control over professional baseball from the players to the owners. As its first president, the new league elected Morgan Bulkeley, president of the Hartford Dark Blues.[3]

"A Startling Coup d'Etat" is how Henry Chadwick described it in a lengthy and vitriolic column in the *New York Clipper*. Although in full agreement that professional baseball was in serious need of reform, he believed that it should have been addressed within the National Association. He decried the secret meeting at which the plans for the National League were hatched as a "star chamber" and "anti–American."[4] But it was too late. The National League was off and running with the best professional clubs and the best players. The National Association couldn't compete and ultimately folded.

For the 1876 season, Candy Cummings was back with the Dark Blues, a member of the brand-new National League. It was the only time in his professional career that he spent more than one season with the same club. But his role with the Hartfords would be somewhat different from the previous year, when he and Tommy Bond shared the honors as the team's regular pitchers. Bond had a good season in 1875 and proved himself to be an excellent hurler. At only 19 years old, he had lots of time to get even better. Cummings had also had a great 1875 season—it was his career best as a pro—but he would be 27 in 1876. The Hartfords saw their future with Bond, so in 1876 they made him their principal pitcher, and Candy Cummings became their change pitcher. There were pre-season indications that Cummings would play right field when he wasn't in the pitcher's box, but that never happened.[5]

Backing up the two pitchers would be catchers Doug Allison and Bill Harbridge, both of whom had been with the team the previous season. Dick Higham, who had been with Chicago and then the Mutuals in 1875, would serve as change catcher.

Allison was particularly suited to Cummings's style of delivery, and the pair worked well together. But none of the team's three backstops was a good target for Bond's swift and erratic delivery. "It is bad enough to have to face the music of a wild delivery," said the *Clipper*, "the result of inability to command the ball; but when the work to be done involves punishment which is in a measure the result of a reckless disregard of the consequences, it becomes doubly arduous…. [C]atcher after catcher had to withdraw from the position, with hands so injured from catching from Bond's delivery as to render them useless for play."[6] Cummings was also difficult to catch, but not as bad as Bond.

Prospects looked good for the Dark Blues in 1876. They had nearly the same players that had brought the club success in 1875. They didn't win the championship then, but they had a year's experience to ponder and remedy managerial mistakes and team weaknesses. Plus they no longer had "that fearful red-legged Boston nine to unnerve them, as was the case last season."[7]

The Dark Blues got off to a good start behind Bond. After losing the regular season opener on April 27 to New York's Mutuals, 8–3, they went on a nine-game winning streak, including four consecutive victories over the severely weakened Boston club, the Red Stockings. Then, from May 23 through August 19, they went 22–12–1 with Bond in the pitcher's box. Six of the wins were shutouts, four against the same team: the Louisville Grays.

Toward the end of the season, the *Springfield [MA] Republican* lauded young Bond, "the best pitcher in the country." "[T]hree years ago," it said, "he was a clerk in a grocery store in Brooklyn, at a salary of four dollars a week—he now easily commands a salary of some $2,000 a year."[8]

From April 27 through August 29, Bond handled all but two of Hartford's National League games; Cummings pitched those, both against Cincinnati. His League debut came on May 30 at Hartford, and he was brilliant. Allowing only three base hits, he spun his club to a 6–0 shutout victory over Cincy's Red Stockings. "His twisting curves puzzled the visitors greatly," said the *Clipper*.[9] According to Connecticut baseball historian David Arcidiacono, manager Bob Ferguson reacted to Cummings' performance in that game with the words that gave Cummings his nickname: "God never gave him any size, but he's the candy."[10]

His outing the following day, however, was quite different: an 8–2 loss. It was a poor display by the Hartford nine all around. Cummings' contribution to the desultory defeat was to serve up 13 base hits to Cincinnati batters. That put him back on the bench, and through August 19, his sole role was to pitch the Dark Blues' games against non–League clubs—such as the Neshanooks of Newcastle, Pennsylvania; the Capital Citys of Indianapolis; and an amateur nine in Bridgeport, Connecticut.

Another non–League club that was mainly Cummings' responsibility was the club from New Haven, called the Elm Citys. A member of the NAPBBP in 1875, the team withdrew the following year, hoping to be admitted into the new National League. But it wasn't, so it played during the 1876 season as an independent professional team.[11] The Hartfords were happy to carry on playing against New Haven even though it was non–League. As Connecticut rivals situated less than 40 miles apart, their matchups drew large crowds, to the financial benefit of both clubs. The two teams played each other ten times over the course of the season, and Cummings pitched in nine of those games. Hartford dropped the first two, to the surprise of everyone, but won six of the remaining eight, with one loss and one tie.

In mid–August, turmoil roiled the Dark Blues.

They were in Boston on August 19 to play the Red Stockings. It was the second of four consecutive games between the two clubs, the final two to take place in Hartford. Up until then, the Hartfords, behind Tommy Bond, had enjoyed a perfect record against the Bostonians, defeating them five times. A couple of those victories were by impressive scores: 15–3 on May 1 and 12–2 on May 19; two others, however, on April 29 and August 18, were one-run cliffhangers.

The game on August 19 was important to both teams. The Chicago White Stockings were maintaining a big lead in the League championship race. Hartford was seeking to stay on course for second place, while Boston was struggling for third. Furthermore, just a week previously, on August 12, the Athletics had hit Bond harder than he'd ever been hit before; 20 Athletics batters reached first base safely on clean hits, contributing to a 15–11 Athletics victory. Although Hartford won their next two tilts, Bond was still smarting from the pounding he received from the Athletics.

The August 19 game didn't go well for the Dark Blues; they lost to the Red Stockings for the first time that season, 13–4. Once again, Bond's pitching was pummeled by opposing hitters. Boston's batters reached first base 16 times on clean hits and scored seven earned runs. Hartford's fielders, for their part, committed 15 errors, five of them by the team's manager and captain, Bob Ferguson. As the *Clipper* put it, the Hartfords "were laid out very cold."[12]

Tommy Bond was angry. Just after the team's return to Hartford, he encountered Ferguson at the United States Hotel downtown. In the presence of the club's president, Morgan Bulkeley, he publicly accused Ferguson of throwing the Boston game. Bond's allegation became public, moving Ferguson to publish a letter in the *Hartford Times* denying that he had sold ball games and insisting that anyone who claimed he did was lying. Bulkeley demanded that Bond prove his charges and offered a reward of $1,300 if he did. But Bond presented no proof. He tried, however, to put the genie back in the bottle by publicly taking back what he had said. In a letter published in the *Hartford Times,* he wrote, "I desire to say that whatever charges of 'crooked' play or willfully losing games were made by me *were entirely unfounded* and made in a moment of excitement, and I cheerfully acknowledge the wrong I have done both to the club and its manager, and make this the only reparation in my power" (emphasis in original).[13] But it was to no avail. The League suspended him and forfeited his salary for the remainder of the 1876 season, and the Hartfords annulled his contract to play in 1877.[14]

There had already been disharmony within the team, bred in part by the presence of the two star pitchers. Bond and Cummings each had partisans among the rest of the squad, and the public squabble between Bond and manager Ferguson created an additional fault line. The discord within the nine, according to the *New York Clipper,* was manifested in a lack of unanimity in support given to the pitchers by the fielders. In solemn tones, the paper cautioned that the situation threatened Hartford's success on the field and the prospects of its securing second place in the National League standings.[15] But there was a bright side to all of this. With Bond gone, Cummings was left as the Hartfords' sole pitcher, and the team seemed to unite behind him.[16]

Following Bond's departure, with Candy Cummings in the pitcher's spot, the Dark Blues won six of the first seven games they played. They split two against Boston, defeating them on August 21 in a 10–4 lopsided affair, and lost a close one, 6–5, the following day. That second game, although close, was poorly played by both teams; between them, they committed 21 errors, Hartford 12 (to which Ferguson—again—contributed five), and Boston nine. The sole earned run was scored by the Reds.[17]

The next five games Cummings pitched were winners, and two of them had special significance. They were both played on the same day, September 9, against Cincinnati, and both were started and completed by Cummings, making him the first pitcher in major league history to hurl a doubleheader. The first game, in the morning, had been re-scheduled from the previous day due to rain. It was won handily by the Dark Blues, 14–4, and featured a nifty triple play in which the choreographer and leading man was Ferguson. The second game was more of a contest, but Hartford was again victorious, 8–4. Over the two games—18 innings—Cummings allowed only a single earned run.[18]

Two games in a single day were "too much for any club," sniffed a Cincinnati paper. "There is danger of rupturing something."[19] It provided no evidence, however, that Cummings or any of the other players involved suffered any such affliction as a result.

Following an 8–7 win over Chicago on September 12, Hartford suffered a string of six defeats at the hands of League clubs. After that, it was clear sailing for Cummings, who pitched the Dark Blues to nine straight victories to finish their League schedule. And those weren't cheap wins. Four of them were shutouts, including an 11–0 embarrassment of Cincinnati on October 9, and others were by convincing scores of 11–2 (vs. Louisville on October 5) and 11–6 (vs. Cincinnati on October 7).

The two final games of the 1876 season were against Boston. They were both resounding victories for Candy Cummings and the Dark Blues: a 5–0 shutout on October 20, followed by an 11–1 win the following day. In that one, the Reds barely escaped being another of Cummings' shutout victims by finally scoring a run (albeit unearned) in the ninth inning.

The Dark Blues put up a good fight for the championship pennant in the National League's inaugural year, but they didn't quite make it. The White Stockings of Chicago achieved William Hulbert's dream and carried off the laurels. They won five more games than Hartford, which took second place. The once-dominant Boston Red Stockings came in fourth, right in the middle of the pack.

Even though Hartford's National League schedule ended with the October 21 game against Boston, Candy Cummings' work wasn't done for the season. Between October 25 and 29, the Dark Blues and the Red Stockings played a four-game series to determine the champion of New England. After defeating the Reds so decisively in the last two games of the League's regular season, the series should have been a cake walk for the Hartfords. But Cummings clearly didn't have his heart in it. Hartford lost all four games, and in only one—the first—was the score close: 8–7. The other three were solid victories by the Red Stockings: 10–5, 12–4, and 13–9. The cold, wintry weather didn't help; it did a job on players' fingers. Errors were abundant and earned runs few in all of the games. But Boston's batters also hit Cummings' offerings pretty hard.[20]

With that, Candy Cummings' fifth year as a professional ballplayer, and his first in the National League, came to an end. Over the course of the season, the Hartfords won 16 League games when he took the ball, five of them shutouts, and lost eight—a .667 percentage. That would be a respectable record if wins and losses were attributed to the pitcher and would place him sixth among National League pitchers in 1876. Cummings' earned run average, 1.67, was slightly higher than his 1.60 ERA the previous year with Hartford, but still excellent.

Doug Allison caught 16 of Cummings' 24 games, and the results showed how effective this pairing was: of those 16 contests with Allison behind the plate, Hartford won 14 and lost only two. Harbridge and Higham had a more difficult time catching Cummings' pitching; the Dark Blues lost all but two of the eight games in which they backed up Allison.

By the time he pitched his final game of 1876, Candy Cummings had just turned 28. The average age of National League pitchers in 1876 was 24.4.[21] So for a professional hurler, Cummings was getting on in years. The 24 National League games that he tossed were only a portion of his workload in 1876; he also pitched a good number of non–League games, not only before he became Hartford's sole pitcher, but also in the rare gaps between League games after Bond left. It was a busy season, and he was beginning to show wear. But he was still one of the top-ranked pitchers in the game. In several statistical categories, he placed among the top five of all National League hurlers: ERA (1.67: third), walks and base hits allowed per inning (1.06: fourth), shutouts (5: fourth), and home runs given up per nine innings (0: first).

The year 1876 would turn out to be Candy Cummings' last winning season. But he was by no means done, and it was time to think about 1877.

16

A Tale of Two Cities

The Dark Blues lost money in 1875 and 1876, due to high player salaries and the small market offered by its home city. The club's stockholders had been funding the deficit. But after ending the 1876 season $3,000 in the red, they were unwilling to keep pouring money into the team. To keep the club afloat, manager Ferguson offered to take a $500 cut in his salary and urged his teammates to make a similar sacrifice. Most did; one of the only hold-outs was Candy Cummings.[1]

In late 1876, Ferguson, who was also a director of the Hartford club, was looking for a bigger stage. He toyed with the idea of renaming the club the Connecticut nine and dividing its games equally between Hartford and New Haven. Eventually, however, he organized the team's relocation to his native Brooklyn. The once baseball-proud city of Brooklyn had not had a major baseball team since the Atlantics disbanded in September of 1875, and it was originally thought that the Hartfords would play under the Atlantic colors. Instead, it took a new name, one that paid homage to the team's Hartford roots, its new home, and the Brooklyn origins of Ferguson and most of its other players; it was called the Hartfords of Brooklyn.[2]

It was thought that Cummings would join the other Hartford players at the club's new base in Brooklyn. But he didn't. His obstinate refusal to agree to Ferguson's call for a franchise-saving reduction of salary couldn't have sat well with the domineering manager. In December, Cummings signed on with a semi-professional club, the Live Oaks from Lynn, Massachusetts, a small city ten miles from Boston on the Bay State's North Shore.[3]

The Live Oaks club was formed in 1873 as an amateur team and turned semi-professional in 1876.[4] The name, referring to the material from which bats were made, was popular at the time and was used by a few amateur teams. The club had been successful, and not only against amateur nines; it even held its own against some big professional clubs.[5] Its pitcher in 1876 had been George "Foghorn" Bradley, a Massachusetts native with a deep, sonorous voice. In August of that year, Boston's Red Stockings, having muddled along with a succession of disappointing hurlers, induced

Foghorn Bradley to break his contract with the Live Oaks and signed him to pitch for the remainder of the season. That left the Lynn team in a bind. With no one to replace Bradley, the club decided to disband, rather than play on with half a squad.[6] Then Candy Cummings became available. He went up to Lynn, reinvigorated the team, and signed on to pitch for them, as well as serve as their manager, in 1877.

Meanwhile, the business of baseball continued to evolve. In its first year, 1876, the National League was not the panacea William Hulbert hoped it would be. Sure, it put the West on the baseball map—and brought Hulbert's White Stockings and the city of Chicago the championship pennant—but it did not rid professional baseball of what ailed it. Weeks after the 1876 season ended, Henry Chadwick, through the columns of the *New York Clipper*, was still railing against dishonesty in the game, and he implored the League to do something about it at its upcoming annual convention. The restoration of public confidence in the integrity of baseball, he wrote, "is of vital importance, not only to [professional players'] financial interests, but to their permanent existence as a class worthy of public support." Despite having mechanisms to punish players for betting on games and crooked play, the League hadn't succeeded in ridding the game of dishonesty. And it wasn't only the players; club officials, too, were frequently dealing in pools on League contests with impunity. There was also a continuing problem of "revolving."[7]

Moreover, membership in the NL didn't immunize clubs from financial precariousness. Over the final month of the 1876 season, not a single League club received sufficient gate receipts from its away games in Hartford, Philadelphia, or Brooklyn to cover its travel and hotel expenses. Three of the eight member clubs—the Hartfords, Philadelphia Athletics, and New York Mutuals—had significant financial problems. Ultimately, the Athletics and Mutuals were expelled from the League, reducing its number to six.[8]

On September 23, L.C. Waite, the secretary of the St. Louis Red Stockings—not a member team of the NL—circulated a letter to other non-League, semi-professional clubs, suggesting that they band together in a new association, for their mutual protection against the League's goal of dominating baseball. After all, argued Waite, the "outside nines"—as the League referred to non-member clubs—had during the season done well in games against NL clubs and had demonstrated that they "can play every bit as pretty a game of ball" as the League teams. They should, he reasoned, therefore attract a good share of the business.[9] Receiving a positive response to his initiative, Waite called for an international convention to be held in Pittsburgh the following February.

That caught the attention of Chicago's William Hulbert. Sensing a threat to the League from the movement for a new rival baseball association, he and White Stockings manager Al Spalding circulated to non–NL clubs a proposal that they become affiliated with the League, without actually being members. Among the advantages of affiliation: a uniform system of playing rules; rules against "revolving," including a prohibition against the raiding of affiliates' players by League clubs; organization of a non–League championship, with League membership offered to the winner; and the ability of affiliated nines to arrange games against League clubs.[10] In early 1877, 13 clubs from the East and the West signed the affiliation agreement with the League, and several more joined over the course of the year. The group came to be known as the League Alliance.[11]

Meanwhile, on February 20, 1877, 21 non–League clubs held their convention in Pittsburgh. One of them was the Lynn, Massachusetts, Live Oaks, represented by their manager, Candy Cummings. The convention organized the International Association of Professional Baseball Clubs—"International" because among the members were two teams from Ontario, the Tecumsehs of London and the Maple Leafs of Guelph. Eighteen clubs joined on the spot, and they elected Cummings to serve as the International Association's first president. At the same time, the convention decided that the IA would adhere to the League Alliance agreement with the National League, enabling International Association clubs to play League nines.[12]

As a rookie manager, Cummings had a lot to do to prepare for the new season. An immediate task was to assemble a squad. He placed this advertisement in the *New York Clipper*:

WANTED—First-Class Ball-Players. Application, stating terms, to be made to WM. ARTHUR CUMMINGS, or to the LIVE OAK B.B. ASSOCIATION, Lynn, Mass.[13]

Cummings put together a team composed of players who had been with the Live Oaks and other Massachusetts semi-pro teams the previous season and a couple who had had experience on former National Association (NAPBBP) clubs.[14] They reported for duty by April 1, and Cummings ordered two hours of practice each day. Meanwhile, he organized the Live Oaks schedule and saw to readying the team's grounds in the city's West Lynn section for the coming season. The grandstand was covered for the comfort of the ladies, who were to be admitted to games free of charge; clubhouse facilities were upgraded; and the playing field was improved. Cummings set strict policies for the ballpark and his team: he banished all pool-selling and gambling from the grounds and required players to comport themselves in a reputable manner. "[T]he manager's aim will be to give tone to the game," said a Boston newspaper, "requiring the players to tread up to the work as gentlemen, so that the taste of the most fastidious will not be offended in witnessing the pastime."[15]

Fans in eastern New England looked forward with excitement to the start of the season. Their focus, however, was on local teams within the New England Base Ball Association, rather than the International Association. (Some New England teams, including the Live Oaks, were members of both the New England Association and the League Alliance). Four clubs, including the Live Oaks, were regarded as particularly strong and poised to wrest the New England championship away from the title holders, a team from Fall River, Massachusetts. (Fall River had been awarded the pennant for 1876 only because all other clubs in the New England Association had disbanded before the end of the season.[16]) Fired up at the prospect of a thrilling competition for the championship, a Fall River newspaper stated, "There will be some 'fun ahead, boys.' Stock has gone up to par again."[17]

But it didn't work out that way, at least for the Live Oaks. The first few weeks of the season were awful for Cummings. His Lynn nine had a miserable losing record through May 9, even though their opponents were mostly semi-professional, amateur, and college teams—hardly baseball dynamos. They lost to the Harvard College team a humiliating three consecutive times. In the first game, on April 12, the Live Oaks committed 17 errors on their way to an 11–3 defeat; their next two losses were only slightly less embarrassing, 6–5 on April 21 and 4–2 a week later. Their record in the International Association competition consisted of two losses to the Manchesters of New Hampshire. One of the Manchester games, on April 26, was a 13-error fiasco resulting in a 14–3 defeat. The only wins the Oaks managed were against a League Alliance team, the Lowells of Lowell, Massachusetts; two minor Boston nines, the Our Boys and the Pioneers; and the Brown University baseball team.

On April 18, the Live Oaks made their first appearance of 1877 against a National League club, the Boston Red Stockings. The Reds shut them out, 7–0. Only two of Boston's runs were earned; the Oaks' 11 errors contributed to the remaining five. Foreshadowing what was to come, the *Boston Globe* offered the understated comment that the team from Lynn was "not proving as strong as was expected."[18] The Lynn fans, who at the beginning of the season were full of optimism about their team, were becoming unhappy and frustrated. By May 4, according to the *Fall River Daily Herald,* they were "growling."

A big problem was poor fielding.[19] But why would a team that, at the beginning of the season, was thought to be so strong, be having such difficulties in the field? The *Boston Globe* offered a reason: "[I]t is very evident," it observed, "that the Oaks are sadly deficient in practice."[20] This failing fell on Cummings, as manager. Either the two hours of practice a day that he ordered was insufficient, or the practice sessions were unproductive, or both. But fielding wasn't the only problem. In the pitcher's box, Cummings had a good game here and there, but in others he was struggling.[21]

After losing to the Lowells on May 9, Cummings and his team began a tour to the West. But their woes continued. First stop was Auburn, New York, where the local nine handed the Live Oaks a 5–3 loss. After that, the Oaks were in Rochester, where they were shut out, 7–0 thanks to 17 Oaks errors, but they turned around and played a "remarkably fine game" to shut out their Rochester hosts, 1–0.[22] Two days in Erie, Pennsylvania, produced two more losses, including another shutout (3–0). Another loss, to the Buckeyes of Columbus, Ohio, was followed by a win at Wheeling, West Virginia. After suffering defeats at Allegheny, Pennsylvania (yet another shutout, 7–0); Erie, Pennsylvania (two losses, including a 13–1 shellacking); and South Adams, Massachusetts (an 8–6 loss), the hapless Live Oaks nine— exhausted from a grueling train trip to seven cities—finally hobbled home in the evening of May 31. In 11 games over 17 days, the Live Oaks had managed to win only two, while losing nine.

Some Live Oaks stockholders, and not a few fans, were wondering whether the team would ever win again. But the players themselves were neither discouraged nor disheartened. On the morning after their return to Lynn, they woke up, headed out to the baseball grounds at West Lynn, and prepared to face their opponents of the day, the Stars of Syracuse, New York. And they shined. Defying the doubters and the bookmakers, who were betting heavily against them, Candy Cummings and his team put on their finest performance of the season. They beat the Stars, 4–1, and that solitary Syracuse run was unearned.[23]

But the success was fleeting. Over the next two-and-a-half weeks, the Live Oaks, and Cummings himself, swung between solid performance and dismal play. During that period, the Oaks scored three wins, all shutouts. But they lost four games, some of them real dogs. Against Indianapolis on June 4, an extraordinary 25 errors by Lynn's fielders, and weak pitching by Cummings, produced a 17–3 defeat. According to the *Clipper*, the Live Oaks' fans were "astonished" by the team's miserable display.[24] On June 13 against the Buckeyes of Columbus, it was pretty much the same; the Oaks went down, 10–1. Five days later, on June 18, the Alleghenys were in town. Cummings started the game but moved to right field. The Lynn team made a game of it but ended up being shut out, 2–0. It was Candy Cummings' final game as a member of the Lynn nine.

His time with the Live Oaks was a great disappointment. He pitched 33 of the 34 games the team played and completed 32. Against International Association clubs, the Oaks won three and lost seven games with him in the pitcher's box; one ended in a tie. When all of the club's 1877 games through June 18 are counted, including those against amateur teams and college boys, those pitched by Cummings resulted in 11 wins, 20 losses, and two ties.[25]

Although Cummings had shown glimpses of his old pitching dominance, it was evident that years of tossing curveballs and rigorous pitching schedules were taking a toll on the 28-year-old. In addition, the realization that, as manager, he bore ultimate responsibility for his team's failings, must have weighed heavily on him. Not long after the June 18 game, he and the Live Oaks agreed to part ways.

At that point in the 1877 season, Cincinnati's National League club, the Red Stockings, was in big trouble. With 15 wins and 42 losses, it was languishing at the bottom of the League table. The team had been playing poorly, suffered from disunity, and was completely demoralized. It was also in financial trouble. It had cancelled its scheduled tour of Eastern cities. Its owners, seeking to reorganize within the same corporate structure, were trying to find financial backers to keep it afloat. But they failed. On June 18—ironically, the same day that Cummings was playing his last game with the Live Oaks—the club's stock company dissolved, and the team was transferred to a new corporate entity. The expectation was that it would retain many of the existing Reds players, hire a couple of new ones, and complete the team's National League schedule.[26]

Cincinnati's pitcher, Bobby Mathews, had left the team, and the newly reorganized club needed a replacement. Initially, it was contemplating hiring a 21-year-old, five-foot-five, 135-pound lefty named Bobby Mitchell, who was pitching for the Champion Citys of Springfield, Ohio, a League Alliance club.[27] But when Cummings became available, they grabbed him instead. Although aging, Cummings was an experienced hurler who still had something to offer. His engagement was probationary, with the expectation of it becoming regular employment if he performed satisfactorily. Cummings would retain his presidency of the International Association, presenting the anomalous situation of the International Association president playing for a League club.[28]

Reflecting the small world of professional baseball in the 1870s, two of Cummings' teammates on his new team were players with whom he'd crossed paths earlier in his career: Lipman Pike, who in 1871 had tried to sign Cummings for the Haymakers of Troy, New York—an episode in Cummings' signing-with-three-teams drama; and Scott Hastings, who was his sometime battery mate on the Baltimore Canaries in 1873. Also on the Cincinnati roster was Jack Manning, a journeyman ballplayer on loan to Cincinnati from the Boston Red Stockings. In his years as a professional, Manning had played mainly in the infield and outfield, but had also done some pitching, chiefly as a reliever.[29]

By July 1, the Reds' full nine had been assembled and was ready to resume where the team's prior incarnation had left off.[30] Its debut was a series at home against the Louisville Grays on July 3 and 4. The Reds lost the opener, 6–3, but they played with greater spirit, unity, and confidence than had been shown by the old Cincinnati nine. Cummings was very effective through seven innings. His team entered the eighth with a 3–2 lead, but his arm wouldn't let him continue whipping in his fast curves. So he slowed down his pace, with disastrous results. He gave up four base hits before recording an out, which contributed to four Louisville runs. The Reds couldn't make up the deficit in the ninth. Despite the loss, the team's solid performance left its fans full of confidence about the hometown nine and feeling that great things were on the horizon.[31]

They didn't have to wait long. One day later, the Reds celebrated the July 4 holiday by bursting to a 10–1 victory over the Grays in front of a huge crowd of Cincinnati's faithful, estimated at between 3,000 and 5,000. Cummings was terrific, allowing not a single earned run to the strongest batting team in the League. Further contributing to his team's victory, he hit a home run in the seventh inning. The Cincinnati fans were jubilant. "A club never played a game through with more spirit, determination, and *eclat,*" exulted the *Cincinnati Commercial Tribune.* "Such was the unity and energy of their play and the daring with which they took chances that after a few innings they had their opponents 'rattled' and disconcerted so that the victory became a foregone conclusion."[32]

The Reds faced Louisville a third time on July 5 and were again victorious, 3–1. Cummings allowed a single earned run in the first inning but held the Grays to zeros for the next eight.[33]

Then they hit a rough patch. Against Boston on July 6, Beantown's hitters struggled against Cummings' pitching for eight innings. In the ninth, however, he fell to pieces and Boston batters unloaded for four singles, a double, and a triple. Further aided by a wild pitch by Cummings, Boston posted six runs that frame and won the game, 10–5.

The teams met again the following day, and Cincinnati again lost the game in the ninth inning. But this time it was not because of Cummings; it was just the breaks of baseball. Throughout that contest, Boston's hitters had been powerless against his pitching. The teams entered the ninth with the score knotted at 2–2. Cincinnati failed to score in the top half of the inning. The bottom half began with two quick Boston outs before their veteran shortstop, Tim Murnane, hit a clean single, then broke for second. Cincy's catcher, Hastings, fired to second but, on a close play, the umpire ruled Murnane safe. Another Boston base hit brought him home for the winning run. The score: Boston 3, Cincinnati 2.[34]

In following games, Cummings and his Reds became erratic. Well-played wins and near-wins were followed by troubling losses;

Cummings alternated between being unhittable and being pounded all over the field.[35]

From the end of July onward, it was downhill for both Cummings and the Reds. They endured a 15–1 lambasting on August 2 by the Chicago White Stockings. On August 4 against the St. Louis Brown Stockings, they squandered a 3–2 lead in the ninth inning. With two out and no one on base, Cummings "completely weakened" and gave up three singles and a double for three St. Louis runs and a 5–3 defeat. On August 6, he was hopeless against St. Louis and lasted only one inning. After giving up five base hits contributing (along with copious Cincinnati errors) to five Browns runs, he was replaced by Manning and moved to center field. Cincinnati lost, 8–2.

Then the Reds hit the road for a lengthy tour of the East that would eventually take them to Brooklyn and Boston. Their first stop was Chicago to play the White Stockings on August 7. For that game, Cummings was relegated to the bench; Manning was given the ball and hurled his team to a 21–7 humiliation. The Reds put Cummings back in the pitcher's box for the next game, also against Chicago, on August 9. He was fine through seven innings but burned out in the final two frames and parlayed a 9–7 lead into a 13–9 defeat.[36]

Following three more losses, Cummings and the Reds faced Hartford again on August 18. Cummings was sailing along into the fourth inning, but then his wrist gave out. He stayed in and pitched through the sixth, only to give up 11 base hits. Finally, in the seventh inning, he was replaced by the second baseman, Amos Booth. It was another loss for the Cincinnatis, 8–5,[37] and it was the last game that Candy Cummings would pitch for the club. The Reds completed their season using Manning, Booth, and Bobby Mitchell as their pitchers.

Through August 18, the Cincinnati club had won only eight games against League teams and lost 29 (including games both before and after its reorganization in June). It had given up on the 1877 season and was looking ahead to the next one. Candy Cummings did not fit into their plans. The club had already signed four players for 1878, and Cummings was not among them.[38] When the Reds returned from their Eastern tour in early September, they revamped their nine. Cummings was out; he was replaced as the team's regular pitcher by Bobby Mitchell.[39]

It was Candy Cummings' worst year as a professional ballplayer. His time with the Live Oaks was disappointing, his service with Cincinnati worse. He pitched 21 complete games for the Reds, including games against League, non–League, and amateur nines, plus an exhibition game. Of those, Cincinnati won eight and lost 13. Including the three additional games in which he started but was replaced, the record drops to eight wins and 16 losses. Against League teams alone, Cincinnati won five and lost 14 with Cummings in the pitcher's box.

Particularly telling as the season wore on was the number of games in which Cummings started off strong but ended up giving away leads and losing games in the late innings. He clearly was weakening. All those years of strain on his arm and wrist from pitching curveballs had taken a toll. He no longer had the stamina to retain his place among the top pitchers in the game.

Also revealing is the *New York Clipper's* 1877 season wrap-up. This feature was a tradition of the paper. At the end of each year, it ran a series of columns reviewing the performance of teams and highlighting the notable players over the recently completed season. In prior years, Cummings had been featured prominently in the review of pitchers. In 1877, the two-part column on "The Pitching of 1877" had an extensive discussion of the curveball, which by then had come into widespread use; but the only mention of Candy Cummings was that he was the one who first introduced the pitch into baseball when he was "the noted pitcher of the Star Club nine or ten years ago."[40] Actually, he had been a member of the Excelsiors when he introduced the curve, but the point is that the *Clipper* regarded him as a player from the past, worthy only of brief mention in an historical context.

After the Big Leagues

Candy Cummings wasn't ready to call it quits. He returned to Brooklyn, where he'd begun his baseball journey over a decade previously, and began scouting around for a team that would take him. In December of 1877, he sent a letter to the club in Buffalo, New York, saying that he'd heard they were looking for a manager for the coming season. "I think I can fill the position with credit for you," he wrote, adding that he could also serve as pitcher and fielder in case of need. Nothing ever came of his query.[1]

In March of 1878, a report in a newspaper in Lynn, Massachusetts—home of the Live Oaks, his team during the first half of 1877—reported that Cummings had been engaged by the Alaskas, a local club in New York City.[2] The paper didn't give a source, and its announcement was probably based on wrong information. Earlier that month, a letter purporting to be from the secretary of the Alaska club was sent to the *New York Clipper*. It gave the names of players selected to play for the team in the upcoming season. Whether Cummings was mentioned in the letter isn't known. One player who was mentioned, however, was Al Nichols, an infielder for the Louisville Grays in 1877, who had been expelled from that club for throwing games. (Gambling and pool-selling remained a problem in professional baseball.[3]) Upon learning of the letter, the Alaskas wrote to the *Clipper* saying that it was a fraud, and that Nichols would not be with the team.[4]

In April, the newly admitted National League club in Milwaukee, called the West Ends, was looking for a change pitcher, as the previous occupant of that position had declared his intention to retire. The *Clipper* announced that the club had hired Cummings. That report, too, turned out to be incorrect. The West Ends were interested in another player for that spot, Mike Golden, and they ended up getting him.[5]

The International Association, of which Cummings remained president until its 1878 convention, was in the ascent, both in terms of members and influence. The National League, in contrast, with its arrogant attitude toward clubs that weren't within the League/League Alliance fold, had made itself highly unpopular. On January 19, 1878, the *New York Clipper* stated:

This season, the League has made war upon the International Association by refusing to recognize clubs belonging to any professional association except the League and the League Alliance.... [B]y a series of arbitrary enactments governing the intercourse of League clubs with non–League clubs, [the League] has rendered itself so obnoxious to the co-operative class of professional clubs, and the less wealthy of the stockholding companies, that a spirit of opposition has been aroused, one result of which will be the establishment of the International Association upon a permanent basis as the regular representative professional association of the country.

One of Candy Cummings' final acts as president of the International Association was to invite clubs—all clubs—to send representatives to the International Association's first annual convention, to be held in Buffalo on February 20. His letter of invitation was addressed to members of the Association as well as the entire "baseball fraternity of the United States and Canada." In it, Cummings presented an image of the IA that sharply contrasted with that of the League, without having to mention the latter group. The International Association, he wrote, "assures the stronger and protects the weaker clubs, and compels clubs and players alike to deal honestly with each other.... [It is] conducted in the interest of the game and the whole baseball fraternity." Contrast this with the League's mission to protect its own. Cummings continued: "All clubs are allowed equal representation in its councils, and possess equal rights before its laws. It is not run in the interest of any club or clique, nor is there recognized in it any preferred class, who are guaranteed any special privileges." Contrast that with the League's according second-class status to members of the League Alliance.[6]

Twenty-six clubs sent representatives to Buffalo for the International Association's convention. "No professional convention ever held," reported the *Clipper*, "had presented so numerous or influential a gathering of professional club representatives." Cummings, who at that point was not a member of any club, did not attend. As the Association's new president, the attendees elected J.W. Whitney of Rochester, New York. The League's convention, held the previous December, had been attended by only six clubs—the entire League membership.[7]

Now back in Brooklyn, Candy Cummings played in a series of exhibition games between "picked nines" of notable professional players in the area. The games were a big treat for local baseball fans, who came to Prospect Park's parade grounds by the thousands see the famous "baseballists" compete. Cummings wasn't particularly effective, but participation enabled him to keep in pitching shape.[8]

His main focus was organizing a new co-operative baseball club in Brooklyn. It was called the Atlantics—taking its name from Brooklyn's storied powerhouse of the 1850s and 1860s, and the not-so-storied team of the

1870s—and its home field was at the Capitoline grounds, in Brooklyn's Western District. The team was to be run by Cummings and Billy Barnie, who had begun his professional career in 1874 with the Hartford Dark Blues, moved to the Westerns of Keokuk, Iowa, and then to the Mutuals of New York City. Cummings would be the team's pitcher and Barnie its catcher.

At the same time, another new club was forming in Brooklyn, run by William Cammeyer, a longtime baseball entrepreneur in the metropolitan region. In the early 1860s, Cammeyer, among his other endeavors, developed and ran Brooklyn's other main baseball venue, the Union grounds, in the city's Eastern District. Pitching for his new Brooklyn nine, and serving as the team captain, was the veteran, Bobby Mathews.[9] The baseball press was excited about a rivalry between the city's two star hurlers. "What with the Atlantic nine of the Western District and Cammeyer's Brooklyn nine for the Eastern," Brooklyn's *Daily Eagle* enthused, "we ought to have some old-time rivalry on the field. It will be Cummings vs. Mathews."[10]

Cummings' Atlantics barely had time to get in a few practice matches and an actual game before they were uprooted. In late April 1878, they were taken over by Ben Douglas. A devoted native son of Connecticut, Douglas had played for, and had otherwise been associated with, several teams in that state. He was responsible for bringing professional baseball to Connecticut. In 1872, he organized the conversion of the Mansfields of Middletown from an amateur club to professional, along with its entry into the National Association of Professional Base Ball Players. After the club folded later in the 1872 season, leaving Connecticut without a professional team, Douglas couldn't abide the lack of representation of his state in the fraternity of professional baseball. He filled the void by organizing the Hartford club, the Dark Blues, in 1874, and remained involved with the team through 1875. After the Hartfords moved to Brooklyn in 1877, Douglas went to Providence, Rhode Island, organized a professional team there, and served as its manager. However, he soon resigned—or was forced out—under controversial circumstances.[11]

Just days after being released by Providence, and harboring a passion to bring professional ball back to his home state, Douglas returned to Connecticut. He leased grounds in both Hartford and New Haven, and then "gobbled up" the Atlantics—Candy Cummings, Billy Barnie, and all—and brought them to Connecticut. The New Haven Hartfords, as they were called, joined the International Association, replacing the team from New Bedford, Massachusetts, and taking over its schedule of IA games. The New Bedfords had withdrawn from the International Association because they were upset with the Association's schedule, which they thought favored Western clubs and deprived them of their share of IA-game revenue. They went on to play mainly local nines.[12]

The New Havens opened the 1878 season on a wet April 27 in New Haven, against the reigning state champions of Connecticut, the club from Waterbury. It was a great beginning. The Cummings-Barnie battery worked well together, and Waterbury's batters could do nothing against Cummings' curveballs. They didn't get a hit through seven innings, and not until the ninth did they manage to score a run. The game ended in a 6–1 victory for the New Havens.[13]

Their first match-up against an International Association team was at Hartford on May 3 against the club from Springfield, Massachusetts. In a hotly contested affair, the New Havens, with Cummings pitching, were again victorious. They were behind, 2–0, after eight innings, but a series of Springfield errors allowed New Haven to score six runs in the ninth for a 6–2 win. The pitcher-catcher combination was again terrific. "Cummings never pitched in better form," said the *Clipper,* "and Barnie caught without any error. They both are working like a piece of machinery."[14]

But Candy Cummings and the New Havens were erratic. After what the *Clipper* called a "brilliant victory" over the Yale College freshmen, 11–3 ("brilliant" seeming excessively exuberant for pros winning over college freshmen), they suffered seven straight defeats. Cummings pitched five of them. Most of his games were close, within a run or two, although one was a 7–0 whitewash by the Cricket club of Binghamton, New York, on May 8.[15] The New Havens were shut out again by the Tecumsehs of London, Ontario, 5–0, on May 18, but Cummings played no part in that one; he was sick with chills and fever.[16] Both the Crickets and the Tecumsehs were International Association clubs. Except for the victory over Springfield on May 3, New Haven lost every one of their IA games from the beginning of the season through May 18.[17]

The team wasn't playing well, and it was failing to attract fans to its games. As a result, the club fell into financial difficulty. In an effort to turn things around, Ben Douglas set about restructuring his squad, adding a few stronger players. He also moved the club's home base from New Haven to Hartford.[18]

Then the team—now called the Hartfords—began a southern tour. They played seven games and won six, although two of those wins were against college nines—Princeton University and Lafayette College of Easton, Pennsylvania—and the others were against lightweight independent clubs. The tour schedule was supposed to include games in Richmond, Virginia, on May 28, 29, and 30. But in a further sign of trouble within the club, it didn't show up, much to the unhappiness of the teams there that had incurred considerable expense advertising those matchups.[19]

Candy Cummings didn't pitch the final three games of the tour. He was out of the lineup altogether in contests against two Washington clubs.

The Hartfords did swell without him, whipping the Eagle club, 17–3, on May 28, and Rosedale, 11–0, on May 29. In the team's first game after its return to Connecticut, against Utica on June 1, Cummings was relegated to right field.[20]

And then he was gone.

A report on May 26 had him going to the Erie club of Pennsylvania. But that was premature; Cummings was still with Hartford at the time. According to one report, manager Douglas had left him behind when the team returned to Hartford from its southern tour.[21] It was an inglorious way to inform Cummings that he'd been sacked. But there was poetic justice of sorts. On July 17, the Hartford club was expelled from the International Association for stiffing Buffalo out of the $75 guarantee due it for a game between the two teams when Buffalo visited New Haven the previous month. That was the end of the Hartford nine. Ben Douglas tried to reorganize the club in Brooklyn, but it didn't go anywhere. He returned to his home in Middletown, Connecticut, and his family's hydraulic pump manufacturing business.[22] Eventually, Hartford's former baseball grounds was abandoned and the property was sold for a trifle.[23]

Candy Cummings wasn't quite ready to hang up his spikes. In late June, he joined a club in Brooklyn called the Witokas and became its captain.[24] A co-operative professional club,[25] the Witokas had been around in 1876 and 1877, playing against local nines in the Brooklyn–New York–New Jersey metropolitan area.

Although the end of Candy Cummings' career was approaching, there was life left in his curveball, and he did pretty well with the Witokas. Then again, the teams he was pitching against were hardly top-of-the-line. They were mostly amateur nines, and even some of the few professional clubs were managed as if they were amateurs.[26] The Witokas' record against these teams was only average. Cummings, however, was again receiving the kind of consistently laudatory press comment such as he hadn't seen for some time. On June 19, for example, the Witokas played a team called the Friendship nine, composed of old players from the Flyaways of New York. Although Witoka lost 3–2, the *Clipper* reported that Cummings "did excellent service for his club in the pitcher's position." On June 27 against the Resolutes of Elizabeth, New Jersey, Cummings's pitching in a 2–1 loss was "worthy of commendation." Reporting on a 3–2 win against the Jersey City team, on July 17, the *New York Times* said, "The Jerseyites could not get the 'hang' of Cummings' effective curve pitching, which was the feature of the game." For its part, the *Clipper* adjudged his pitching "perfect." He was "splendid" against Jersey City again on July 27.[27]

Candy Cummings did have some bad days, but they were rare. One was on August 5 against the Pittsfield, Massachusetts, team, which pummeled his pitching for 18 base hits on its way to an easy 11–2 victory.[28] Maybe he was thinking about other things.

In late July, a new International Association club was organizing in Albany, New York. Cummings ended up signing on with the team in early August.[29] Accompanying him was Billy Barnie, the catcher who had worked well with him on the New Havens earlier in the year.

Cummings pitched fewer than ten games for the Albanys. In the club's debut, against Pittsfield on August 14, he was very effective. Avenging his poor showing against Pittsfield earlier in the month when he was with the Witokas, he gave up only four base hits and held Pittsfield scoreless until the eighth inning, when they scored their only two runs of the game. The final score: Albany 3, Pittsfield 2. Cummings pitched well again when the two teams met again five days later. Over an exciting 13 innings, he gave up only two scattered runs, for another Albany victory, 4–2.[30]

That 13-inning marathon took a heavy toll on the nearly 30-year-old Cummings. Less than 24 hours later, the Albanys had to host the nine from New Bedford. None of the Albanians was in good shape to play. Cummings was particularly hurting. He was "very badly off," said the *Clipper*, "in fact, he was hardly able to pitch at all."[31] The team was soundly defeated, 10–4.

Cummings recovered to pitch a few more games in August and into September, but with mixed results. Meanwhile, Albany had beefed up its team with a few new players. Among its hires was a pitcher, Morrie Critchley. The 6' 1", 190-pounder, called "Jumbo" for obvious reasons, had been with a few teams in New York state, most recently the International Association club in Hornellsville. Critchley gradually took over the pitching duties for Albany and finished the season with a great record.[32]

Candy Cummings' final appearance for Albany was on September 10 at home against the club from Worcester, Massachusetts. His team lost, 3–2, but he gave up only five base hits. The *Clipper* (on September 21, 1878) called his pitching one of the "features of the contest."

There was some talk that Cummings would pitch for the balance of the season for the Alaska club of New York City.[33] But that didn't happen. With his fine performance on September 10, he ended the 1878 season on a high note. It was his last game as a professional baseball player.

The Skipper

The team in Albany, for which Candy Cummings pitched a few games in 1878, did well over the two months that it existed. On the field, it won 30 games, lost ten, and tied one. Financially, it turned a profit, ending the season with a $5,000 surplus in its treasury.[1] So the club was looking good for 1879.

A group of the city's prominent gentlemen, eyeing the Albany club's financial success, saw dollar signs. There was, they believed, money to be made from professional baseball in New York State's capital city. Seeking to cash in, they organized a second team in Albany and called it the Capital City Base Ball Club. It was formally incorporated on December 14, 1878.[2] Could Albany, with a population of around 90,000,[3] support two professional ball clubs?

As for Candy Cummings, it was tough to admit to himself that his days as a professional ballplayer were over. Perhaps what convinced him was his near-collapse during that 13-inning ordeal on August 19, 1878, against Pittsfield. At any rate, he knew that, after years of consistent punishment tossing his twisting curves and pacers, his body simply wouldn't allow him to continue—not at the high standards that he set for himself and that others had become familiar with. But he was by no means ready to leave the game.

Managing a team was one option. His stint as manager of the Live Oaks had been anything but successful, but maybe the ever-driven Cummings felt a need to purge himself of that experience and prove to himself and others that he could succeed. Plus, managing would keep him on the playing field, in the game, and directly involved in day-to-day baseball action, from which he couldn't even contemplate removing himself. And it would provide an income. Before the year was out, he signed on with the still-organizing Capital City club as the team's skipper.[4]

Cummings remained actively involved in the affairs of the International Association. He represented the Capital Citys at the Association's convention in Utica, New York, in February 1879. His term as the IA's president was over, but he chaired the convention during its debate on the report of the judiciary committee, and was proposed, but was not elected, to serve on the scheduling committee. One of the actions taken by the Association at its convention was to change the "International" in its name to "National," as its only remaining Canadian member, the Tecumsehs of Ontario, had disbanded the previous August due to financial difficulties.[5] It became the National Base Ball Association (NBBA).

Cummings spent the early months of 1879 assembling his team. He put together a nine composed of several notable players, including Doug Allison, his successful catcher with the Hartford Dark Blues, and Dick Higham, another ex-Hartford backstop, as well as four veterans of the Boston Red Stockings: Andy Leonard, Jack Manning, Tim Murnane, and Harry Schafer. Their pitcher would be Fred Corey, who worked five games for the Providence, Rhode Island, National League club in 1878. That Cummings was able to attract quality players was perhaps a reflection of the regard in which he was held within the baseball community. The *Buffalo Express* liked the lineup. "This material ought to do some good work," it said, "and with right support from the Albanians, they will undoubtedly do the city credit."[6]

It was assumed that the new club would join the Association. Cummings, however, had other plans. He wanted to join the National League, and he wrote to its secretary to express his interest. From one perspective, that seemed strange, given Cummings' role in the founding of the Association and having served as its first president. We don't know why he wanted to join the League, but there were certainly motivations. First, League teams were in cities with large populations that could produce decent turnouts for ball games; most Association clubs were in less-populated places. In addition, two strong New York teams that were members of the IA in 1878, Buffalo's Bisons and the Syracuse Stars, jumped to the League in 1879.[7] The loss of these teams, especially the Buffaloes, which had won the IA pennant in 1878, threatened to weaken the competition within the Association, potentially lessening popular interest and adversely affecting game attendance. One more upstate New York team, the Trojans of Troy, was admitted to the League in 1879, and the Capital Citys' rival club in Albany was angling to join.[8]

The admission of Troy gave rise to another situation that might have given Candy Cummings pause. Under the rules of the League, no member team could play in the city of another League team, or in an area within five miles of that city, until all League championship games had been completed. The city of Troy abutted Albany, and the Trojans' five-mile exclusive zone encompassed the grounds of the Capital Citys. This meant that the Capital Citys could not host any League team until late in the baseball season and would be deprived of the revenue opportunities of games earlier than that.[9]

There was, however, another hitch to Candy Cummings' interest in joining the League—the 50-cent admission price to League games. Cummings wanted greater flexibility with pricing. As one newspaper observed, "the custom of the League has always been to charge an admission of 50 cents, and any attempt to break in on this rule is pretty sure to be regarded with disfavor." It cautioned Cummings to "take a little time for meditation" on this point before pursuing the matter.[10] Maybe he did, because he never pushed for admission into the League. The Capital Citys became a member of the Association, as did the other Albany club.[11]

By early April 1879, everything seemed to be in place for a promising season for the Capital City nine. The players had been hired and were expected to do the city credit. Extensive work was underway to prepare the club's grounds, and it was hoped that it would be ready in time for the beginning of the season. The plans called for a new playing surface, for which a large amount of gravel had to be brought in, then rolled and sodded. A new, 2,000-seat grandstand was to be erected. Other novel ball park features were to be incorporated, such as an entrance and exit for carriages, and reserved space from which carriage occupants could have an unobstructed view of the field. Amid all these preparations, Candy Cummings was confident of his team's chances in the race for the Association pennant.[12]

The Capital Citys started off well enough. For the season opener, on April 22, they made the short trip to Troy, where they lost a closely-contested game to the Trojans, 2–1. Cummings' team batted and fielded well, and pitcher Corey held the home team to one run through eight innings. In the ninth, he gave up two base hits which produced Troy's game-winning run. A Utica, New York, newspaper liked what it saw in the visitors from Albany. "For the Capital Citys," it said, "we can safely say they fully come up to the expectations of their supporters."[13]

Meanwhile, a Rochester businessman, Asa T. Soule, was trying to revive professional baseball in his city; its club the previous season had disbanded. Soule's company manufactured Dr. Soule's Hop Bitters, a patent medicine that, according to its advertisement, cured "all diseases of the stomach, bowels, blood, liver, kidney and urinary organs."[14] In mid–April, before the NBBA's season had officially begun, Soule dispatched one of his company's officials, Joe Simmons, to Albany to entice the Capital City nine to relocate to Rochester. They didn't bite; but Simmons kept on trying.[15]

Back in Albany, with the 1879 season still in its infancy, serious trouble was brewing within the Capital Citys. The club's grand home grounds were still not completed, and the team couldn't practice. To make matters worse, the club was losing money, and players were not being paid. Internal dissension arose. The team was failing to win. Of its first six contests, it lost five and won only one.[16]

On May 10, newspapers broke the double-barreled news that the Capital Citys had released their manager, Cummings, along with a few players, and that the team was moving to Rochester. Asa Soule had bought it—papers were signed on May 9—and he got it at a bargain-basement price. For the team, its equipment and uniforms, he shelled out only $500. He would pay the Capital City players the salaries due them up to May 1, as well as advances for their services with the new club. In the end, all ten players who had made up the Capital Citys signed on to play for Rochester. Cummings would not be joining them.[17] Right after the move, and without Cummings, the club went on a winning streak.[18]

Soule named the team the "Hop Bitters." Calling his club by the brand of his product met with widespread derision. He was said to be using the team as an advertising gimmick, his players reduced to sandwich-board barkers.[19] One paper reacted with a spoof announcement of upcoming games: "'The Gargling Oils' of Lockport will, on to-morrow, cross bats with 'Cleveland's Baking Powders' of Albany; on the following day the 'Magic Ointments' of Boston will play the 'Singer Lock-Stitchers' of New York," and so on.[20]

Rumors as to what happened with the Capital City club started to fly. One newspaper reported that it had been organized merely for speculation, and that its backers had been lured into investing by extravagant promises that went unfulfilled.[21] There was also talk of fraud on the part of certain directors, and crooked play by players, in relation to some of the games.[22] Two Albany papers implicated Cummings in nefarious machinations in relation to the move of the club to Rochester. The *Albany Argus* claimed that, at the Association's convention back in February, he had hatched "some kind of a scheme" to have the Capital Citys transferred to Rochester.[23] The *Albany Morning Express* alleged that certain members of the club were guilty of "crooked business" in relation to the move, and that Cummings was the ringleader.[24]

The truth, however, is murky. Was the team's move to Rochester anything more than a legitimate business decision, or was something more sinister involved? The Albany papers made Cummings the villain. They were clearly livid at the loss of the club to Rochester, and, as the team's manager, Cummings was an identifiable and available target. But does it make sense to believe that, after the Capital City directors, all of whom were rooted in Albany, had hired him, he would turn on them and instigate a move to Rochester? What would he gain by doing that? He wasn't in league with the directors; they had initially balked at Asa Soule's efforts to move the club.[25] And he wasn't in cahoots with Soule, since when Soule finally purchased the club, he left Cummings out in the cold. If Cummings played any sort of role at all in the move, it seems unlikely that it was for personal gain. He had his faults—such as petulance and obstinacy, as well as naiveté in business matters—but dishonesty was not one of them. Cummings, wrote baseball columnist Sam Crane in 1912, "was not over popular ... with a certain class of ballplayers who were mixed up in rather doubtful diamond transactions. He himself was as honest a player as ever lived, and he never hesitated in telling any player he was suspicious of just what he thought of him, and he invariably hit the nail on the head—the truth hurt.... He was thoroughly appreciated and admired by the better element of players and lovers of the game, and he was always in demand."[26]

As for the implications of players in game-fixing, the *New York Clipper* regarded it disapprovingly as "some very loose talk" about men of "unblemished integrity."[27]

Probably the most trustworthy glimpse into what really went on with the Capital Citys was given by one of its players, Tim Murnane. Murnane, who in the 1870s had played with five NAPBBP and National League clubs, including the Boston Red Stockings, was reaching the end of his noteworthy career as a professional player. He was certainly a man of integrity. In its bio of him in 1879, the *Clipper* said, "He possesses qualities seldom found in the baseball arena, is an honorable, faithful player, and has had a most creditable record with each of the clubs with whom he has been connected."[28] Murnane wrote a letter to the *New York Clipper,* published in its May 31, 1879, edition. Clearly indignant about the "loose talk" about his teammates alluded to by the *Clipper,* he insisted that the charges of crooked play were "too absurd for our contradiction." The team's defeats, he said, were due merely to "the uncertainty of the game." He also pointed out that, without grounds to practice on, the newly formed nine wasn't able to cohere into a functioning unit.

Murnane also revealed his disgust with the Capital Citys' executives, and in doing so, lent some credence to the allegations attributing to them a share of the blame for the club's problems. "I think the officers of the club," he wrote, "with one or two exceptions, were a lot of politicians who, seeing they could not make [the club] pay, got scared, and, to make themselves 'solid' with the Albany people, slandered us."

There clearly was unhappiness within the Capital City team. Murnane pointed out that the players, not being paid, responded by refusing to practice even after the club had secured grounds. Further, the Capital Citys' captain and right fielder, Dick Higham, was given to publicly browbeating and threatening his players on the field.[29] Problems like these reflected on Cummings, as manager. It was his responsibility to maintain discipline, control his players, and do what he could to deal with their legitimate grievances.

Candy Cummings' experience as skipper of the Live Oaks in 1877 had not been positive; his brief stint at the helm of the Capital Citys was worse. Cummings, once one of the game's top pitchers, was simply not a manager.

After pitching in a couple of exhibition games in Albany, Cummings landed a job with a newly organized independent club in Hudson, New York, as manager and pitcher. Once again, however, he heedlessly raised hackles and got himself embroiled in controversy. In mid–June, he tried to move the team to Albany, where it would be called (of course) the "Capital Citys."[30] Feeling like jilted brides, the Hudsonites directed their wrath toward Cummings. Their hometown newspaper snorted, "we hope that he will be so disgusted with Hudson as never to have a desire to visit us again. He is a sort of Canadian thistle, good for nothing but to be uprooted and cast out upon the highway, or words to that effect."[31] In the end, however, the club remained in Hudson—but without Candy Cummings.

In early July, Cummings was back in the New York metropolitan area, pitching for a local New York City nine. He was essentially a rental for the New Yorks, hired to help the team in the race for the championship of the Metropolitan Association. (This association was a group of co-operative clubs from the region.) Cummings pitched a few games, then resigned three weeks later, complaining that the team had failed to give him proper support. He returned after a few days to pitch again for the New Yorks, but his brief sulk came at a bad time. The team, weakened by his absence, lost a couple of games and irretrievably lost ground to its main competitor, the Flyaways of New York. The Flyaways ended up winning the pennant, with the New Yorks runners-up.[32]

And with this, Candy Cummings closed out the 1870s. It was a decade that saw him rise to become one of the premier pitchers in baseball. In Francis Richter's listing of the best players of each decade, Cummings and Al Spalding were hailed as the greatest pitchers of the 1870s.[33] It was also a time in which the curveball, which Candy Cummings conceived and introduced into baseball in the 1860s, came into widespread use. By the end of the decade, a pitcher who couldn't toss a decent curve wasn't worth his salt. The latter years of the 1870s also witnessed Candy Cummings' decline. The constant strains and stresses to which he subjected his arm, wrist, and shoulder took their inevitable toll. And his managerial stints were failures. All of this was difficult for Cummings to face. He was becoming cranky,

But a new decade was about to commence, and Candy Cummings had some decisions to make.

19

(Semi-)Retirement
from Baseball

It's tough for a guy to retire at age 31, especially with a young family to support. It's tough to leave a career that has been one's life since his teens and that has brought such satisfaction, joy, adulation, and fame as baseball brought to Candy Cummings. He knew it was time to bow out; but he did it slowly.

In 1880, he was back in Brooklyn. Candy, Mary, and their five-year-old child, Arthur, were probably living with Candy's parents and four of their other children. While he was trying to figure out what he wanted to do, he took a job as a jewelry agent in New York City.[1]

But Cummings, once baseball's top pitcher, couldn't give up the game entirely. He pitched several games for an amateur club in Brooklyn called the Nameless, helping them in their quest for the championship of the Long Island Amateur Association.[2] He also played on a nine composed of men in the New York jewelry business. One of his outings was quite a grand affair. July 6 was the day of the fourth annual reunion and baseball match between the New York jewelers and those of Providence, Rhode Island. At 6:00 a.m., the New Yorkers met their Providence guests at the East River dock and escorted them to their Manhattan hotel. After breakfast, the two teams, both led by marching bands and accompanied by their respective entourages of supporters numbering in the hundreds, paraded through lower Manhattan and up Broadway, thence to a boat landing on the Hudson. They all climbed aboard a ferry for the quick trip across the river to the ball fields at Hoboken, New Jersey. The game was, according to the *New York Herald*, "most admirably contested," the pitchers for the two teams being the main feature. Cummings didn't disappoint. He allowed only a single base hit and led his nine to a 4–2 victory. Play was brought to a close after six and a half innings to allow the assemblage, now 500 strong, to board a steamer and sail 12 miles up the Hudson to the Palisades Mountain House, a stately, elegant Victorian hotel overlooking the New Jersey cliffs. There, with views of Manhattan and New York harbor as a backdrop, the entire group was treated to a lavish dinner. After a long and exhausting but satisfying day, the travelers made it back to Manhattan by 7:00 p.m.[3]

By 1883, Candy Cummings and his family had moved into their own home. It was at 661 Carroll Street, a typical Brooklyn brownstone.[4] But after a year or so, they were packing moving boxes again, relocating to Athol, Massachusetts, then a town of just under 5,000 inhabitants, 70 miles west of Boston in the north-central part of the state.[5] Originally within a vast region of forests and meadows inhabited by Native Americans, the area comprising the town had been part of a 30,000-acre tract purchased from the natives in 1720 by Captain Zacharia Field, an officer in the King's army who lived to the west, alongside the Connecticut River. He got it for the equivalent of around $600 in today's dollars, and then, as required by law in the Province of Massachusetts Bay, turned it over to the provincial government. The first colonial settlers began to arrive in the township of Pequoig, as Athol was first called, in 1735. It was formally incorporated as a town in 1760 with the name Athol, in recognition of a member of the Scottish noble family Atholl who settled there and became one of its principal landowners.

In its early days, Athol was a poor agricultural village. The mid- and late-1700s saw the establishment of small-scale mill operations, exploiting the ample water power provided by the Millers River and other waterways running through the town. The 19th century brought the industrial revolution, and, in mid-century, manufacturing in Athol began to explode. In the 1880s, the L.S. Starrett Company, a machine tool manufacturer, built what would become the town's largest factory. It, and other factories like it, gave rise to Athol's nickname, "tool town." The Starrett Company exists to this day.[6]

It's not clear what drew Candy Cummings to settle in Athol, rather than returning to his roots in Ware. In terms of population, the two towns were about the same size; the 1880 United States Census puts Athol at 4,817 inhabitants and Ware at 4,307.[7] Also, at that time, both towns were booming, thanks to their mills and factories, although the industrial sector was somewhat larger in Athol. There were members of Candy's extended Cummings family still living in Ware, and Candy's parents, as well as Candy himself, would visit there from time to time. But there were also familial links to Athol. Candy's pedigree traced back to the same Scottish Atholl nobility that gave the town its name, and at least one family within the larger Cummings clan lived in Athol in the second half of the 18th century.[8]

Once in Athol, Cummings set himself up in the house painting, interior decorating, and wallpapering business.[9] When he was growing up in Brooklyn, his father was a successful wallpaper manufacturer and merchant, so the trade was not unfamiliar to him.[10]

But he was itching to be back in baseball. In May 1884, he lent a hand to a team in Waltham, Massachusetts, 60 miles east of Athol on the outskirts of Boston. The Waltham club was a charter member of the Massachusetts State Association. (Both the club and the State Association were formed in March 1884, and both were short-lived; the Walthams disbanded on July 21, and the State Association didn't last beyond 1884.[11])

Candy Cummings pitched a game for Waltham on May 7, against a club in Lawrence, Massachusetts. If the fans in attendance came expecting to witness a pitching clinic from the old master, they were disappointed. Both Cummings and the pitcher for Lawrence were hit hard by opposing batters; each hurler gave up 19 hits. When the slugfest ended, Cummings' team emerged the victor by the narrow margin of 20–19.[12]

Not long afterward, Cummings joined an independent semi-pro club in his new hometown, Athol. He started well. Pitching in an exhibition game between two picked nines on Decoration Day, May 30, he "twirled the sphere very effectively" and led his side to a 15–2 victory. A day later, when his Athol club faced a team from nearby Royalston, Massachusetts, he struck out 12 Royalston batters to secure an 18–10 win.[13] But against a team from Gardner, Massachusetts, on June 7, he essentially lost the game in the sixth and seventh innings when he gave up seven runs, enabling Gardner to erase Athol's lead and eke out a 12–11 win. The Athol newspaper was bitter. It was convinced that the umpire, who was from Gardner, had handed the game to his townsmen through his "most outrageously unfair decisions." The paper punctuated with sarcasm its accusation that the ump had bet on the game: He "is known to have had a good deal of money at stake—that is, a good deal for a Gardner man (two dollars and a half)."[14]

Cummings bounced back, albeit temporarily. He had a good outing on June 20 against another Athol team, the Actives. In what was called "the best game of ball ever played in Athol," he twirled a three-hit, one-run gem for a 3–1 victory[15] He was enjoying his success and the adulation of his fans. But his hurting body wouldn't allow him to sustain it. The ensuing Independence Day holiday period was an utter disaster. On July 4, he gave up 14 base hits to a team from Orange, Massachusetts, called the New Homes. That, together with his fielders' 16 errors, sank Athol to a crushing 14–2 defeat. New Homes plated nine of its 14 runs in Cummings' first three innings—a truly miserable performance by the one-time greatest pitcher in baseball. But it was far worse when the two teams met the following day. Candy Cummings was savagely pummeled by New Homes batters, and in the first five innings, he gave up 20 runs. At that point, he was mercifully pulled from the pitcher's box and finished the last four frames in right field, where he could do no further harm. The Athol second baseman took over pitching duties. It was the last time Cummings, the future Hall of Famer, pitched for an organized baseball team. Six days later, on July 11, when the Athols hosted a team from the town of Millers Falls, Cummings was in the lineup, but not as pitcher; he was assigned first base. After that, the Athols hired a new hurler, producing in their fans "high hopes that they will acquit themselves with credit the rest of the season."[16]

With that, at the age of 35, Candy Cummings quietly took his leave from organized baseball.

Ninth Inning

With his playing days behind him, Candy Cummings devoted much of his time to developing his painting and wallpapering business, which he initially operated out of his home in Athol.

Meanwhile, his devoted wife, Mary, was having health problems. In May 1895, he put his business on hold and returned with Mary and their son, Arthur, to Brooklyn for an extended stay.[1] Candy perhaps thought it best for Mary to be near family and better medical care.

Mary succumbed to her illness on January 15, 1896, at a Brooklyn

House at 375 Pequoig Ave., Athol, Mass., where Candy Cummings resided from 1906–1910 with his son and daughter-in-law, Arthur and Lottie, and their son Glenn (photograph by the author).

**Candy Cummings' attic room at the Cummings residence, 375 Pequoig Ave.,
Athol, Mass (National Baseball Hall of Fame and Museum).**

hospital. Her grieving widower brought her remains back to Athol. She
was buried in a local cemetery, in the presence of her family as well as several friends who had made the journey up from Brooklyn to pay their last
respects.[2]

After the funeral, Candy and his son, Arthur, who by then had become
a pianist and music teacher, resumed their lives in Athol. Arthur married a
local girl, Lottie Thompson, in a spring wedding in April 1896. The couple
set up their household in Athol, and nine months later, they produced Candy's only grandchild, a boy they named Glenn. Candy lived with the young
family.[3]

Baseball was never far from Candy Cummings' heart, and the old
ball-tosser remained a popular figure with players and fans alike. He was
invited to participate in a baseball game commemorating Harry Wright Day,
held on April 13, 1896. Wright, one of the most highly esteemed men in the
game, had earned a formidable reputation as a successful player and manager, most notably with Cincinnati's, and then Boston's, Red Stockings. Even
more importantly, he was universally respected as a gentleman. Wright died
on October 3, 1895, and in 1937 was elected to the Hall of Fame.[4]

In homage to Wright and his contributions to baseball, the National League organized the ball game to raise funds for the erection of a memorial at his gravesite in Bala Cynwyd, Pennsylvania. The competing squads were the Harvard College team and a picked nine captained by John Morrill, who for many years had been a player and manager with Boston's National League clubs. Morrill asked Cummings to pitch for his side; his other pitcher was Cummings' old teammate, Tommy Bond. The game was played at Boston's South End Grounds, newly rebuilt just three years after it fell victim to a raging fire that began in a debris-filled area below the wooden right field seats.[5]

Cummings and Bond entertained the crowd by pitching as they did in the old days, underhand and straight-armed. Cummings,

Harry Wright. One of the game's great players and managers, most notably with Cincinnati's and then Boston's Red Stockings, Wright was one of the most highly esteemed men in baseball. He was elected to the Baseball Hall of Fame in 1937. In 1896, Candy Cummings pitched in an old-timers game held in homage to Wright and his contributions to baseball (A.G. Spalding Baseball Collection. New York Public Library Digital Collections).

now graying and with a handlebar moustache, worked two innings. It was reportedly his first time pitching since his retirement from baseball, and he'd had only a half-hour practice before the game, so he was shaky at the beginning. Showing the Harvard boys his curveball, he gave up two hits and two walks for three runs in the fourth inning. But he settled down in the fifth to hold the collegians scoreless. Morrill's nine ended up defeating Harvard, 14–10. But that was beside the point. The event raised enough money to erect a stately monument for Wright, bearing the inscription "The Father of Baseball."[6] One can imagine an aging Henry Chadwick nodding his approval of sharing that title with Harry Wright.

Not a lot of famous people have come from Athol. Unless you count Dave Bargeron, a member of the rock group Blood, Sweat and Tears, who was born there, Candy Cummings was the only nationally renowned personality ever to live in the town. The townsfolk were well aware that in their midst was one of the most famous players of his era, a pitcher who had a transformative effect on the game of baseball. The editor of an Athol monthly, the *Cottager,* knew, and he believed that Candy Cummings' story would be a draw for his readership:

> Strong interest ever attaches to the personality of one who makes a discovery that changes the whole current of any pursuit, custom, calling or amusement in which large numbers of the human family are concerned. A great percentage of Americans are interested in baseball, and consequently, in the man who practically revolutionized the game by the discovery or invention of the "curve" ball, thereby adding a scientific element and elevating batting from a mere exercise of brute force to a play of the wits.[7]

"He is a good talker," explained the editor, "and would be a highly acceptable companion to any baseball enthusiast, for he can chat by the hour on ball history." So he asked Cummings to record his reminiscences in a series of articles for the *Cottager.* The first one, about his conception and development of the curveball, was published in the November 1897 issue. He produced five subsequent pieces, chronicling his career from his early days in Brooklyn until his retirement from the game, and providing recollections of his experiences and encounters along the way.

Writing largely from memory decades after the events he described, he was a bit shaky on some of the details, although, in the main, his recollections are supported by the factual record. Also, Cummings had a tendency to omit some of the less flattering episodes of his career and to gloss over others. However, his *Cottager* series provides a rare firsthand account of Candy Cummings' discovery of the curveball and of his baseball career.

Cummings wasn't a self-promoter by nature. On the contrary, he was, according to the editor of the *Cottager,* "a quiet, modest man,"[8] an assessment that echoed those of several other commentators who knew Cummings. His six-article *Cottager* series was his first foray into writing, and he was asked to write those pieces by the paper's editor. If he were seeking a broad audience for tooting his own horn, the readership of a small-town newspaper was not it. His contributions to the *Cottager* were moderate in comparison to the full-length autobiographies produced (often with the help of experienced authors) by some big-name major leaguers.

Apart from the *Cottager* series, and interviews given to sportswriters, Cummings penned three short articles about his invention of the curveball, one in 1908 for *Baseball Magazine,* another that appeared in 1912 in a book by Elwood A. Roff titled *Base Ball and Base Ball Players,* and yet another in 1921 for the *Pittsburgh Press.*[9] They were written at a time when controversy was simmering over who deserved credit for inventing the pitch (see Chapter 8). Candy Cummings was rightly proud of his accomplishment and wanted to set the record straight. Plus, he was not one to remain silent when he felt that he had been wronged. When other ex-pitchers wrote to newspapers claiming credit for the curveball, Cummings was compelled to respond in kind.

In 1898, Cummings was on the move again, but this time it was only temporary. He relocated to Fitchburg, another north-central Massachusetts town, around 30 miles east of Athol, to work with a paint and wallpaper wholesaler/retailer named George Z. Page. Page had gone bankrupt in 1896, and his entire stock-in-trade was sold at auction. In 1898, however, he opened a new shop and was back in business. It seems that Page hired Cummings to handle the wallpapering side of his business, allowing Page to devote his time to setting up his new store.[10] It was a good opportunity for Cummings, still a novice at business, to learn tips of the trade.

After a year or so, Cummings returned to Athol and opened his own shop downtown. He placed this ad in the Athol newspaper: "W.A. Cummings, the well known painter and paper hanger, has returned to Athol and is located at 456 Main St. He is an experienced and skilled person, and can always be depended upon to give a thorough job."[11] Performing his work with his customary diligence, Cummings was gaining a reputation for fine workmanship.[12]

Location of Candy Cummings' house painting and wallpapering business at 456 Main St., Athol, Massachusetts, as it was in 2018. Cummings began this business after his retirement as an active baseball player (photograph by the author).

Meanwhile, Candy Cummings retained his ties with the baseball world. He loved meeting up with other players from the past and reminiscing about baseball as it was in the good old days, and he was a welcome visitor when he dropped by baseball meetings and conventions. Appearing at the National League's annual assembly held from late February to early March 1899, he was received as one of baseball's elder statesmen. "Arthur is one of the historic landmarks of baseball," observed the *Washington Post,* almost with reverence, "and now in the lusty autumn of his life he browses in the pasture of reminiscences and tells how battles on the baseball heather were won and lost." He cut a reserved, unimposing figure. "Tall and gray, quiet of attire and speech,"

Candy Cummings, possibly taken in 1905 (National Baseball Hall of Fame and Museum).

said the *Post,* "Arthur looks the practical man of mercantile life rather than an ex-athlete."[13] Circled by players and stars from the old days, Cummings, together with Al Spalding, regaled them with anecdotes from times past.[14]

Into his 60s, a regular event on Candy Cummings' calendar was the annual Old-Timers Day at Peddocks Island, one of the several picturesque islands that embellish Boston Harbor. The gathering brought together former ball players and other baseball devotees for companionship, reminiscences, and an old-timers ball game.

His first Old-Timers Day was in 1907, and he didn't miss one for several years afterward.[15] He was a focus of attention at these events. In its account of Old-Timers Day 1909, *Sporting Life* said of Cummings, "he can well claim the honor of being the most interesting character in base ball at the present time." Cummings would usually pitch three innings, using his straight-arm, underhand delivery, and showed he still had some of his old stuff. "He amazes the boys with his remarkable curve," marveled *Sporting Life* in 1911. "Past his 65th year [actually, he was 62] he can still pitch good ball. He has perfect control."[16]

1, Tom Smith. 2, Bobby Wheelock. 3, Jerry Hurley. 4, Dick Pearce. 5, Arthur Cummings. 6, Mose Chandler. 7, Leo Smith. 8, Joe Hornung. 9, Tom Bond. 10, John Merrill. 11, Jack Manning. 12, Billy Hawes. 13, Arthur Irwin. 14, Connie Murphy. 15, Tom McCarthy. 16, John Irwin. 17, Jerry McNamara. 18, George Dovey, President, Boston National League Club. 19, George Wood. Between 19 and 20, James A. Gallivan. 20, Tim Murnane. 21, Capt. Bill ... aly. 22, Mash Murray. Between 22 and 23, Pat Hartnett. 23, Joe Burns. 24, Ed. Shaughnessy. 25, Charley Farrell. 26, "Nuf Ced" McGreevey. 27, Sam Crane. 28, "Patsy" Sheppard. 29, George H. Lloyd. 30, J. C. Morse. 32, "Mike" Regan, "Royal Rooter."

Old-Timers Day at Peddock's Island, Boston, Massachusetts, 1908. Candy Cummings is in the first row, fifth from the left, wedged in between Dickie Pearce and Mose Chandler. The Old-Timers Day at Peddock's Island was an annual event in the early 1900s. Cummings took part in several of them. From *Baseball Magazine* **2:1 (1908), p. 42 (courtesy of LA Foundation).**

As the years advanced, Candy Cummings stopped subjecting his body to pitching in competitions, but he continued to be an enthusiastic fan and observer of the game. Reported the Springfield, Massachusetts *Republican* in 1914, "Mr. Cummings enjoys the game to-day as much as ever, and he likes nothing better than to get the daily paper and look over the box scores of the big league games and read the accounts of the matches. And he is well posted on all the teams."[17] In 1921, the *Sporting News* noted that "he is still a fan, keeps close tabs on all the ball clubs and their chances for the pennant."[18]

He was also called upon to umpire occasionally, and he attended ball games as a spectator when he could. While in Brooklyn for his parents' wedding anniversary in 1914, he went over to Ebbets Field to watch Brooklyn's National League club, the Superbas, take a doubleheader from the Philadelphia Phillies. At the stadium, he was welcomed by Charles Ebbets, half-owner and president of the Superbas, who showed his pleasure at Cummings' visit by giving him a pass to Ebbets Field.[19]

ARTHUR CUMMINGS, CURVE BALL DISCOVERER

Veteran Snapped on the Roof of The Republican Building Illustrating His Old Underhand Pitching Pose

"Arthur Cummings, curve ball discoverer," during a visit to the *Springfield [MA] Republican*. The image appeared in the March 9, 1919, issue of the newspaper. It was sub-captioned: "Veteran Snapped on the Roof of the Republican Building Illustrating His Old Underhand Pitching Pose" (NewsBank, Inc., and the American Antiquarian Society.

In 1921, he was at Boston's nine-year-old Fenway Park to catch a game between the Red Sox and the St. Louis Browns. Not a single error was committed in that one, and Cummings, who had been used to playing when fielders wore no gloves and errors were in double digits, wasn't terribly keen on that aspect of the evolving game. He was quoted as saying, "It was too perfect, too mechanical." Errors, he said, were part of the game; they added to the excitement.[20]

Candy Cummings's parents lived to a ripe old age. In 1918, they celebrated their 74th wedding anniversary. They were looking forward to their diamond 75th the following summer, when they would be surrounded by children, grandchildren, great-grandchildren, and even a couple of great-great-grandchildren.[21] But by then, William B. was gone. He died in Brooklyn on December 19, 1918, at

Cummings family plot at Aspen Grove Cemetery, Ware, Massachusetts. Candy's grave is second to the right of the large Cummings stone marker (photograph by the author).

the age of 96. After William's death, his widow, Mary, moved to the Borough of Queens to live with her daughter Edith and son-in-law Frank Beall, and Frank's mother. Mary, aged 95, passed away in Brooklyn on April 19, 1922.[22]

Candy Cummings was living in Athol when his parents died. After attending their funerals in Brooklyn, he brought their remains back to Ware for burial in the Cummings family plot.

Not long before William's death, Candy's son, Arthur, and his family had moved to Lansing, Michigan. He went there to work as a salesman at Grinnell Brothers, a renowned piano manufacturer and seller of musical instruments and supplies. With locations in several cities in Michigan and elsewhere, Grinnell's was in its day the world's largest manufacturer of pianos and the biggest purveyor of musical instruments in the United States. Arthur was with the Lansing store until 1921, when he transferred to the company's recently opened outlet in Toledo, Ohio.[23]

Candy, meanwhile, remained in Athol. Now in his 70s and living alone, he was still plying his wallpapering trade. In 1919, he received a large commission to wallpaper homes in a new residential development that was being constructed in town. Then, around 1922, probably just after his mother's death, he left Massachusetts and moved out to Toledo to live with Arthur and his family.[24]

On May 17, 1924, a fine spring day in Toledo with temperatures in the high 50s, Candy Cummings drew his last breath. He was 75 years old. His Toledo death certificate records the cause of death as senile dementia, with a contributory cause of exhaustion. His burial record, however, states that he died of Bright's disease, a chronic inflammation of the kidneys also known as nephritis.[25] The *Brooklyn Daily Eagle* mourned his passing: "Another old-timer has heard the inevitable decision of the One Great Umpire."[26]

Candy Cummings' grave marker at Aspen Grove Cemetery, Ware, Massachusetts (photograph by the author).

Candy's son, Arthur, brought his remains back to the town of Candy's birth, Ware, Massachusetts. On May 20, 1924, he was buried in the town's historic and beautiful Aspen Grove Cemetery. He lies in the Cummings family plot atop a gently sloping hill among many of his siblings and other members of his family, all presided over by his parents, William Brackenridge Cummings and Mary Parker Clark. A simple stone bearing only the name "Arthur" marks his grave.

21

Monuments

At the time of Cummings' death, there existed no national institution to memorialize baseball's most outstanding players or other persons who made the greatest contributions to the game. They were lauded by tributes in the press, commemorative baseball games, structures at their grave sites, and other singular manifestations of high esteem. *The Sporting News*—known as the "Bible of Baseball"—considered that Candy Cummings was deserving of accolades no less than those that had been accorded to other luminaries of the sport. Less than three weeks after his death, the paper declared:

> It is doubtful if there is any ball player's memory which deserves more to be commended and honored by such feeble tokens as man may devise, than that of Arthur Cummings, pitcher, of olden times, who only recently passed to the great beyond....
> So, while we moderns remember our Ruths and our Sislers, and award them diplomas, and are to honor them in some way or another by a monument, all baseball can rightfully demand that the name of a player such as Arthur Cummings be perpetuated in some way that shall be commendable, for here was an individual who absolutely changed the course of baseball into a new channel.[1]

For years, there had been an imaginary baseball hall of fame. Sportswriters would write that this, that, or another player who had a particularly good day on the diamond had played himself into the hall of fame.

The imaginary became a reality in 1935, when the real National Baseball Hall of Fame and Museum was founded. For the Hall's physical location, the founders chose Cooperstown, a rural village in central New York State at the southern end of picturesque Otsego Lake, surrounded by wooded hills. The town had been founded by the father of the American author James Fenimore Cooper, who lived in Cooperstown for nearly his entire life and used the region as a setting for many of his novels.

Cooperstown was selected as the site of the Baseball Hall of Fame and Museum because it was believed that Abner Doubleday had invented baseball there in 1839.[2] We now know, however, the game wasn't invented by

Doubleday, or for that matter, any other individual; it has a much longer and more complex history (see Chapter 3).

The mission of the Hall of Fame and Museum is "preserving history, honoring excellence, connecting generations."[3] Today, it houses more than 40,000 artifacts, including major league players' gloves, uniforms, and bats, and other baseball paraphernalia and mementos, and its library and archives are filled with over a million documents, images, and media. At the core of the Hall of Fame is the Plaque Gallery, the pantheon of baseball's immortals. Hundreds of thousands of people visit the Hall each year to learn about baseball's past and present, and, through its exhibits, establish an intimate connection with their favorite teams and players.

The greatest monument to any big-league baseball player is a bronze plaque, bearing the player's likeness and a brief description of his contribution to the game, in the Plaque Gallery. It is baseball's highest honor—definitive affirmation that the player reached the pinnacle of his profession. Of the more than 19,700 players who have taken the field for big-league teams since 1876, the year the National League was formed, fewer than 250 of them have received that honor.[4]

Candy Cummings' plaque at the Baseball Hall of Fame and Museum (National Baseball Hall of Fame and Museum).

The Hall elected its first immortals in 1936. They were Babe Ruth, Ty Cobb, Christy Mathewson, Walter Johnson, and Honus Wagner. Three years later, on June 12, 1939, the Hall's imposing colonial-style red brick building on Cooperstown's Main Street was dedicated, and baseball's best, 26 of them—the original five plus those elected in subsequent years—were formally inducted. Among them was W.A. "Candy" Cummings, one of 13 pioneer stars of the game from the 19th century chosen by a joint commission of the National and American Leagues.

A crowd of over 10,000 people jammed

Cooperstown's Main Street that day to witness the splendid dedication and induction pageant, called the Cavalcade of Baseball; countless others listened in on their radios. It was a gala celebration of the centennial of Doubleday's supposed invention of baseball in Cooperstown. The exercises opened with the singing of "Take Me Out to the Ball Game," followed by speeches from

Plaque in front of Candy Cummings' grave marker, Aspen Grove Cemetery, Ware, Massachusetts. It was placed there in 2012 by the Town of Ware to commemorate its famous native son (photograph by the author).

the commissioner of baseball, Kenesaw Mountain Landis; the presidents of the National and American Leagues; and other dignitaries. There was a solemn ceremony to honor the memory of 12 inductees who were no longer living. Candy Cummings was among them. So were such greats as Cap Anson, Henry Chadwick, Charles "Old Hoss" Radbourn, Al Spalding, and George Wright. As each name was announced, a drum roll sounded in salute.[5]

Plaques for each of the freshly minted Hall of Famers were unveiled in the Hall's Plaque Gallery. Candy Cummings' cites his transformative contribution to our national pastime:

> Pitched first curve ball in baseball history. Invented curve as amateur ace of Brooklyn Stars in 1867. Ended long career as Hartford pitcher in National League's first year, 1876.

Yes, Candy Cummings was the first hurler to pitch a curveball in competition and thus introduce it into the game of baseball, and he did it in 1867, as the plaque says—but he was with Brooklyn's Excelsiors then, not the Stars. That was clarified in the short biography of Cummings prepared by the Hall of Fame that now appears on its website. Also, his professional career didn't end with the Hartfords in 1876. Nor was that his final year in the National League; for part of 1877 he played for another NL club, Cincinnati's Red Stockings. This, too, has been clarified in his Hall of Fame bio. But those minor points in no way detract from the enormity of the honor of Candy Cummings' inclusion among the highly select group of baseball immortals—baseball's best-of-the-best.

Trophy awarded posthumously to Candy Cummings at his induction into the Western Massachusetts Baseball Hall of Fame, 2019 (photograph by the author).

In October 2012, the Town of Ware established its own monument to Candy Cummings by installing a commemorative stone at his gravesite. The marble marker refers to him as the "Father of the Curveball" and to his induction into the Baseball Hall of Fame in 1939. Underscoring the indisputable link between Candy Cummings and the town, the dedication ceremony was attended by local residents and town officials, as well as their representatives in the Massachusetts legislature.[6] It was a fitting homage to Ware's native son who left town, enriched the national pastime, and then came home.

Candy Cummings' most recent tribute came in 2019, when he was inducted into the Western Massachusetts Baseball Hall of Fame. Founded in 2014 to honor the best and brightest baseball figures in the region and to celebrate the area's long and deep baseball traditions, the Western Massachusetts Hall is under the patronage of the Valley Blue Sox, a Holyoke-based team that plays in the New England Collegiate Baseball League.[7]

At the Hall's induction ceremony, Candy Cummings' trophy was accepted on his behalf by the author. It is displayed in the Valley Blue Sox front office in Springfield, Massachusetts.

22

Candy's Legacy

Candy Cummings' contribution to our national pastime was immense. *The Sporting News* summed it up this way, shortly after his death in 1924:

> He changed all the art of pitching. There is no individual ball player in the history of the sport whose influence has been so great upon pitchers and pitching as that of Cummings. He gave to the pitchers such opportunities for strategy and rightful deception as they never had possessed from the moment the first ball was thrown in Abner Doubleday's rudely constructed diamond at Cooperstown, N.Y.[1]

The myth that Mr. Doubleday invented baseball in Cooperstown has since been debunked. But the central point made by *The Sporting News* cannot be gainsaid. It is as true today as it was in 1924. The game has evolved dramatically since the 1860s and 1870s, when Candy Cummings was in the pitcher's spot. And his debut of the curveball on that autumn afternoon in 1867, in Cambridge, Massachusetts, was a seminal event in that evolution. As Francis Richter wrote, "[H]e made a monumental discovery by the invention and perfection of the curve ball. This discovery had [a] fundamental effect on the game, as it revolutionized pitching and therefore profoundly affected all other departments of the game."[2]

Candy Cummings' curveball transformed baseball from a hitter's game to a contest between pitcher and batter; from a game in which the pitcher merely catered to the batter's desires to one in which the pitcher employed skill, strategy, and deception to prevail in the battle between moundsman and batsman; from a game in which the pitcher's job was to enable the batter to hit the ball to one in which the pitcher does what he can to prevent the batter from hitting it, or to induce the batter to hit it where it can be fielded and do no damage, or even force a double play. Cummings introduced science into pitching; he saw the promise of putting a spin on the ball. His wrist-twist delivery begot a gradual relaxation of the rules regarding pitching, from stiff-armed, underhand, horseshoes-like tossing to throwing in whatever manner the human body could devise. Cummings' curveball was a model for the development of other types of breaking pitches that are still employed to deceive the batter.

But Cummings's contribution to baseball was so much more than the curveball. In his day, he was one of baseball's biggest stars—a top pitcher of his era. Henry Chadwick and others considered him the best. From his early days onward, he created excitement on the ball fields and in the press, and he attracted fans to baseball grounds to see him play. His years as a professional were stellar. The compilation by baseball-reference.com of his appearances on leaderboards in key pitching categories during his years with the National Association of Professional Base Ball Players (NAPBBP) and National League (1872–1877) shows the following:

> Fewest walks per 9 innings: first among all pitchers in 1875; his career record places first among those of big-league pitchers of all time.
> Most strikeouts: first in 1875; second in 1872 and 1874; third in 1873.
> Most strikeouts per 9 innings: four seasons in top 5.
> Strikeouts to walks ratio: first in 1875; four seasons in top 5.
> Most shutouts: first in 1872 and 1875; five seasons in top 4.
> Fewest home runs allowed per 9 innings: first in 1875 and 1876; four seasons in top 5; his career record places fourth among those of big-league pitchers of all time.
> Earned run average (ERA): four seasons in top 5. (Nemec's *Great Encyclopedia of Nineteenth Century Major League Baseball* places him in the top 5 in five seasons.[3])
> Winning percentage: four seasons in top 4. (Nemec places him in the top 5 in five seasons.)
> Fewest hits allowed per 9 innings: three seasons in top 4.
> Fewest walks + hits per inning: five seasons in top 5.

Added to all that, Candy Cummings was a pioneer of his sport. He served as the first president of baseball's first minor league—the International Association of Professional Base Ball Clubs; he played at the dawn of professional baseball and at the founding of the National League.

Candy's was a life well-lived and a career well-pursued. There can be no doubt that his baseball achievements and contributions to the game were worthy of the honors, monuments, and accolades bestowed upon him. Since so many of the tributes to him came long after he was around to bask in them, it seems fitting that he should get the final word here:

> I get a great deal of pleasure now in my old age of going to games and watching the curves, thinking that it was through my blind efforts that all this was made possible.[4]

Chapter Notes

Chapter 1

1. Harold C. Burr, "Candy Cummings," *Sporting News,* November 19, 1942.

2. William J. Ryczek, *Baseball's First Inning: A History of the National Pastime Through the Civil War* (Jefferson, NC: McFarland, 2009), 8.

3. "The First to Curve. How Arthur Cummings Made the Discovery," *Sporting Life,* April 11, 1896.

4. Sam Crane, "Arthur Cummings," *New York Journal,* December 29, 1912.

5. William C. Alden, *The Physical Features of Central Massachusetts,* United States Geological Survey, Bulletin 760–B (Washington: Government Printing Office, 1924).

6. Commonwealth of Massachusetts, Department of Conservation and Recreation, *Ware Reconnaissance Report* (June, 2009), 4; Dennis A. Connole, *The Indians of the Nipmuck Country in Southern New England, 1630–1750: An Historical Geography* (Jefferson, NC: McFarland, 2001), 7–10; William Hyde, *An Address, Delivered at the Opening of the New Town-Hall, Ware, Mass., March 31, 1847* (Brookfield, MA: Merriam and Cooke, 1847), 6, 15, 42 (available online at https://archive.org/details/addressde livered00hyderich); Arthur Chase, *History of Ware, Massachusetts* (Cambridge, MA: University Press, 1911), 4 (available online at https://archive.org/details/history waremass00chasgoog); Donald Duffy, "Ne Namas Eck Or The Place of Fish," in Ware Historical Society, *History of Ware, Massachusetts, 1961–2011* (Salem, MA: Higginson Book Co., 2012), 58–84; Nipmucks: Ives Goddard, "The 'Loup' Languages of Western Massachusetts: The Dialectical

Diversity of Southern New England Algonquian," 125, in Monica Macaulay *et al,* eds., *Papers of the Forty-Fourth Algonquian Conference* (Albany, NY: SUNY Press, 2016), 104–138.

7. Commonwealth of Massachusetts, Massachusetts Historic Commission, *MHC Reconnaissance Survey Town Report—Ware* (1982), 6, 7, 11; Chase, *History of Ware, Massachusetts,* 7–10, 224–226.

8. *MHC Reconnaissance Survey Town Report—Ware,* 10–11; *Ware Reconnaissance Report,* 4–5; Chase, *History of Ware,* 219–221.

9. John Warner Barber, *Historical Collections, Being a General Collection of Interesting Facts, Traditions, Biographical Sketches, Anecdotes, &c., Relating to the History and Antiquities of Every Town in Massachusetts* (Worcester, MA: Warren Lazell, 1844), 343–344 (available online at https://archive.org/details/ historicalcolle00barbuoft).

10. U.S. Secretary of State, *Census for 1820* (Washington: Gales & Seaton, 1821); Seventh Census of the United States: 1850, Appendix (Washington: Robert Armstrong, Public Printer, 1853); *MHC Reconnaissance Survey Town Report—Ware,* 10–11.

11. *MHC Reconnaissance Survey Town Report—Ware,* 13.

12. Record of birth of William A. Cummings, in Jay Mack Holbrook, *Massachusetts Vital Records to 1850: Ware 1735–1893,* vol. 3, "Births, Marriages, Deaths, 1844–1852, Births in Ware 1848–1849," 31.

13. Rev. George Mooar, *The Cummings Memorial: A Genealogical History of the Descendants of Isaac Cummings, an Early Settler of Topsfield, Massachusetts* (New York: B.F. Cummings, 1903), 434 (available

online at https://archive.org/details/cumm
ingsmemorial00inmooa).

14. Albert Oren Cummins, *Cummings Genealogy. Isaac Cummings, 1601–
1677 of Ipswich in 1638 and Some of His
Descendants* (Montpelier, VT: Argus and
Patriot Printing House, 1904) (available online at https://archive.org/details/
cummingsgenealog00cumm).

15. Cummins, *Cummings Genealogy*; website of the Isaac Cummings Family Association, http://www.isaaccummings
family.org/about.php. Candy Cummings'
direct ancestral line is given in Stephen R.
Katz, "The Story of the Portraits of Mr. and
Mrs. William Brackenridge Cummings of
Ware, Massachusetts, and Brooklyn, New
York," *MASSOG: A Genealogical Journal for
the Commonwealth of Massachusetts* 41, no.
2 (Massachusetts Society of Genealogists,
2016–2017), 50–61.

16. Marietta Clark, *et al, Isaac Cummings of Topsfield, Mass., and Some of His
Descendants* (Topsfield: Topsfield Historical Society, 1899) (available online at
https://archive.org/details/isaaccumming
soft00clar; George Francis Dow, *History of
Topsfield, Massachusetts* (Topsfield: Topsfield Historical Society, 1940), 273 (available online at https://archive.org/details/
historyoftopsfie00dowg); www.ancestry.
com, *U.S. and Canada, Passenger and Immi-
gration Lists Index, 1500s-1900s*.

17. Charles E. Jefferson, *Congregationalism* (Boston: Pilgrim Press, 1910), 17, 22,
24 (available online at https://archive.org/
details/congregationali00jeffgoog).

18. James F. Cooper, *Tenacious of Their
Liberties: The Congregationalists in Colonial
Massachusetts* (New York: Oxford Univer-
sity Press, 1999), 5.

19. Jefferson, *Congregationalism*, 29.

20. Cummins, *Cummings Genealogy*,
24–25; Mooar, *Cummings Memorial*, 33.

21. Chase, *History of Ware*, 58–70,
133–134, 136, 141ff, 160, 205, 249–250;
Mooar, *Cummings Memorial*, 33; Bernice
Amsden Warnick, *Ancestors and Descendants of Jonathan Nichols Amsden and Amelia Jane Smith* (Santa Maria, CA.: Bernice
Amsden Warnick, 1978), 71.

22. Hyde, *An Address*, 28, 41, 55, 56;
Mooar, *Cummings Memorial*, 313–314.

23. Record of birth of William A.
Cummings.

24. Cornelia A. Gould, *Genealogy

of the Descendants of James Breakenridge, Who Emigrated from Ireland, July,
1727* (Ware, MA: Charles W. Eddy, 1887),
5–12 (available online at https://archive.
org/details/genealogyofdesce1887goul);
Charles Knowles Bolton, *Scotch Irish Pioneers in Ulster and America* (Boston: Bacon
& Brown, 1910), 193 (available online at
https://archive.org/details/scotchirish
00boltrich); Chase, *History of Ware*, 133,
159, 250–51; Hyde, *An Address*, 28–29, 49,
55.

25. Chase, *History of Ware*, 224, 237,
251.

26. City Clerk, Hartford, Conn., Marriages, Births, Deaths, 1797–1855, 205,
https://familysearch.org/pal:/MM9.3.1/
TH-1971-43943-8409-12?cc=2448940.

Chapter 2

1. 1850 U.S. Census, New York City,
16th Ward, New York County, New York,
251, Dwelling no. 430, Family no. 1143;
*Doggett's New York City Street Directory for
1851* (New York: John Doggett, Jr., 1851),
378.

2. B.T. Pierson, *Directory of the City of
Newark for 1851–1852* (Newark, NJ: Holbrook's Steam Press, 1851), 100; Pierson,
*Directory of the City of Newark for 1852–
1853* (Newark, NJ: A. Stephen Holbrook,
1852), 107; Pierson, *Directory of the City of
Newark for 1853–1854*, 108.

3. *Return of Births in the City of Newark, County of Essex, State of New Jersey,
from the first day of May 1851 to the first day
of May 1852*, 113.

4. 1850 U.S. Census, Ware, roll 321, p.
406B; 1855 New York State Census, Brooklyn, 2nd E.D., 6th Ward, household 1048,
stating that the family had been residing
there for three years.

5. *Smith's Brooklyn Directory for the
Year Ending May 1st, 1857* (Brooklyn:
Charles Jenkins, 1856), 76.

6. Brooklyn/Queens Waterfront,
"Wallabout Bay/Navy Yard," https://sites.
google.com/site/brooklynqueenswater
front/neighborhood-histories/wallabout-
bay-navy-yard.

7. Harold Coffin Syrett, *The City of
Brooklyn, 1865–1898* (New York: Columbia Univ. Press, 1944), 13 ff (available
online at https://archive.org/details/

cityofbrooklyn180000syre); James L. Terry, *Long Before the Dodgers: Baseball in Brooklyn, 1855–1884* (Jefferson, NC: McFarland, 2002), 7–8.

8. Thirteen/WNET, "History of Brooklyn," http://www.thirteen.org/brooklyn/history/history3.html; "Mass Transit, Brooklyn Style," http://www.brooklynwaterfronthistory.org/story/mass-transit-brooklyn-style; New York City Landmark Preservation Commission, *Carroll Gardens Historic District: Designation Report* (1973), http://www.nyc.gov/html/lpc/downloads/pdf/reports/CARROLL_GARDENS_HISTORIC_DISTRICT.pdf, 2.

9. Work in telegraph office: 1855 NY State Census, King's County, Brooklyn, 2nd ED, 6th Ward, family no. 1048; *Brooklyn City Directory for the Year Ending May 1, 1856* (Brooklyn: William H. Smith, 1855), 95; beginning of commercial telegraphy: Edwin Wiley and Irving E. Rines, *Lectures on the Growth and Development of the United States* 9 (New York: American Educational Alliance, 1915), 245–7; Economic History Association, "History of the U.S. Telegraph Industry," https://eh.net/encyclopedia/history-of-the-u-s-telegraph-industry.

That William B. Cummings was working in a telegraph office in New York is surmised from the Newark City Directories cited above, stating that he worked in New York, and the 1855 New York State census (after the family had moved to Brooklyn), giving his occupation as cashier in a telegraph office (1855 NY State Census, King's County, Brooklyn, 2nd E.D., 6th Ward, family no. 1048).

10. Figures from the U.S. Census of 1840 and 1870. A small portion of this increase was due to the consolidation of Brooklyn and the villages of Williamsburg and Bushwick in 1855.

11. *Brooklyn Daily Eagle*, February 16, 1869.

12. *Ibid.*

13. Website of the Plymouth Church, http://www.plymouthchurch.org/history; "Plymouth Church of the Pilgrims," https://www.atlasobscura.com/places/plymouth-church-of-the-pilgrims?utm_source=atlas-forum&utm; Andy McCue, "Branch Rickey," SABR BioProject, https://sabr.org/bioproj/person/6d0ab8f3; Ephemeral New York, "The Piece of

Plymouth Rock in a Brooklyn Church," https://ephemeralnewyork.wordpress.com/2015/07/20/the-piece-of-plymouth-rock-in-a-brooklyn-church.

14. http://newenglandsociety.org; *Constitution and By-Laws of the New-England Society in the City of Brooklyn* (Brooklyn: E.B. Spooner, Printers, 1847).

15. *Brooklyn Daily Eagle*, February 16, 1869.

16. Clay Lancaster, "Carroll Gardens/Brooklyn /Long Island/New York. An Architectural Evaluation" (May 23, 1970), unpublished manuscript in the files of the Brooklyn Historical Society; Citizens for New York City, *The Neighborhoods of Brooklyn*, 2nd ed. (New Haven, CT: Yale University Press, 2004).

17. *Carroll Gardens Historic District: Designation Report*, 1, 2.

18. *Brooklyn Daily Eagle,* July 16, 1873; "Old Brooklyn Farm Lands," *Brooklyn Daily Eagle,* July 19, 1896; "Carroll Gardens Brooklyn History," http://carrollgardenshistory.blogspot.com/2009/03/bergen-hill.html.

19. Richard Butt, *Map of the City of Brooklyn, and the Village of Williamsburgh, showing the Size of Blocks and Width of Streets as Laid Out by the Commissioners, the Old Farm Water Line, and All Recent Changes in Streets* (1846); *Brooklyn Daily Eagle*, January 28, 1851.

20. Jeanette Jeanes, "A History of Carroll Gardens" (1970), unpublished manuscript in the files of the Brooklyn Historical Society; *Carroll Gardens Historic District: Designation Report*, 2.

21. William Perris, *Maps of the City of Brooklyn*, 2nd ed., vol. 2 (1860–1861).

22. William Perris, *Maps of the City of Brooklyn* (1855).

23. Clay Lancaster, "Carroll Gardens/Brooklyn/Long Island/New York. An Architectural Evaluation" (May 23, 1970), unpublished manuscript in files of the Brooklyn Historical Society.

24. *New York Evening Post,* November 20, 1854.

25. South Brooklyn Network, "Carroll Gardens," https://www.southbrooklyn.net/neighborhood/carroll-gardens.

26. Luciano Iorizzo, *Al Capone: A Biography* (Westport, CT: Greenwood Press, 2003), 24–26; "Carroll Gardens."

27. 1855 NY State Census, King's

County, Brooklyn, 2nd E.D., 6th Ward, family no. 1048; *Smith's Brooklyn City Directory for the Year Ending May 1st, 1856* (Brooklyn: William H. Smith, 1855), 95; *Brooklyn City Directory for the Year Ending May 1st, 1858* (Brooklyn: J. Lain) (hereafter shortened to "Lain's Brooklyn Directory ... [year]"), 82; Lain's Brooklyn Directory 1859, 84; 1860, 90; 1862, 93; 1864, 104; 1866, 106; 1869, 136; obituary of William B. Cummings, *Brooklyn Daily Eagle,* December 21, 1918.

28. 1865 New York State Census, King's County, Brooklyn, 4th Ward, Family no. 310; 1870 U.S. Census, Brooklyn, King's County, NY, Ward 22, 29.

29. Obituary of William B. Cummings, *Brooklyn Daily Eagle,* December 21, 1918.

30. Syrett, *The City of Brooklyn, 1865–1898,* 22.

31. Stephen R. Katz, "The Story of the Portraits of Mr. and Mrs. William Brackenridge Cummings of Ware, Massachusetts, and Brooklyn, New York," *MASSOG: A Genealogical Journal for the Commonwealth of Massachusetts* 41, no. 2 (Massachusetts Society of Genealogists, 2016–2017), 50–61.

32. *Manual of the South Congregational Church, Brooklyn, N.Y.* (New York: Blakeman and Mason, 1859) (in the Brooklyn Historical Society's South Congregational Church of Brooklyn collection 1986.020).

33. *Ninetieth Anniversary: South Congregational Church, Brooklyn, N.Y.* (in the Brooklyn Historical Society's South Congregational Church of Brooklyn collection 1986.020).

34. A. Emerson Palmer, *The New York Public School. Being a History of Free Education in the City of New York* (New York: MacMillan, 1905), 214, 215; Department of Public Instruction, *Sixth Annual Report of the Superintendent of Schools of Brooklyn, New-York, for the Year Ending January 31, 1861* (Brooklyn: L. Darbee, 1861), 55; Department of Public Administration, *Twelfth Annual Report of the Superintendent of Schools for the Year Ending January 31, 1867* (Brooklyn: L. Darbee, 1867), 33–34.

35. Palmer, *The New York Public School,* 217; Ferris G. Bergen, "The Department of Public Education," in Henry R. Stiles, ed., *Civil Political, Professional and Ecclesiastical History and Commercial and Industrial Record of the County of Kings and the City of Brooklyn, N.Y. from 1683–1884* vol. 1 (New York: W.W. Munsell, 1884), 615; *Brooklyn Daily Eagle,* July 9, 1869, 2.

36. Mark Pestana, "Candy Cummings Debuts the Curve," in Bill Felber, ed., *Inventing Baseball: The 100 Greatest Games of the Nineteenth Century* (Phoenix: Society for American Baseball Research, 2013), 60–62.

37. *Brooklyn Daily Eagle,* August 24, 1865.

Chapter 3

1. Marshall D. Wright, *The National Association of Base Ball Players 1857–1870* (Jefferson, NC: McFarland, 2000), 7–8; *New York Clipper,* May 8, 1858; Randall Brown, "1837.1 The Evolution of the New York Game—An Arbiter's Tale," *Base Ball: A Journal of the Early Game* 5, no. 1 (Spring 2011), 81–84.

2. The Knickerbocker rules are printed in Henry Chadwick, *Beadle's Dime Base-Ball Player for 1860* (New York: Irwin P. Beadle, 1860), and in *The Base Ball Player's Pocket Companion* (Boston: Mahew & Baker, 1859), available online at https://archive.org/stream/ TheBaseBallPlayersPocketCompanion ContainingRulesAndRegulationsFor/ Baseball.

3. *Boston Traveler,* May 18, 1858; *Springfield [MA] Republican,* May 19, 1858; the rules are printed in *The Base Ball Player's Pocket Companion,* and *Spirit of the Times,* March 18, 1865; Larry McCray, "1829.2. The Rise and Fall of New England-Style Ballplaying," *Base Ball: A Journal of the Early Game* 5, no. 1 (Spring 2011), 69–72.

4. John Thorn, *Baseball in the Garden of Eden* (New York: Simon & Schuster, 2011), 26, 31–32, 38, 43, 46–48, 59; Ryczek, *Baseball's First Inning,* 39–40, 114; *Connecticut Courant* (Hartford), April 9, 1853; *Brooklyn Daily Eagle,* April 8, 1896, and May 28, 1900; *Brooklyn Junior Eagle,* April 16, 1911; Illinois: *Sangamo Journal* (Springfield), June 14, 1834; Indiana: *Indiana Democrat* (Indianapolis), May 10, 1837; Missouri: *Sporting News,* November 2, 1895; Ohio: *New York Clipper,* June 26, 1858; Montana: *Helena Weekly Herald,* April 14, 1887.

5. Thorn, *Baseball in the Garden of Eden*, 4, 31, 59; Ryczek, *Baseball's First Inning*, 37.

6. *Brooklyn Daily Eagle*, July 20, 1871; *New York Sunday Telegraph*, October 8, 1899.

7. Thorn, *Baseball in the Garden of Eden*, 26.

8. Richard Hershberger, "A Reconstruction of Philadelphia Town Ball," *Base Ball: A Journal of the Early Game* 1, no. 2 (Fall 2007), 28–43; also available on John Thorn's baseball blog, https://our game.mlblogs.com/a-reconstruction-of-philadelphia-town-ball-f3a80d283c07.

9. The rules are printed in Henry Chadwick, ed., *Beadle's Dime Base-Ball Player for 1866* (New York: Beadle, 1867). They are also available online at http://vbba. org/rules-and-customs/beadles-1867.

10. Henry Chadwick, *The Game of Baseball* (New York: George Munro, 1868), 15, 51; Thorn, *Baseball in the Garden of Eden*, 74, 122; Harvey Frommer, *Old-Time Baseball: America's Pastime in the Gilded Age* (Lanham, MD: Taylor Trade Publishing, 2006), 32.

11. *Boston Herald*, June 15, 1857; *Boston Transcript*, September 10, 1858, and May 8, 1860; Thorn, *Baseball in the Garden of Eden*, 112.

12. *Boston Transcript*, September 10, 1858.

13. *Boston Transcript*, May 8, 1860.

14. *Constitution and By-Laws of the New England Association of National Base Ball Players*, 5–7 (Boston: Wright & Potter, 1866), available online at https://www.goo gle.com/books/edition/Constitution_and_ By_laws_of_the_New_Engl/0bwVAAAAY AAJ?hl=en&gbpv=1&dq=%22Constitution +and+By-Laws+of+the+New+England+As sociation+of+National+Base+Ball+Players; *Boston Herald*, November 9, 1865; *New York Sunday Mercury*, November 22, 1865.

15. *Massachusetts Weekly Spy* (Worcester, MA), April 11, 1860; *National Aegis and Gazette* (Worcester, MA), July 20, 1867.

16. *Spalding's Official Base Ball Guide for 1915* (New York: American Sports Publishing, 1915), 48.

17. Steve Light, "Baseball Came of Age During American Civil War," https:// baseballhall.org/discover/baseball-came-of-age-during-civil-war; *New York Clipper*,

May 4 and January 11, 1861, and August 12, November 11, and December 23, 1865; *Brooklyn Daily Eagle*, July 5, 1861 and March 30, 1864; *Chicago Tribune*, November 18, 1861.

18. David Dyte, "1845.4 Baseball in Brooklyn, 1845–1870: The Best There Was," in *Base Ball: A Journal of the Early Game* 5, no. 1 (Spring 2011): 98–102.

19. Richard Hershberger, "The Antebellum Growth and Spread of the New York Game," in *Base Ball: A Journal of the Early Game* 8 (2014): 134–149; Terry, *Long Before the Dodgers*, 18–19.

20. Chadwick, *The Game of Baseball*, 156–157; Wright, *The National Association of Base Ball Players*, 54–56; Terry, *Long Before the Dodgers*, 29; Charles A. Peverelly, *Book of American Pastimes* (New York: Charles A. Peverelly, 1866), 357 (available online at https://babel.hathitrust.org/cgi/ pt?id=nyp.33433082423470; Dyte, "1845.4 Baseball in Brooklyn"; Craig B. Waff, "1860.60 Atlantics and Excelsiors Compete for the 'Championship,' July 19, August 9, and August 23, 1860," in *Base Ball: A Journal of the Early Game* 5, no. 1 (Spring 2011), 139–142 (also available at https:// ourgame.mlblogs.com/atlantics-and-excelsiors-compete-for-the-championship-1860-55b9bfb89217); Richard Hershberger, "Did New York Steal the Championship of 1867 from Philadelphia?" in Morris Levin, ed.: *The National Pastime: From Swampoodle to South Philly: Baseball in Philadelphia and the Delaware Valley*, Society for American Baseball Research 2013, 22–27 (also available online at https:// sabr.org/research/did-new-york-steal-championship-1867-philadelphia).

21. *New York Sunday Mercury*, April 7, 1861, and October 15, 1865.

22. *Brooklyn Daily Eagle*, August 4, 1863.

23. *New York Clipper*, May 8, 1858; Wright, *The National Association of Base Ball Players*, 55, 139, 186.

24. Wright, *The National Association of Base Ball Players*, 54; Waff, "1860.60 Atlantics and Excelsiors"; Andrew Schiff, "Henry Chadwick," SABR BioProject, http://sabr. org/bioproj/person/436e570c.

25. *Brooklyn Daily Eagle*, September 2, 1865. This passage appeared in an "Epistle" written for the *Eagle* by Corry O'Lanus, a *nom de plume* taken from the legendary Roman general named Coriolanus and the

Shakespearean play of that name. O'Lanus published a collection of his "Epistles" in Corry O'Lanus, *Corry O'Lanus: His Views and Experiences* (New York: G.W. Carleton, 1867); the quoted passage appears on pp. 74–75.

26. Waff, "1860.60 Atlantics and Excelsiors"; Francis C. Richter, *Richter's History and Records of Baseball* (Philadelphia: Francis C. Richter, 1914), 14; Wright, *The National Association of Base Ball Players*, 94–95, 188.

27. Peverelly, *American Pastimes*, 400–401. That the founders were in commerce and the financial industry has been derived from researching, in census reports and other primary sources, the backgrounds of the club's officers in 1854 and 1855 listed by Peverelly.

28. W.A. Cummings, "Baseball in the Sixties. With the Excelsiors," in *The Cottager* (Athol, MA), May, 1898. This was one of a series of reminiscences written by Cummings in 1897 and 1898 for *The Cottager*, a weekly publication in Athol, Massachusetts, herein referred to as the "Cummings *Cottager* series"; Ryczek, *Baseball's First Inning*, 60.

29. *Philadelphia Sunday Mercury,* February 17, 1867. A transcription of the article is at https://protoball.org.

30. W.A. Cummings, "Baseball in the Sixties and Seventies. A Tour with the Star Club of Brooklyn," Cummings *Cottager* series, July, 1898; Syrett, *The City of Brooklyn, 1865–1898,* 16.

31. *Brooklyn Daily Union,* May 2, 1866.

32. *Brooklyn Daily Eagle,* August 24, 1860; *New York Clipper,* September 1, 1860; Albert G. Spalding, *America's National Game* (New York: American Sports Publishing, 1911), 83–85; Craig B. Waff, "No gentlemen's game, Excelsior of South Brooklyn vs. Atlantic of Bedford," in Felber, *Inventing Baseball,* 28–31; Dyte, "1845.4 Baseball in Brooklyn, 1845–1870."

33. *Brooklyn Daily Eagle,* April 30 and October 30, 1860; Brian McKenna, "Asa Brainard," SABR BioProject, http://sabr.org/bioproj/person/a151ac94.

34. *Brooklyn Daily Union,* May 2, 1866.

35. Richter, *Richter's History and Records of Baseball,* 14; *Brooklyn Daily Eagle,* August 24, 1865, and January 5, 1866.

36. *Brooklyn Daily Eagle,* October 16, 1865; *New York Herald,* March 31, 1867.

37. *New York Clipper,* October 6, 1860.

38. *Boston Evening Transcript,* July 10, 1862; *Boston Evening Traveller,* October 4, 1867.

39. *The Age* (Philadelphia), October 31, 1865.

40. *Leavenworth [KS] Evening Bulletin,* March 23, 1868.

41. "He Pitched the First Curve Ball," *Brooklyn Daily Eagle,* April 26, 1896.

42. *Sporting News,* February 20, 1897; *Brooklyn Daily Eagle,* August 5 and September 3, 1895, April 26, 1896, and August 16, 1897.

43. *Brooklyn Daily Eagle,* December 3, 1861, and November 10, 1862.

44. *Brooklyn Daily Eagle,* February 5, 1861, February 24, 1862, January 13, 1865, and January 25, 1867; *New York World,* February 5, 1861; and a newspaper clipping, probably from the *Brooklyn Eagle* around 1868, found in Henry Chadwick's Scrapbooks in the *Spalding Baseball Collection, 1845–1913, bulk (1860–1900),* microform reel 8, New York Public Library, Manuscripts and Archives Division.

45. Lancaster, "Carroll Gardens/Brooklyn /Long Island/New York. An Architectural Evaluation"; *Discover Smith Street: A Walking Tour and Guide Book—A Joint Project of the Merchants' Association of Smith Street, N.Y.C. Board of Education, and Prospect Park Environmental Center* (booklet in the files of the Brooklyn Historical Society).

46. *New York Herald,* March 31, 1867. Some clubs with home grounds at Carroll Park at various times—Excelsior: *New York Herald,* June 22, 1860; Star: *Brooklyn Daily Eagle,* September 24, 1861; Vernon: *ibid.,* May 19, 1859; Esculapian, Olympic: *ibid.,* September 28, 1859; Exercise: *ibid.,* April 7, 1862; Charter Oak: *New York Evening Express,* August 25, 1859; Marion: *Brooklyn Daily Eagle,* April 6, 1861; Waverly: *ibid.,* October 1, 1861; Hamilton: *ibid.,* October 3, 1861; Typographicals: *ibid.,* May 15, 1866; Independent, Mohawk, Powahattan: *New York Clipper,* April 6, 1867. Game every day in 1862: *Brooklyn Daily Eagle,* March 27, 1862.

47. *Brooklyn Daily Eagle,* June 26, 1865; *New York Tribune,* March 30 and April 9, 1867. Clubhouses: *Brooklyn Daily Eagle,* April 7, 1862; *Brooklyn Daily Eagle,* August 19, 1863.

48. *New York Clipper,* March 23, 1867.

49. *Brooklyn Daily Eagle,* November 19 and 21, December 5, 1861, and June 15, 1864.

50. Candy Cummings, "How I Pitched the First Curve," first published in *Baseball Magazine* 1 (September 1908), and reprinted in various places since then, including Jeff Silverman, ed., *Classic Baseball Stories* (Guilford, CT: The Lyons Press, 2003), 69–73.

51. William Arthur Cummings, "Story of the Curve Ball," in Elwood A. Roff, *Base Ball and Base Ball Players,* 225–231 (Chicago: E.A. Roff, 1912), available online at https://babel.hathitrust.org/cgi/pt?id=loc.ark:/13960/t56d6ps7d&view=1up&seq=5.

52. Sergey Kadinsky, *Hidden Waters of New York City* (New York: Countryman Press, 2016), 185–192; Dorothy Miner *et al,* "Gowanus Canal Corridor," Columbia University Historic Preservation, Studio II (Spring 2008) (available online at https://semspub.epa.gov/work/02/122510.pdf); United States Environmental Protection Agency (EPA), "Gowanus Canal, Brooklyn, NY," https://cumulis.epa.gov/supercpad/SiteProfiles/index.cfm?fuseaction=second.Cleanup&id=0206222#bkground; United States Environmental Protection Agency, "Record of Decision: Gowanus Canal Superfund Site, Brooklyn, Kings County, New York," https://casedocuments.darrp.noaa.gov/northeast/gowanus/pdf/GowanusROD.pdf.

Soon after completion of the Gowanus Canal, it attracted more and more manufacturing facilities. But the canal was a victim of its own success: it became massively polluted with industrial and other waste. It got so bad that, in 2013, the United States Environmental Protection Agency declared the canal a "Superfund Site" and commenced a project to clean it up.

53. W.A. Cummings, "The 'Curve' Ball. The Inventor Tells All About It," in the Cummings *Cottager* series, November 1897.

54. "Arthur Cummings Talks Over His Discovery of Curve Ball."

55. In addition to the pieces in *The Cottager* and *Baseball Magazine,* Cummings related the story in, among other places: "He Pitched the First Curve Ball"; "Inventor of Curve Tells of Old Times," *Duluth [MN] Herald,* February 17, 1912; "William Arthur Cummings, the Inventor of the Curve Ball Tells About its Early Use," *Denver Post,* August 17, 1912; "Arthur Cummings Tells How He Discovered the Curve Ball," *The Mixer and Server: Official Journal of the Hotel and Restaurant Employees International Alliance and Bartenders International League of America"* (Cincinnati, Ohio) 21, no.10 (October 15, 1912): 61; "Arthur Cummings Talks Over His Discovery of Curve Ball"; and in *Spalding's Official Base Ball Guide for 1915,* 48.

56. *Boston Globe,* April 21, 1895; "The Curve Ball. The Discoverer of the Art of Curve Pitching," *Sporting Life,* May 4, 1895.

57. "The First to Curve."

58. "Pitched First Curve," *Washington Post,* March 6, 1899.

59. "The First to Curve."

60. E.J. Edwards, "The House Painter Who Invented the Curved Ball," *Idaho Statesman* (Boise, ID), May 7, 1910.

61. Peter Morris, *A Game of Inches: The Story Behind the Innovations that Shaped Baseball* (Chicago: Ivan R. Dee, 2010), 88.

62. "He Pitched the First Curve Ball"; "Arthur Cummings Tells How He Discovered the Curve Ball"; "William Arthur Cummings," *New York Clipper,* July 8, 1871.

63. Chadwick, *The Game of Baseball,* 42; Terry, *Long Before the Dodgers,* 18; Warren Goldstein, *Playing for Keeps: A History of Early Baseball* (Ithaca, NY: Cornell University Press, 1989), 45; *Brooklyn Daily Eagle,* March 14, 1864.

Chapter 4

1. Falley's academic year began in May. Rev. W. Dempster Chase, ed., *History and Reunion of Falley Seminary* (Fulton, NY: Morrill Brothers, 1890), 8 (available online at https://babel.hathitrust.org/cgi/pt?id=mdp.39015075902927.

2. Crisfield Johnson, *History of Oswego County, New York* (Philadelphia: L.H. Everts, 1877), 225– 241 (available online at https://archive.org/stream/historyofoswegoc00john); John C. Churchill, ed., *Landmarks of Oswego County, New York* (Syracuse, NY: D. Mason, 1895), 773–826 (available online at https://archive.org/stream/landmarksofosweg00chur); J. Calvin Smith, *Smith's Rail Road, Steam Boat & Stage Route Map of New England, New-York*

and Canada (New York: J. Calvin Smith, 1858); *New Railway Map of the United States* (New York: G.W. & C.B. Colton, 1867) (available online at https://www.loc.gov/resource/g3701p.rr000480).

3. The Erie Canal, "Boats on the Erie Canal," http://eriecanal.org/boats.html.

4. Chase, *Falley Seminary*, 6, 23.

5. National Society, Sons of the American Revolution, Application for Membership of George F. Falley 2nd (1944); Mrs. Edward Hitchcock, Sr., *The Genealogy of the Hitchcock Family* (Amherst, MA: Carpenter and Morehouse, 1894), 234 (available online at https://archive.org/details/genealogyofhitch00hitc); "Grover Cleveland's Local Ancestry," *Springfield [MA] Republican,* August 17, 1884.

6. Chase, *Falley Seminary*, 20 ff.; Johnson, *History of Oswego County*, 234.

7. *Fulton [NY] Patriot*, October 13, 1981; *Oswego [NY] Commercial Advertiser*, July 1, 1864.

8. Chase, *Falley Seminary*, 7.

9. *Catalogue of the Officers and Students of Falley Seminary, Fulton, Oswego County, N.Y., for the Academic Year Ending June 29, 1865* (Fulton, NY: Patriot and Gazette Caloric Power Press Print, 1865); ditto *for the Year Ending June 28, 1866; Oswego [NY] Commercial Advertiser*, various dates in 1864 and 1866.

10. Chase, *Falley Seminary*, 11.

11. Willard H. Torbert, "Seminary Life," in Chase, *Falley Seminary*, 64, 66.

12. Chase, *Falley Seminary*.

13. Letter from Cummings to Tim Murnane, editor of the *Boston Globe*, quoted in *Sporting Life*, April 11, 1896.

14. *New York Clipper*, March 23, 1861; *New York Sunday Mercury*, January 20 and April 7, 1861; *New York World*, June 5, 1861.

15. *Rules and Regulations of the Game of Base Ball, adopted by the National Association of Baser-Ball Players*, 1860, section 1, and subsequent iterations of the rules.

16. This account is based on the following sources: W.A. Cummings, "Base Ball in 1864–1865. The Games for the Silver Ball," in the Cummings *Cottager* series; *Oswego [NY] Daily Palladium*, September 13, 16, 22, 25, and 28, 1865. Cummings' article, written more than 30 years after the events, contains some inaccuracies.

17. *Oswego [NY] Daily Palladium*, September 28, 1865.

18. *Oswego [NY] Daily Palladium*, October 21, 22, 23, and 30, 1865.

19. *Oswego [NY] Daily Palladium*, May 18 and 21, 1866.

20. In his article "Story of the Curve Ball" in Roff, *Base Ball and Base Ball Players*, at 225–231, Cummings reprinted a piece by Buster McKinstry that, according to Cummings, appeared in the *Fulton [NY] Patriot*, November 24, 1909. As I have not been able to locate that issue of the *Fulton Patriot*, I cannot confirm that McKinstry's article appeared there.

21. *Fulton [NY] Times*, June 8, 1910; *Oswego [NY] Palladium–Times*, August 25, 1925.

22. The comings and goings of the silver ball related in these paragraphs are based on: *Fulton [NY] Times*, June 8, 1910; *Fulton [NY] Patriot*, May 18 and 25, 1921, November 26, 1924, and June 20, 1935; *Oswego [NY] Palladium*, May 16, 1921; *Daily Sentinel* (Rome, NY), August 27, 1927; *Otsego Farmer* (Cooperstown, NY), March 17, 1939; *Oswego [NY] Palladium–Times*, June 17, 1939; *The Freeman's Journal* (Cooperstown, NY), July 12, 1939; Letter of Jesse A. Morrill to Alexander Cleland, chairman of the Hall of Fame committee overseeing the construction of the Hall's new premises, dated December 18, 1936, viewable at www.cooperstown expert.com/player/candy-cummings; note of Jesse A. Morrill, July 5, 1939, in Arthur Cummings: Pitcher Scrapbook, 1866–1939, accession no. BL–139–39, call no. BA SCR 175, National Baseball Hall of Fame Library, Cooperstown, NY.

23. *The American Printer* 37, no. 6, New York, (February 1904): 466.

Chapter 5

1. W.A. Cummings, "Baseball in the Sixties. Experience in Junior Clubs," in the Cummings *Cottager* series, March 17, 1898. His stint with the Star juniors was likely in the summer of 1865: In his article "Experience in Junior Clubs," he mentioned that most of the club's players were 17-year-old schoolboys—Cummings was 16 in the summer of 1865—and played all the games they could before school opened; his only intervening summer vacation between his terms at Falley would have been in 1865.

2. Cummings, "Experience in Junior Clubs."

3. Fleitz's most recent entry about Candy Cummings is in Bill Nowlin and Emmet R. Nowlin, eds., *20-Game Losers* (Phoenix: Society for American Baseball Research, 2017), 284–287. Other entries are in David L. Fleitz, *Ghosts in the Gallery at Cooperstown* (Jefferson, NC: McFarland, 2004), 18–31, and "Candy Cummings," SABR BioProject: https://sabr.org/bioproj/person/99fabe5f.

4. *New York Sunday Mercury,* July 30 and August 30, and September 10, 1865.

5. Cummings, "Experience in Junior Clubs."

6. John Thorn, "Jim Creighton," SABR BioProject, http://sabr.org/bioproj/person/2d2e5d16; McKenna, "Asa Brainard"; *Brooklyn Daily Eagle,* October 20, 1862.

7. Ryczek, *Baseball's First Inning,* 56–57.

8. McKenna, "Asa Brainard."

9. *Brooklyn Daily Eagle,* August 15, 1866; *New York Sunday Mercury,* August 19, 1866.

10. *Brooklyn Daily Eagle,* August 15, 1866.

11. W.A. Cummings, "Baseball in the Sixties. With the Excelsiors," in the Cummings *Cottager* series, May 1868.

12. Henry Chadwick, *Beadle's Dime Base Ball Player for 1871* (New York: Beadle, 1871), 9–10.

13. *Brooklyn Daily Eagle,* August 18, 1866.

14. Thorn, *Baseball in the Garden of Eden,* 67.

15. *New York Sunday Mercury,* August 26, 1866.

16. *Newark [NJ] Daily Advertiser,* August 15, 1866.

17. "He Pitched the First Curve Ball."

18. Cummings, "Baseball in the Sixties. With the Excelsiors"; *New-York Daily Tribune,* August 29, 1866; *New York Clipper,* September 8, 1866.

19. *New York Sunday Mercury,* August 26, 1866.

20. *New York Clipper,* September 8, 1866.

21. *New York Daily Tribune,* August 29, 1866.

22. *Brooklyn Daily Eagle,* September 18, 1866.

23. Principal sources for the account of the southern tour include Peverelly, *America's Pastimes,* 414–415; Cummings, "With the Excelsiors"; and the following newspapers: *Washington [D.C.] Evening Star,* September 19 and 20, 1866; *Washington [D.C.] National Republican,* September 19, 1866; *New York Herald,* September 19, 1866; *New York Clipper,* September 29, 1866. Particular points and quotations are given their own source citations.

24. Peverelly, *America's Pastimes,* 443.

25. https://www.nps.gov/nr/travel/wash/dc36.htm; http://www.abrahamlincolnonline.org/lincoln/sites/willards.htm.

26. Peverelly, *America's Pastimes,* 414.

27. Joel D. Treese, "Baseball and the White House in the Nineteenth Century," https://www.whitehousehistory.org/baseball-and-the-white-house-in-the-nineteenth-century.

28. *New York Herald,* August 19, 1866.

29. *Washington [D.C.] Evening Star,* September 19, 1866.

30. *New York Clipper,* September 29, 1866.

31. *Ibid.*

32. *Washington [D.C.] Evening Star,* September 19, 1866.

33. *Ibid.*

34. Cummings, "With the Excelsiors."

35. *Chicago Tribune,* July 18, 1872 (quoting from the *New York World*); *Boston Globe,* June 8, 1891; *Sporting Life,* November 16, 1895, and April 11, 1896; *Sporting News,* February 20, 1897; "William Arthur Cummings, the Inventor of the Curve Ball"; "Cummings First Pitcher to Hurl a Curve Ball," *Duluth [MN] News Tribune,* January 17, 1920 (this piece also appeared in several other newspapers and journals in 1912 and 1913); *Lexington [KY] Leader,* July 31, 1920.

36. David Fleitz, "Candy Cummings," SABR BioProject, http://sabr.org/bioproj/person/99fabe5f; *Sporting Life,* July 16, 1898.

37. *Sporting Life,* July 16, 1898.

38. David Arcidiacono, "The Hartford Dark Blues," *Hog River Journal* 1, no. 3 (Summer 2003); Harold Burr, "Candy Cummings," *Sporting News,* November 19, 1942.

39. *Cincinnati Enquirer,* August 3, 1877.

40. *Chicago Tribune,* January 12, 1879.

41. *Sporting News,* August 13, 1898.

42. *New York Daily Tribune,* April 9 and 29, 1867; *Brooklyn Daily Eagle,* May 14, 1867; *New York Clipper,* June 8, 1867.

43. W.A. Cummings, "Baseball in the Sixties and Seventies, A Tour with the Star Club of Brooklyn," in the Cummings *Cottager* series, July 1898; 1870 U.S. Census, Brooklyn, King's County, NY, Ward 22, p. 29.

44. *Brooklyn Daily Eagle,* October 24, 1867.

45. *Brooklyn Daily Eagle,* June 17, July 30, August 17, and September 14, 21, and 24, 1867; *New York Clipper,* August 10, 1867.

46. *Brooklyn Daily Eagle,* August 17, 1867.

47. *Brooklyn Daily Eagle,* August 24 and September 11, 14, and 24, 1867.

48. *New York Clipper,* October 3, 1867.

Chapter 6

1. *Boston Herald,* October 5, 1867; *Brooklyn Daily Union,* October 7, 1867.

2. Wright, *The National Association of Base Ball Players,* 133, 154.

3. *Boston Daily Journal,* June 3 and August 24, 1867.

4. Fred H. Harrison, *Athletics for All. Physical Education and Athletics at Phillips Andover Academy, 1778–1978* (Andover, MA: Phillips Academy, 1983), 23–27; https://www.andover.edu/Athletics/Teams/BBBV/Pages/Alumni.aspx; *Frank Leslie's Illustrated Newspaper* (New York), August 11, 1866; Pestana, "Candy Cummings Debuts the Curve; William Ryczek, "The 1867 Nationals of Albany, Part 2 (August 5, 2013)," website of the National Pastime Museum, https://www.thenationalpastimemuseum.com/article/1867-nationals-albany-0; *Bridgeport [CT] Evening Farmer,* March 7, 1910; "Modern Stars Wonderful, But They Have Nothing on Old-Timers in His Opinion," *Rockford [IL] Morning Star,* July 14, 1912.

5. *Boston Evening Traveler,* October 7 and 8, 1867; *Boston Press and Post,* October 10, 1867.

6. *Boston Herald,* October 8, 1867.

7. "William Arthur Cummings, the Inventor of the Curve Ball Tells About its Early Use."

8. "William Arthur Cummings, the Inventor of the Curve Ball Tells About its Early Use"; Cummings, "The 'Curve' Ball. The Inventor Tells All About It"; "The First to Curve. How Arthur Cummings Made the Discovery"; "He Pitched the First Curve Ball"; Frommer, *Old-Time Baseball,* 129.

9. "William Arthur Cummings, the Inventor of the Curve Ball Tells About its Early Use"; Cummings, "The Inventor Tells All About It"; Frommer, *Old Time Baseball,* 129; and Pestana, "Candy Cummings Debuts the Curve."

10. Cummings, "How I Pitched the First Curve."

11. William Arthur Cummings, "How I Invented the First Curve Ball," *Pittsburg Press,* June 26, 1921.

12. "The Curve Ball. The Discoverer of the Art of Curve Pitching"; "The First to Curve. How Arthur Cummings Made the Discovery"; "The 'Curve' Ball—The Inventor Tells All About It."

13. "Cummings of Brooklyn Fired First Curve," *Brooklyn Daily Union,* May 25, 1918.

14. John H. Gruber, "The Development of the Playing Rules," *Sporting Life,* January 8, 1916.

15. Henry Chadwick, *Haney's Base Ball Players' Book of Reference for 1869* (New York: Peck & Snyder, 1869), 29.

16. "Arthur Cummings Talks Over His Discovery of Curve Ball."

17. Henry Chadwick, ed., *DeWitt's Base-Ball Guide for 1873* (New York: DeWitt, 1873), 62–63. Chadwick had previously published his discussion of pitching versus throwing in the *New York Clipper,* February 17, 1872.

18. Chadwick, ed., *DeWitt's Base-Ball Guide for 1873,* 63.

19. *New York Clipper,* December 18, 1869.

20. Henry Chadwick, *The Base-Ball Players' Book of Reference for 1867* (New York: J.C. Haney, 1867), 12–13, 41.

21. Chadwick, ed., *DeWitt's Base-Ball Guide for 1873,* 63.

22. Cummings, "How I Invented the First Curve Ball."

23. "He Pitched the First Curve Ball"; "Arthur Cummings Tells How He Discovered the Curve Ball"; "Cummings Tells Story of Early Days of Curve Ball," *Sporting News,* December 29, 1921; "The First to Curve."

24. *Boston Herald*, October 8, 1867; *Harvard College Advocate* 4, no. 2 (October 22, 1867): 25; *Brooklyn Daily Union*, October 9, 1867.

25. *New York Clipper*, November 2, 1867.

26. Chadwick, *The Game of Baseball*, 34.

27. *Brooklyn Daily Eagle*, June 22 and 29, 1868.

Chapter 7

1. Quoted by Henry Chadwick in "The Art of Pitching in Baseball," *Scientific American* 55, no. 5 (July 31, 1886): 71. The quotation is from the editor of the *Grand Rapids World*, a newspaper that cannot now be located.

2. Morris, *A Game of Inches*, 95.

3. *Boston Advertiser*, October 25, 1877.

4. "A Letter of Mr. Isaac Newton, Professor of the Mathematicks in the University of Cambridge; containing his New Theory about Light and Colors," reproduced in the website of The Newton Project, http://www.newtonproject.ox.ac.uk/view/texts/normalized/NATP00006.

5. G. Magnus, *Über die Abweichung der Geschosse; Über eine auffallende Erscheinung bei Rotierenden Körpern* (Berlin: Ferd. Dümmler's Verlags-Buchhandlung, 1852) (available online at https://reader.digitale-sammlungen.de/en/fs1/object/display/bsb10909033_00001.html). Among the many modern-era physicists to analyze the operation of the Magnus force upon the curveball are Alan Nathan, Professor Emeritus of Physics at the University of Illinois, whose extensive work on this and other aspects of the science of baseball can be viewed on his website, The Physics of Baseball: http://baseball.physics.illinois.edu/nathan-papers.html; and Robert K. Adair, Professor Emeritus of Physics at Yale, author of *The Physics of Baseball*, cited below.

6. *Catalogue of the Officers and Students of Falley Seminary ... 1865*, 23; A. Ganot and William G. Peck, *Introductory Course of Natural Philosophy for the Use of Schools and Academies, Edited from Ganot's Popular Physics by William G. Peck* (New York: Barnes and Burr, 1865), available online at https://babel.hathitrust.org/cgi/pt?id=nyp.33433069107732.

7. Cummings, "Story of the Curve Ball."

8. *Ibid*.

9. Cummings, "How I Pitched the First Curve."

10. "Base Ball Science," *Scientific American* 37, no. 20 (November 17, 1877): 312.

11. Specific incidents are related by Morris in *A Game of Inches*, 94–96.

12. "Origin of Curves," *Current Literature, A Magazine of Record and Review* 23 (January–June 1898), 557–558.

13. *Boston Advertiser*, October 25, 1877. A good description of the experiment was given in the *Cincinnati Gazette*, October 22, 1877.

14. Chadwick, *The Art of Pitching and Fielding*; Edward J. Prindle, *The Art of Curved Pitching* (Philadelphia: A.J. Reach, 1886); W.F. Hopkinson, "The Theory of the Curve Ball," *Outing* 10, no. 2 (May 1887): 98–103.

15. "Baseball's Curve Balls," *Life* 11, no. 11 (September 15, 1941): 83–89.

16. Robert K. Adair, *The Physics of Baseball* (New York: HarperCollins, 2002), 51.

17. Frank L. Verwiebe, "Does a Baseball Curve?" *American Journal of Physics* 10 (April 1942): 119–120; Richard M. Sutton, "Baseballs Do Curve And Drop!" *American Journal of Physics* 19 (August, 1942), 201.

18. Quoted in a number of places, including David Kagan, "The Physics of the Curveball—A Short History" (March 3, 2014), https://www.fangraphs.com/tht/tht-live/the-physics-of-the-curveball-a-short-history, which also provides a concise summary of the various scientific studies on the physics of the curveball.

19. Peter J. Brancazio, "The Physics of a Curveball," *Popular Mechanics* 174, no. 4 (April 1997): 56–57.

20. *Weekly Trenton [NJ] Times*, August 30, 1883; Creighton: *Brooklyn Daily Eagle*, August 6, 1860; *New York Clipper*, December 15, 1877; John Thorn, "Pitching: Evolution and Revolution," https://ourgame.mlblogs.com/pitching-evolution-and-revolution-efd3a5ebaa83. McBride: *Boston Globe*, February 10, 1889.

21. Mike Fast, "What the Heck Is PITCHf/x?" http://baseball.physics.illinois.edu/FastPFXGuide.pdf, reprinted from Joe Distelheim et al, eds., *The Hardball Times*

Baseball Annual, 2010 (Skokie, IL: Acta Sports, 2010).

22. Data taken from the PITCHf/x tool on www.brooksbaseball.net.

23. *New York Journal,* January 8, 1912.

24. "Arthur Cummings Talks Over His Discovery of Curve Ball."

25. *New York Times,* August 22, 1873.

26. *Sporting News,* June 19, 1924.

27. *Rules and Regulations as Amended by the National Association of Base-Ball Players, December 8th, 1869,* Rule Second, printed in Henry Chadwick, ed., *Beadle's Dime Base-Ball Player for 1870* (New York: Beadle & Co., 1870), 20.

28. Henry Chadwick, ed., *DeWitt's Base-Ball Guide for 1870* (New York: DeWitt, 1870), 17.

29. *Rules and Regulations as adopted by the Amateur National Association of Base-Ball Players, March 16, 1871,* Rules Second and Third, printed in Henry Chadwick, ed., *The Dime Base Ball Player* (New York: Beadle & Co., 1871), 93–94.

30. *The Rules of Base-Ball for 1872, as Adopted by the Professional and Amateur Associations, in March, 1872,* rules Second and Third, printed in Henry Chadwick, ed., *Beadle's Dime Base Ball Player for 1872* (New York: Beadle & Co., 1872), 89–91; Henry Chadwick, ed., *The Dime Base Ball Player for 1873,* 41.

31. *Constitution and Playing Rules of the National League of Professional Base Ball Clubs, 1884* (Chicago: A.G. Spalding, 1884), Playing Rules 24–28.

32. Morris, *A Game of Inches,* 17–20; *Constitution and Playing Rules of the National League of Professional Base Ball Clubs, 1889* (Chicago: A.G. Spalding, 1889(?)), Playing Rules 43 and 44.

33. Richter, *Richter's History and Records of Baseball,* 243.

34. *New York Clipper,* December 2, 1876.

35. A.G. Spalding and Lewis Meacham, eds., *Spalding's Official Base Ball Guide for 1878* (Chicago: A.G. Spalding), 7.

36. *Chicago Tribune,* November 23, 1879.

37. *Canton [OH] Daily Depository,* October 8, 1885.

38. Tyler Kepner, *A History of Baseball in Ten Pitches* (New York: Anchor Books, 2019), 149.

39. Kepner, *A History of Baseball in Ten Pitches*; Martin Quigley, *The Crooked Pitch: The Curveball in American Baseball History* (Chapel Hill, NC: Algonquin Books, 1984).

Chapter 8

1. W.A. Cummings, "More Baseball History. Close of Mr. Cummings' Reminiscences," in the Cummings *Cottager* series.

2. 1870 U.S. Census, Brooklyn, Kings County, New York, 52.

3. *New York Times,* July 21, 1900.

4. *Hawaii, Certificate of Special Rights of Citizenship,* James G. Spencer, July 23, 1894.

5. Letters to the editor from Joseph McElroy Mann, W.J. Henderson, and "Yale," *New York Times,* June 10, 1900.

6. *New York Sun,* March 15, 1918.

7. Alphonse C. Martin, "McSweeney of Mutuals First to Pitch Curve," *New York Sun,* March 17, 1918.

8. *New York Sun,* March 31, 1918.

9. https://www.baseball-reference.com/players/s/startjo01.shtml; New York State Census, 1855, Brooklyn, 9th Ward, Kings County, New York.

10. *Brooklyn Daily Eagle,* October 12, 1864; *New York Clipper,* April 3, 1869; https://sabr.org/latest/19th-century-overlooked-legend-nominees-2012.

11. *Boston Globe,* November 10, 1895.

12. *Sporting Life,* August 6, 1898.

13. *Brooklyn Daily Eagle,* August 15 and 29, 1866, and August 24, 1867.

14. Henry Chadwick, "Old Time Baseball," *Outing* 38, no. 4 (July 1901): 420–422.

15. Henry Chadwick, *The Art of Pitching and Fielding* (Chicago: A.G. Spalding & Bros., 1885), 11 (available online at https://archive.org/details/artofpitching fie00chad); Henry Chadwick, *How to Play Base Ball* (New York: A.G. Spalding & Bros., 1889), 31.

16. John Thorne, "George Wright," SABR BioProject, https://sabr.org/bioproj/person/5468d7c0; https://baseballhall.org/hall-of-famers/wright-george.

17. T.H. Murnane, "The Curve Ball," *Sporting Life,* March 25, 1911.

18. *New York Clipper,* September 3, 1870, and September 5, 1874.

19. The quotes are from the *Lexington [KY] Leader,* July 31, 1920. Essentially

the same column was in "Cummings First Pitcher to Hurl a Curve Ball," although in that column, it is unclear as to who was being quoted.

20. *New York Clipper,* September 2, 1871; *Brooklyn Daily Eagle,* October 9, 1871.

21. "Cummings First Pitcher to Hurl a Curve Ball."

22. Alfred H. Spink, *The National Game* (St. Louis: National Game Publishing, 1910), 41.

23. Bill McMahon, "Al Spalding," SABR BioProject, https://sabr.org/bioproj/person/b99355e0; Francis C. Richter, ed., *The Reach Official American League Baseball Guide for 1918* (Philadelphia: A.J. Reach, 1918), 251.

24. *Illinois State Journal* (Springfield), May 4, 1895.

25. *New York Clipper,* June 4 and 11, 1870.

26. John B. Foster, ed., *Spalding's Official Base Ball Guide, 1915* (New York: American Sports Publishing, 1915), 48.

27. The *Brooklyn Union* article was reproduced in Cummings, "Close of Mr. Cummings' Reminiscences," which gives the date as May 9, 1870. That date cannot be verified against the May 9, 1870, issue of the *Union* since that issue no longer exists; however, it is assumed to be correct as it is the same date as the *New York Tribune's* report. The *Union* article was also reproduced in William Rankin's letter in the *New York Times* on September 29, 1900, and in Cummings' letter in the August 20, 1898 issue of *Sporting Life.* The latter, however, dates the article as July 9, 1870, an obvious error since it doesn't appear anywhere in the *Union* on that date.

28. *Wilkes' Spirit of the Times,* August 27, 1870.

29. "Reminiscences of a Ball Player," *New York Times,* June 2, 1900.

30. Letter to the Editor from W.J. Henderson, *New York Times,* June 10, 1900.

31. *New York Times,* June 10, 1900.

32. Adrian Constantine Anson, *A Ball Player's Career* (Chicago: Era Publishing, 1900), 33.

33. Frank Presbrey and James Hugh Moffatt, comp., *Athletics at Princeton: A History* (New York: Frank Presbrey Co., 1901), 99 (available online at https://archive.org/details/athleticsatprin00presgoog).

34. *Record of the Class of Eighteen Hundred and Seventy-Six, Princeton,* no. ix (1876–1911), 87–89.

35. U.S. Passport Application for Charles Hammond Avery, no. 6343, May 28, 1886; *Fifty-Five Yale, Supplementary Record, 1889–1895,* 131; Richard M. Hurd, *A History of Yale Athletics* (New Haven, CT: R.M. Hurd, 1888), 105 (available online at https://archive.org/details/historyofyaleath00hurduoft/).

36. General Joshua L. Chamberlain, ed., *Universities and Their Sons* 5 (Boston: R. Herndon, 1900), 412 (available online at https://archive.org/details/b29000 35x_0005/page/412?q=%22Charles+Hammond+Avery%22).

37. Jean-Pierre Caillault, comp., *The Complete* New York Clipper *Baseball Biographies* (Jefferson, NC: McFarland, 2009), 408–409.

38. Peverelly, *The Book of American Pastimes,* 386; Henry Chadwick, *The Base Ball Player's Book of Reference* (New York: J.C. Haney, 1867), 107; Henry Chadwick, *Beadle's Dime Base Ball Player for 1873,* 24; Caillault, *The Complete* New York Clipper *Baseball Biographies,* 408.

39. *Lexington [KY] Leader,* July 31, 1920.

40. *New York Clipper,* December 15, 1877.

41. For example, "The First Pitcher to Throw Curves—His Fancy Wrist Action," *Arizona Republican,* June 5, 1911; Martin, "McSweeney of Mutuals First to Pitch Curve."

42. *Brooklyn Daily Eagle,* June 22, 1865, and August 15, 1866.

43. *New York Sun,* March 17, 1918.

44. *Worcester [MA] Daily Spy,* September 8, 1893.

45. J.E. Edwards, "The House Painter Who Discovered the Curve Ball," *Desert Evening News* (Salt Lake City), March 12, 1910; *Idaho Statesman* (Boise), May 7, 1910.

46. *New York Clipper,* October 28, 1876; *Hartford Courant,* October 26 and 28, 1876; *Boston Advertiser,* October 28, 1876; *Boston Journal,* October 30, 1876.

47. *New York Clipper,* September 22, 1860.

48. Presbrey and Moffatt, *Athletics at Princeton,* 84; J.C. Kofoed, "Early History of Curve Pitching," *Cleveland Leader,* August 22, 1870, reprinted in *Baseball Magazine* 15,

no. 4 (August 1915): 55–57; Henry Chadwick, *The Base Ball Player's Book of Reference*, 101–102; John Montgomery Ward, *Base-Ball: How to Become a Player* (Philadelphia: Athletic Publishing Co., 1888) (e-book): "Curve Pitching"; Chadwick, *The Art of Pitching and Fielding*, 10; Ryczek, *Baseball's First Inning*, 180–181.

49. Henry Chadwick, *American Base Ball Manual* (London: George Routledge and Sons, 1874), 51.

50. *Boston Globe*, June 8, 1891; *Sporting Life*, April 11, 1896.

51. Murnane, "The Curve Ball."

52. *Ibid.*

53. *Weekly Trenton [NJ] Times*, August 30, 1883.

54. Brian McKenna, "Bobby Mathews," SABR BioProject, https://sabr.org/bioproj/person/e7ad641f.

55. William J. Ryczek, *Blackguards and Red Stockings* (Jefferson, NC: McFarland, 2016), 4–5; Caillault, *The Complete New York Clipper Baseball Biographies*, 411; *Cleveland Leader*, May 6, 1871.

56. *New York Times*, August 22, 1873.

57. *Sporting Life*, August 6, 1898; "Pitched First Curve"; "Arthur Cummings Talks Over His Discovery of Curve Ball"; *Springfield [MA] Daily News*, October 31, 1913; *Reach's Official Base Ball Guide for 1897* (Philadelphia: A.J. Reach, 1897), 101; McKenna, "Bobby Mathews."

58. "Pitched First Curve."

59. *New York Sun*, March 17, 1918.

60. Spalding, *America's National Game*, 484; Anson, *A Ball Player's Career*, 33.

61. *Boston Globe*, February 10, 1889, June 8, 1891, and November 10, 1895; *Sporting Life*, April 11, 1896, and March 25, 1911; Foster, ed., *Spalding's Official Base Ball Guide 1915*, 49.

62. *Sporting News*, November 4, 1909; *Lexington [KY] Leader*, July 31, 1920.

63. Goldsmith's birth certificate gives his birth date as May 15, 1856 (David Fleitz, "Fred Goldsmith," SABR BioProject, https://sabr.org/bioproj/person/99c4a5f5); the 1860 and 1870 U.S. Censuses for New Haven, CT, as well as the certificate of his marriage to Rowena Brooks (his first wife), are consistent with that; however, other dates have been given, including by Goldsmith himself. On occasion he reported his birth date as 1852, and his death certificate gives it as May 15, 1852.

64. David Arcidiacono, "Fred Goldsmith: A Closer Look," *Base Ball: A Journal of the Early Game* 6, no. 2 (Fall 2012), 70–82.

65. *Boston Traveler*, October 13, 1874.

66. *Springfield Republican*, September 25, 1875; *Sporting News*, August 13, 1898.

67. *Sporting Life*, August 6 and 20, 1898.

68. *Sporting News*, August 13, 1898.

69. Philip N. O'Hara, "Survivor of Pioneer Days on Diamond Describes Game and Players of Five Decades Ago for Fans of Modern Age," *Detroit Free Press*, November 23, 1924.

70. *Sporting News*, March 30, 1939.

71. *New York Post*, March 30, 1939.

72. *Ibid.*

73. *Brooklyn Daily Eagle*, March 29, 1939.

74. "Origin of Curves"; *Cincinnati Gazette*, October 22, 1877.

75. Cummings, "The 'Curve' Ball. The Inventor Tells All About It."

76. *Brooklyn Daily Eagle*, October 25, 1885, and June 15, 1896; *New York Clipper*, January 17, 1880, reprinted in Caillault, *The Complete New York Clipper Baseball Biographies*, 114–115.

77. *Brooklyn Daily Eagle*, December 18, 1887, December 23, 1900, and April 20, 1908.

78. Arcidiacono, "Fred Goldsmith"; Fleitz, "Fred Goldsmith."

79. Arcidiacono, "Fred Goldsmith"; *Benham's New Haven City Directory and Annual Advertiser, 1875–'76* (New Haven: J.H. Benham, 1875), 163.

80. Examples include college pitchers Frank Henry (*New York Clipper*, October 10, 1863; *Philadelphia Inquirer*, May 25, 1919; Presbrey and Moffatt, *Athletics at Princeton*, 84); E. Davis (Presbrey and Moffatt, *Athletics at Princeton*, 67 and 84); Alvah Hovey (*Dallas Morning News*, April 14, 24, and 30, 1923).

81. *Sporting News*, November 4, 1909.

Chapter 9

1. *New York Clipper*, August 10 and October 19, 1867.

2. *New York Clipper*, October 19, 1867.

3. *Brooklyn Daily Eagle*, November 5, 1868.

4. *Brooklyn Daily Eagle*, August 18,

1864. This article refers to the newly organized Mohawks as a "junior" club, but this evidently was a mistake. There was already a junior club called the Mohawks, which had been operating for a few years and continued to do so.

5. *Brooklyn Daily Eagle,* August 8, 1867, and February 13, 1868. The latter article called the move by Tracey and Lennon from Excelsior to Mohawk a rumor, but subsequent game reports show them with Mohawk.

6. *Brooklyn Daily Eagle,* February 13, 1868.

7. *Brooklyn Daily Eagle,* June 24, 1868.

8. *New York Clipper,* June 13 and July 4, 1868; *New York Herald,* August 15, 1868.

9. *Brooklyn Daily Union,* May 2, 1866.

10. Figures from Wright, *The National Association of Base Ball Players,* 186.

11. *Brooklyn Daily Eagle,* June 22, 1868.

12. *Brooklyn Daily Eagle,* February 13, 1868.

13. *Brooklyn Daily Eagle,* June 29, 1868.

14. Peter Morris, et al, eds., *Base Ball Founders: The Clubs, Players and Cities of the Northeast that Established the Game* (Jefferson, NC: McFarland, 2013), 153.

15. *Brooklyn Daily Eagle,* April 2 and September 5, 1868.

16. *Brooklyn Daily Eagle,* May 4, 1864; January 24 and May 1, 1866; April 26 and September 16, 1867; April 18, September 25, and October 7, 1873; and April 2 and 28, 1880; Spink, *The National Game,* 10; Ryczek, *Baseball's First Inning,* 199–200; http://www.projectballpark.org/history/na/capitoline.html.

17. *Brooklyn Daily Eagle,* February 17, 1865; April 2 and 11, and May 18, 1868; May 18 and June 1, 1869; letter dated May 15, 1964, from unknown writer to F.J. Consolozio, Philadelphia, PA, copy in Brooklyn Historical Society, Brooklyn Scrapbooks, vol. 163, insert between pp. 75–76.

18. *New York Clipper,* August 22, 1868.

19. *New York Herald,* August 15, 1868.

20. Wright, *The National Association of Base Ball Players,* 206.

21. *Brooklyn Daily Eagle,* August 29, 1868; *New York Clipper,* September 5 and October 24, 1868.

22. *Brooklyn Daily Eagle,* September 14, 1868.

23. Wright, *The National Association of Base Ball Players,* 206.

24. *Brooklyn Daily Eagle,* October 7 and 27, 1868; *New York Clipper,* October 31, 1868.

25. In the 1860 version of the NABBP's *Rules and Regulations of the Game of Baseball, 1860,* the rule is in sec. 36.

26. Morris, *A Game of Inches,* 462–463.

27. Morris, *A Game of Inches,* 464; Morris, *Base Ball Founders,* 80–81; William J. Ryczek, *When Johnny Came Sliding Home* (Jefferson, NC: McFarland, 1998), 19–21; Roger I. Abrams, *Playing Tough: The World of Sports and Politics* (Boston: Northeastern University Press, 2013), 31–33.

28. Thorn, "George Wright."

29. Spalding, *America's National Game,* 119–123.

30. The report of the convention is in Chadwick, *Beadle's Dime Base Ball Player, 1869* (New York: Beadle, 1869), 44ff.

31. Chadwick, *Beadle's Dime Base Ball Player, 1869,* 133.

32. Morris, *A Game of Inches,* 463–465; *Richter's History and Records of Baseball,* 38–40; Chadwick, *Beadle's Dime Base Ball Player, 1869,* 43, 46, 48; *New York Clipper,* January 23, 1869.

33. Morris, *A Game of Inches,* 464; Abrams, *Playing Tough,* 33; *New York Clipper,* April 10, 1869.

34. *Chicago Tribune,* January 16, 1872.

35. *New York Clipper,* April 10 and 17, 1869.

36. *New York Clipper,* April 3, 1869.

37. *New York Herald,* April 11, 1869; *New York Clipper,* May 1, 1869.

38. *New York Clipper,* May 1, 1869; Chadwick, *Beadle's Dime Base Ball Player, 1870,* 65. The *New York Clipper,* on June 26, 1869, gave the score as 56–22; Chadwick may be more accurate.

39. *Brooklyn Daily Eagle,* June 21, 1869.

40. *New York Clipper,* June 26, 1869.

41. *Brooklyn Daily Eagle,* June 21, 1869.

42. *New York Clipper,* August 21, 1869; *Brooklyn Daily Eagle,* October 4, 1869.

43. *Brooklyn Daily Eagle,* July 20, 1869.

44. *Brooklyn Daily Eagle,* October 1, 1869; *New York Clipper,* October 9, 1869.

45. *Wilkes' Spirit of the Times,* October 30, 1869.

Chapter 10

1. *Lain's Brooklyn Directory 1870,* 144, 559; New York City (Manhattan) Marriage Certificate No. 1371; *Church Records and General Register, North Presbyterian Church* (New York: Nathan Lane, 1854); *Manual of the North Presbyterian Church in the City of New York* (New York, John A. Gray, 1858), 5 (available online at https://archive.org/stream/manualofnorth pre00nort_0); Brooklyn, NY, Marriage Certificate No. 1143; New York City Marriage Records, 1829–1940, https://www.familyse arch.org/ark:/61903/1:1:24MX-VHS.

2. From a clipping of an article in Henry Chadwick's scrapbooks; no date or source given.

3. *Brooklyn Daily Eagle,* March 11, 1870.

4. *New York Clipper,* April 2, 1870.

5. Morris, *Base Ball Founders,* 98; *Brooklyn Daily Eagle,* May 16, 1862; letter dated May 15, 1964, from unknown writer to F.J. Consolozio, Philadelphia, Penn., copy in Brooklyn Historical Society, Brooklyn Scrapbooks, vol. 163, insert between pp. 75–76.

6. *New York Herald,* May 8, 1870.

7. *Wilkes' Spirit of the Times,* December 31, 1870.

8. *Ibid.*

9. *New York Sunday Mercury,* May 8, 1870.

10. *New York Tribune,* May 9, 1870.

11. *Brooklyn Daily Eagle,* May 9, 1870.

12. *Brooklyn Daily Eagle,* May 16, 1870.

13. *New York Clipper,* May 28, 1870.

14. *New York Clipper,* June 25, 1870.

15. *New York Herald,* June 19, 1870.

16. *New York Clipper,* July 23, 1870.

17. From a clipping of an article in Henry Chadwick's scrapbooks; no date or source given.

18. Cummings, "Baseball in the Sixties and Seventies. A Tour with the Star Club of Brooklyn."

19. *New York Clipper,* July 2, 1870.

20. Cummings, "Baseball in the Sixties and Seventies."

21. *New York Times,* July 6, 1870.

22. *Brooklyn Daily Eagle,* July 13, 1870.

23. *New York Clipper,* December 28, 1872, and March 8, 1873.

24. Morris, *A Game of Inches,* 288–280;

Ryczek, *Blackguards and Red Stockings,* 19; *New York Clipper,* August 25, 1877.

25. *Rockford [IL] Gazette,* August 1, 1872.

26. *Rockford [IL] Gazette,* April 26, 1896.

27. *Brooklyn Daily Eagle,* August 5, 1870.

28. *Brooklyn Daily Eagle,* August 8, 1870.

29. *Washington [D.C.] Evening Star,* July 7, 1870.

30. Peter Morris, *Catcher: How the Man Behind the Plate Became an American Folk Hero* (Chicago: Ivan R. Dee, 2009), 43–48.

31. From a clipping of an article in Henry Chadwick's scrapbooks; no date or source given.

32. *Wilkes' Spirit of the Times,* August 27, 1870.

33. *Wilkes' Spirit of the Times,* January 20, 1871.

34. *Brooklyn Daily Eagle,* September 12, 1870.

35. From a clipping of an article in Henry Chadwick's scrapbooks, no date or source given; *Boston Journal,* November 3, 1970.

36. *Brooklyn Daily Eagle,* November 17, 1870.

37. *Brooklyn Daily Eagle,* September 20, 1870.

38. *Wilkes' Spirit of the Times,* October 1, 1870.

39. *Brooklyn Daily Eagle,* March 24, 1871.

40. *Brooklyn Daily Eagle,* April 26, 1871.

41. *New York Sunday Mercury,* May 21, 1871.

42. *New York Clipper,* June 3, 1871.

43. *Brooklyn Daily Eagle,* May 27, 1871.

44. *New York Clipper,* June 10, 1871; *Brooklyn Daily Eagle,* June 21, 1871.

45. *New York Herald,* May 31, 1871.

46. *New York World,* May 31, 1871; *Cincinnati Inquirer,* May 31, 1871.

47. *Brooklyn Daily Eagle,* May 31, 1871.

48. *New York Clipper,* June 10, 1871.

49. *New York Tribune,* June 5, 1871.

50. *New York Sunday Mercury,* June 4, 1871.

51. *New York Clipper,* June 17, 1871.

52. *New York Clipper,* July 1, 1871.

53. *New York World,* June 21, 1871.

54. *Brooklyn Daily Eagle,* June 21, 1871.

55. *New York Clipper,* August 6, 1870.

56. *New York Clipper,* October 2, 1869; June 25, July 2, and July 9, 1870; July 8, 1871.

57. *New York World,* August 2, 1871.

58. Cummings, "Close of Mr. Cummings' Reminiscences"; *New York Tribune,* August 14, 1871; *New York World,* August 16, 1871.

59. *New York Clipper,* September 2, 1871; Cummings, "Close of Mr. Cummings' Reminiscences."

60. *Chicago Tribune,* August 22, 1871.

61. *Brooklyn Daily Eagle,* August 23, 1871; *New York Clipper,* September 2, 1871.

62. Cummings, "Close of Mr. Cummings' Reminiscences."

63. *Ibid.*

64. *Brooklyn Daily Eagle,* August 24, 1871.

65. *New York Sunday Mercury,* August 27, 1871; Cummings, "Close of Mr. Cummings' Reminiscences."

66. *New York Clipper,* September 2, 1871.

67. *Cincinnati Daily Inquirer,* August 27, 1871.

68. *New York Herald,* September 17, 1871.

69. *New York Clipper,* October 7, 1871.

70. *New York Clipper,* October 14, 1871.

71. Cummings, "Close of Mr. Cummings' Reminiscences."

Chapter 11

1. Ryczek, *Blackguards and Red Stockings,* 12–13; *New York Clipper,* February 20, 1869.

2. Chadwick, *Beadle's Dime Base Ball Player, 1870,* 45–46.

3. Quoted by Ryczek in *Blackguards and Red Stockings,* 13.

4. Ryczek, *Blackguards and Red Stockings,* 14.

5. "A National Association of Amateur Base Ball Players Established," *New York Clipper,* March 25, 1871.

6. "The Professionals in Council," *New York Clipper,* March 25, 1871.

7. *Ibid.*

8. *Chicago Tribune,* August 22, 1871, and September 10, 1876; *New York Clipper,* December 28, 1872.

9. *New York Journal,* December 29, 1921.

10. Cummings' letter was published in the *New York Clipper* on January 27, 1872 (he had sent a similar, but not exact, version to the *Brooklyn Daily Eagle,* which published it on January 15); the Haymakers' reply appeared in the *Clipper* on February 24.

11. *Harrisburg [PA] Daily Patriot,* October 9, 1871.

12. *Brooklyn Daily Eagle,* January 18, 1872; "The Profits of Ball Tossing," *West Meriden [CT] Daily Republican,* September 25, 1872.

13. *Brooklyn Daily Eagle,* January 15, 1872.

14. *New York Clipper,* January 20, 1872.

15. *Brooklyn Daily Union,* August 9, 1872; *New York Clipper,* August 17, 1872.

16. *New York Clipper,* January 20, 1872.

17. Brian McKenna, "Steve Bellàn," SABR BioProject, https://sabr.org/bioproj/person/78dbf37d.

18. *New York Clipper,* May 18, 1872.

19. McMahon, "Al Spalding."

20. *New York Daily Herald,* April 30, 1872.

21. *Brooklyn Daily Eagle,* May 22, 1872; *Brooklyn Daily Union,* July 5, 1872, which contains the quote.

22. *New York Clipper,* June 22, 1872.

23. *New York Clipper,* October 12, 1872.

24. *Boston Journal,* September 23, 1872.

25. *Brooklyn Daily Eagle,* May 9, 1872; *New York Clipper,* May 18, 1872.

26. *New York Clipper,* September 14, 1872.

27. This data is based on newspaper accounts of individual games, the Mutuals' 1872 regular season game log (which excludes exhibition games and games against amateur clubs) in www.retrosheet.org, and the Mutuals' 1872 record published in the *New York Clipper* on November 23, 1872 (which includes exhibition and amateur club games). The *Clipper* listing includes 51 championship games and

13 "exhibition games" against professional clubs; it omits the following five additional championship games and one additional exhibition game against professional clubs for which box scores have been found: June 15: Cleveland 11, Mutual 4 (*Clipper,* June 22, 1872); July 20, 1872: Mutual 11, Athletic 6 (*Clipper,* July 27, 1872); July 27: Mutual 26, Mansfield 9 (*New York Times,* July 28, 1872); August 5: Mutual 14, Mansfield 3 (*Clipper,* August 10, 1872); August 13: Boston 4, Mutual 2 (*Clipper,* August 24, 1872); and October 12 (exhibition game): Athletic 11, Mutual 5 (*Clipper,* October 19, 1872). The *Clipper* listing also includes, possibly in error, an exhibition game on July 30, 1872 (Mutual 11, Troy 2) that is questionable: no record of that game has been found, and the *Eagle* of July 29, 1872 and the *Clipper* of August 3, 1872, announced that the Troy club had disbanded. Different figures given in *Beadle's Dime Base Ball Player* and in baseball-reference.com result from the fact that both sources omit some games.

28. Figures extrapolated from data in ESPN's MLB Team Stats, http://www.espn.com/mlb/stats/team/_/stat/pitching/year/2018/split/127.

29. Frank J. Williams, "All the Record Books are Wrong," https://sabr.org/journal/article/all-the-record-books-are-wrong/ (1982); Frank Vacarro, "Origin of the Modern Pitching Win," https://sabr.org/journal/article/origin-of-the-modern-pitching-win/ (2013).

30. *New York Clipper,* March 15, 1879. Chadwick made the same points, in almost the same words, on other occasions, including in his book, *The Art of Pitching and Fielding,* 9–10.

31. *New York Clipper,* December 28, 1872.

32. *New York Clipper,* June 8, 1872.

33. *Philadelphia Inquirer,* June 10, 1872; *New York Clipper,* June 15, 1872.

34. *Brooklyn Daily Eagle,* July 15, 1872

35. *New York Clipper,* December 28, 1872.

36. *New York Clipper,* March 15, 1879.

37. *Brooklyn Daily Eagle,* March 22, 1872; *New York Clipper,* April 20, 1872.

38. *New York Clipper,* November 23, 1872.

39. *New York Clipper,* December 14, 1872.

40. www.retrosheet.org.

41. *New York Clipper,* December 28, 1872.

Chapter 12

1. *New York Herald,* October 11, 1872; *Buffalo [NY] Commercial,* October 31, 1872.

2. *Washington [D.C.] National Republican,* September 13, 1873; "The Profits of Ball Tossing."

3. https://www.britannica.com/topic/American-colonies/Land-policy-in-New-England-and-Virginia#ref1268500; Casey Egan, "The Surprising Irish Origins of Baltimore, Maryland," https://www.irishcentral.com/roots/history/the-surprising-irish-origins-of-baltimore-maryland; *New York Clipper,* May 4, 1872.

4. *New York Clipper,* May 4, 1872; *Chicago Inter-Ocean,* May 30, 1872; https://www.threadsofourgame.com/1872-lord-baltimore-baltimore.

5. *New York Clipper,* March 8, 1873.

6. *New York Clipper,* December 21, 1872, and March 8, 1873.

7. *New York Clipper,* November 10 and December 15, 1877.

8. *Washington [D.C.] Capital,* April 20, 1873; *New York World,* April 22, 1873.

9. *New York Clipper,* May 3, 1873.

10. Baseball-reference.com.

11. *New York Clipper,* December 21, 1872.

12. *New York Clipper,* May 17, 1873.

13. www.retrosheet.org.

14. *New York Clipper,* May 17, 1873.

15. *New York Clipper,* May 17 and August 16, 1873.

16. *New York World,* June 10, 1873.

17. *Washington [D.C.] Capital,* September 14, 1873; *Spirit of the Times,* October 4, 1873.

18. *New York World,* September 13, 17, and 20, 1873; *Baltimore Sun,* September 17, 1873; *Washington [D.C.] Capital,* September 28, 1873.

19. *New York World,* September 6, 1873; *Washington [D.C.] Capital,* September 14, 1873; *New York Clipper,* September 10 and October 18, 1873.

20. *Spirit of the Times,* October 4, 1873.

21. *New York Clipper,* January 31, 1874.

22. *Washington [D.C.] Capital,* September 28, 1873.
23. McKenna, "Asa Brainard."
24. *New York Clipper,* January 10 and 31, 1874.
25. *New York Clipper,* February 28, 1874.
26. *New York Daily Graphic,* February 10, 1874.
27. https://www.american-rails.com/couplers.html.
28. United States Patent Office, Patent No. 149,376 (April 7, 1874), issued to William A. Cummings.
29. https://www.american-rails.com/couplers.html.

Chapter 13

1. *New York Clipper,* April 11, 1874.
2. *New York Clipper,* August 30, 1873.
3. *New York Clipper,* April 11, 1874.
4. *New York Clipper,* April 19, 1873.
5. *New York Clipper,* February 21, 1874.
6. *Spirit of the Times,* September 23, 1873.
7. *New York Clipper,* February 28, 1874.
8. *New York Clipper,* April 25, 1874.
9. *New York Clipper,* August 8, 1874.
10. *Chicago Inter-Ocean,* June 16, 1874; *New York Clipper,* June 27, 1874.
11. *New York Clipper,* June 27, 1874.
12. *Ibid.*
13. *New York Clipper,* May 30, 1874.
14. *New York Clipper,* July 11, 1874.
15. *New York Clipper,* May 16, 1874.
16. Record of Christening of Arthur R. Cummings, "New York Births and Christenings, 1640–1962," www.familysearch.org; Marriages Registered in the Town of Athol, Mass. For the Year 1896; United States World War I Draft Registration Cards, 1917–1918, Michigan, Arthur Roberts Cummings; 1875 New York State Census, King's County, Brooklyn Ward, 23, p. 35.
17. *New York Clipper,* October 31, 1874.
18. *New York Herald,* November 1, 1874.
19. *New York Clipper,* November 28, 1874.
20. Henry Chadwick, ed., *Beadle's*

Dime Base Ball Player for 1875 (New York: Beadle and Adams, 1875), 44.
21. *Chicago Tribune,* July 16, 1874.
22. https://www.mlb.com/official-information/umpires/timeline.
23. *New York Clipper,* September 12, 1874.
24. *New York Clipper,* March 6 and 20, 1869; *New York Sunday Mercury,* February 28, 1869; *New York Tribune,* June 23, 1869.
25. *Chicago Tribune,* July 16, 1874.
26. *Chicago Inter-Ocean,* July 16, 1874.
27. *New York Clipper,* September 19, 1874, and March 13, 1875.
28. *New York Clipper,* May 16, July 4, and August 1, 1874.
29. *Boston Advertiser,* October 27, 1874.
30. *Boston Advertiser,* October 27, 1874; *Hartford Courant,* October 29, 1874; *New York Clipper,* November 7, 1874.
31. *New York Clipper,* January 9, 1875.

Chapter 14

1. David Arcidiacono, *Major League Baseball in Gilded Age Connecticut* (Jefferson, NC: McFarland, 2010), 91–92; *Middletown [CT] Daily Constitution,* August 14, 1872.
2. Arcidiacono, *Major League Baseball in Gilded Age Connecticut,* 94–98; *Middletown [CT] Daily Constitution,* March 28, 1874; *Hartford Courant,* April 10, 1874; *New York Clipper,* May 22, 1875.
3. *New York Clipper,* November 14, 1874.
4. Brian McKenna, "Bob Ferguson," SABR BioProject, https://sabr.org/bioproj/person/df8e7d29;Arcidiacono, *Major League Baseball in Gilded Age Connecticut,* 108, 133–134; *St. Louis Globe–Democrat,* June 25, 1875; *St. Louis Republican,* August 1, 1875.
5. Chris Rainey, "Tommy Bond," SABR BioProject, https://sabr.org/bioproj/person/c0089818#sdendnote1anc.
6. *Chicago Tribune,* October 25, 1874.
7. *Hartford Courant,* October 31, 1875.
8. *New York Herald,* November 1, 1874.
9. *Waterbury [CT] Daily American,* November 2, 1874.
10. *Chicago Tribune,* December 6, 1874.

11. *New York Clipper,* January 30, 1875; *St. Louis Republican,* January 31, 1875.

12. Arcidiacono, *Major League Baseball in Gilded Age Connecticut,* 136.

13. *Hartford Courant,* August 21, 1875.

14. *New York Clipper,* July 10, 1875.

15. *New York Clipper,* January 1, 1876.

16. Richard Puff, "Douglas L. Allison," in Frederick Ivor-Campbell, ed., *Baseball's First Stars* (Cleveland: Society for American Baseball Research, 1996), 2; Charles F. Faber, "Doug Allison," SABR BioProject, https://sabr.org/bioproj/person/dc86c546; Ryczek, *Blackguards and Red Stockings,* 20.

17. *Hartford Courant,* June 24, 1875.

18. *New York Clipper,* April 24, 1875.

19. *New York Clipper,* February 6 and April 10, 1875.

20. *Ibid.*; Arcidiacono, *Major League Baseball in Gilded Age Connecticut,* 112–113; *St. Louis Republican,* August 1, 1875.

21. *Hartford Courant,* April 26, 1875; *New York Clipper,* May 1 and 8, 1875.

22. John Thorn, "George Wright," SABR BioProject, https://sabr.org/bioproj/person/5468d7c0.

23. This description of the game and its aftermath is from the *Boston Advertiser,* May 19, 1875; *Boston Journal,* May 19, 1875; *Hartford Courant,* May 19, 1875; and *New York Clipper,* May 29, 1875.

24. https://marktwainhouse.org/about/mark-twain/biography.

25. Website of the Mark Twain Project, University of California at Berkeley, https://www.marktwainproject.org/xtf/view?docId=letters/UCCL11895.xml;query=baseball;searchAll=;sectionType1=;sectionType2=;sectionType3=;sectionType4=;sectionType5=;style:letter;brand=mtp#1.

26. *Hartford Courant,* May 20, 1875.

27. *New York World,* May 28, 1875; *Schenectady [NY] Evening Star,* August 2, 1875.

28. *New York Clipper,* May 29, 1875.

29. Games on June 17, July 5, and September 25, 1875: *New York Clipper,* June 26, July 17, and October 9, 1875.

30. *Hartford Courant,* October 30, 1875.

31. Henry Chadwick, ed., *The Dime Base Ball Player, for 1876* (New York: Beadle and Adams, 1876), 38.

32. *New York Clipper,* May 29, 1875.

33. *New York Clipper,* November 21, 1874.

34. Chadwick, *The Dime Base Ball Player, for 1876,* 38.

35. Figures calculated from game and run-scoring statistics at www.retrosheet.org.

36. Morris, *A Game of Inches,* 17–20.

37. *Chicago Tribune,* June 20, 1875.

38. Game account based on descriptions by the *Chicago Tribune,* June 20, 1875, *Hartford Courant,* June 21, 1875, *New York Clipper,* June 26, 1875, and *Chicago Post and Mail,* reprinted in the *New York Clipper* on July 3, 1875. The *Post and Mail's* description differs from the others in that it had Devlin scoring on Burdock's wide throw to first, while in the others Devlin made it a far as third and was driven home by the next batter, Hines.

39. *Chicago Tribune,* June 20, 1875.

40. *New York Clipper,* June 26, 1875.

41. *Chicago Tribune,* June 20, 1875.

42. Quoted by David Arcidiacono in "The 'Model' Game: Hartford vs. Chicago," in Felber, *Inventing Baseball,* 93–94.

43. *New York Clipper,* September 18, 1875.

44. *New York Clipper,* November 6 and December 11, 1875.

45. *New York Clipper,* May 15, 22, and 29, and October 16, 1875; *Hartford Courant,* June 11 and 15, and October 19, 1875.

46. United States Patent Office, Patent No. 194,996 (September 11, 1877), issued to William A. Cummings.

47. Arcidiacono, *Major League Base Ball in Gilded Age Connecticut,* 107 ff.; Irv Goldfarb, "Morgan Bulkeley," SABR BioProject, https://sabr.org/bioproj/person/73d7237a.

48. https://www.newenglandhistoricalsociety.com/candy-cummings-invented-curveball/.

49. https://www.american-rails.com/couplers.html.

Chapter 15

1. 1870 U.S. Census, vol. 1, Population of Civil Divisions Less than Counties, Table III, 137.

2. Tom Melville, *Early Baseball and the Rise of the National League* (Jefferson, NC: McFarland, 2001), 70–78; Arcidiacono, *Major League Baseball in Gilded Age Connecticut,* 147–150; Michael Haupert,

"William Hulbert and the Birth of the National League," SABR BioProject, https://sabr.org/research/william-hulbert-and-birth-national-league; *Chicago Tribune,* October 24, 1875; *New York Clipper,* January 22, 1876.

3. *Chicago Tribune,* October 24, 1875; "The Proceedings at the Grand Central," *New York Clipper,* February 12, 1876.

4. "National League of Professional Clubs: A Startling Coup d'Etat," *New York Clipper,* February 12, 1876.

5. *Columbian Register* (New Haven, CT), November 27, 1875; *New York Clipper,* February 5, 1876.

6. *New York Clipper,* December 30, 1876.

7. *New York Clipper,* April 8, 1876.

8. *Springfield [MA] Republican,* September 9, 1876.

9. *New York Clipper,* June 10, 1876.

10. Arcidiacono, *Major League Baseball in Gilded Age Connecticut,* 161. Burr, "Candy Cummings."

11. *Bridgeport [CT] Standard,* February 29, 1876; *Chicago Daily News,* April 13, 1876.

12. *New York Clipper,* August 26, 1876.

13. *Hartford Times,* September 2, 1876.

14. *Hartford Courant,* August 25, 1876; *Springfield [MA] Republican,* September 9, 1876; *New York Clipper,* September 16, 1876.

15. *New York Clipper,* September 2, and October 14 and 28, 1876.

16. *New York Clipper,* December 2, 1876; *St. Louis Globe–Democrat,* September 7, 1876.

17. *New York Clipper,* September 2, 1876.

18. *Cincinnati Enquirer,* September 10, 1876; *New York Clipper,* September 16, 1876.

19. *Cincinnati Enquirer,* September 10, 1876.

20. *Hartford Courant,* October 26 and 28, 1876; *Boston Advertiser,* October 28, 1876; *Boston Journal,* October 30, 1876.

21. www.baseball-reference.com.

Chapter 16

1. *Chicago Tribune,* December 24, 1876.

2. *New York Clipper,* November 25 and December 23, 1876; *Hartford Courant,* December 15, 1876.

3. *New York Clipper,* September 16, November 25, and December 16, 1876; *Hartford Courant,* December 15, 1876.

4. *New York Clipper,* August 12, 1876; *Lynn [MA] Evening Item,* June 28, 1895.

5. *New York Clipper,* July 17, 24, and 31, 1875, and August 12, 1876.

6. *Lowell [MA] Citizen,* August 23, 1876; *Providence Press,* August 28, 1876.

7. *New York Clipper,* December 2, 1876.

8. *New York Clipper,* September 30, October 21, and December 16, 1876; *Chicago Tribune,* December 24, 1876.

9. *New York Clipper,* October 21, 1876.

10. *St. Louis Globe-Democrat,* January 15, 1877; *New York Clipper,* January 20 and 27, 1877.

11. Brock Helander, "The League Alliance," https://sabr.org/bioproj/topic/league-alliance.

12. *St. Louis Globe-Democrat,* February 23, 1877; *New York Clipper,* March 3 and June 23, 1877.

13. *New York Clipper,* January 27, 1877.

14. *Lowell [MA] Citizen,* February 19, 1877.

15. *Boston Journal,* March 19, 1877.

16. *Fall River [MA] Herald,* February 2, 1877.

17. *Fall River [MA] Herald,* March 24, 1877.

18. *Boston Globe,* April 19, 1877.

19. *New York Clipper,* June 2, 1877.

20. *Boston Globe,* April 26, 1877.

21. Good games: vs. Fall River: *Fall River [MA] Herald,* May 5, 1877; vs. Indianapolis: *Boston Journal,* June 5, 1877; vs. Harvard College: *Boston Journal,* June 13, 1877; struggling: vs. Manchesters: *Boston Globe,* April 27, 1877; vs. Auburn (NY), and Erie (PA): *New York Clipper,* May 26, 1877; vs. Buckeyes: *Boston Advertiser,* June 14, 1877, and *New York Clipper,* June 23, 1877.

22. *New York Clipper,* May 16, 1877, and *New York Clipper,* May 26, 1877.

23. *Boston Journal,* June 2, 1877; *Lowell [MA] Citizen,* June 2, 1877; *New York Clipper,* June 9, 1877.

24. *Boston Journal,* June 5, 1877; *New York Clipper,* June 16, 1877.

25. Win-loss figures are based on the interim International Association standings

reported in the *New York Clipper,* June 23, 1877, and reports of individual games. The *Clipper* accounting does not reflect games that ended in ties. Baseball-reference.com gives Candy Cummings' record against International Association clubs as 1 win, 7 losses.

26. *Cincinnati Gazette,* June 18 and 19, 1877.

27. www.retrosheet.org; *New York Clipper,* June 23, 1877.

28. *Cincinnati Commercial Tribune,* July 1, 1877; *Chicago Tribune,* July 1, 1877.

29. David Nemec, "Jack Manning," SABR BioProject, https://sabr.org/bioproj/person/fbd233f7.

30. *Cincinnati Commercial Tribune,* July 1, 1877.

31. *Cincinnati Gazette,* July 4, 1877; *Chicago Tribune,* July 4, 1877.

32. *Cincinnati Commercial Tribune,* July 5, 1877; *Cincinnati Gazette,* July 5, 1877; *New York Tribune,* July 10, 1877.

33. *New York Clipper,* July 14, 1877.

34. *Cincinnati Gazette,* July 9, 1877; *New York Clipper,* July 14, 1877.

35. *Chicago Tribune,* July 14 and 15, 1877; *Cincinnati Commercial Tribune,* July 22, 1877; *Cincinnati Gazette,* July 13 and 25, 1877; *New York Clipper,* July 21 and 28, and August 4 and 11, 1877.

36. *Chicago Tribune,* August 5, 1877; *Cincinnati Commercial Tribune,* August 10, 1877; *New York Clipper,* August 11 and 18, 1877.

37. *New York Clipper,* August 25, 1877.

38. *New York Clipper,* August 18, 1877.

39. *New York Clipper,* November 10, 1877.

40. *New York Clipper,* December 8 and 15, 1877.

Chapter 17

1. Letter dated December 20, 1877, from W.A. Cummings, 650 Warren St., Brooklyn, to Directors of the Buffalo Base Ball Association. A copy of the letter is in the archives of the Hall of Fame (Player File: Cummings, William Arthur, 1872– / compiled by the National Baseball Hall of Fame Library, Cooperstown, NY).

2. *Lynn [MA] Evening Item,* March 19, 1878.

3. *Brooklyn Daily Eagle,* February 3, 1878.

4. *Brooklyn Daily Eagle,* March 12 and 13, 1878; *New York Clipper,* March 30, 1878.

5. *New York Clipper,* March 23, April 6, and April 13, 1878.

6. *New York Clipper,* January 19, 1878.

7. *New York Clipper,* March 2, 1878; Henry Chadwick, ed., *The Dime Base Ball Player for 1878* (New York: Beadle and Adams, 1878), 81.

8. *New York Clipper,* March 23 and 30.

9. *New York Clipper,* April 20, 1878.

10. *Brooklyn Daily Eagle,* April 7, 1878; *Buffalo [NY] Commercial Gazette,* April 24, 1878.

11. David Arcidiacono, "Ben Douglas," SABR BioProject, https://sabr.org/node/26039; *Rhode Island Press* (Providence), December 29, 1877; *New York Clipper,* February 2, 1878; *Chicago Tribune,* April 21, 1878.

12. *New York Clipper,* April 27 and May 11, 1878, and November 27, 1880; *Lowell [MA] Daily Citizen,* May 1, 1878.

13. *New York Clipper,* May 4 and 11, 1878.

14. *New York Clipper,* May 11, 1878.

15. *New York Clipper,* May 18, 1878.

16. *Boston Globe,* May 20, 1878.

17. *New York Clipper,* July 27, 1878.

18. *New York Clipper,* May 18, 1878; *Chicago Tribune,* May 19, 1878; *Boston Journal,* May 20, 1878; *Memphis [TN] Daily Appeal,* May 24, 1878.

19. *New York Clipper,* June 8, 1878.

20. *Washington [D.C.] National Republican,* May 29, 1878; *Washington [D.C.] Evening Star,* May 30, 1878; *New York Clipper,* June 8 and 15, 1878.

21. *Brooklyn Daily Eagle,* June 17, 1878; *New York Clipper,* June 22, 1878.

22. *New York Clipper,* July 27 and September 14, 1878; *New York Times,* July 9, 1878; Arcidiacono, "Ben Douglas."

23. *Rochester [NY] Democrat and Chronicle,* May 12, 1879.

24. *Chicago Tribune,* June 30, 1878; *New York Clipper,* July 6, 1878.

25. *Brooklyn Daily Eagle,* July 23 and October 25, 1877.

26. *Brooklyn Daily Eagle,* June 20 and 23, 1878.

27. *Brooklyn Daily Eagle,* June 20, 1878; *New York Clipper,* June 29, July 6 and 27, and August 3, 1878; *New York Times,* July 18, 1878.

28. *New York Clipper,* August 24, 1878.

29. *Buffalo [NY] Commercial Gazette,* August 5, 1878; *New York Clipper,* August 24, 1878.

30. *New York Clipper,* August 24 and 31, 1878.

31. *New York Clipper,* August 31, 1878.

32. https://www.baseball-reference.com/bullpen/Morrie_Critchley; *Sporting Life,* January 18, 1908, and March 19, 1910.

33. *New York Herald,* September 7, 1878.

Chapter 18

1. *New York Clipper,* November 2 and December 14, 1878.

2. *New York Clipper,* November 2, 1878; *Albany [NY] Times,* December 14, 1878.

3. 1870 U.S. Census, vol. 1, Population of Civil Divisions Less than Counties, Table III, https://www2.census.gov/library/publications/decennial/1880/vol-01-population/1880_v1-11.pdf?#.

4. *New York Clipper,* November 2, 1878; *Chicago Tribune,* January 12, 1879.

5. *Buffalo Express,* February 20, 1879; *Cincinnati Inquirer,* February 21, 1879; *New York Clipper,* March 1, 1879.

6. *Buffalo Express,* March 29, 1879.

7. *New York Clipper,* December 14, 1878.

8. *Chicago Tribune,* January 12, 1879.

9. *Albany [NY] Argus,* May 1, 1879.

10. *Chicago Tribune,* January 12, 1879.

11. *New York Clipper,* March 1, 1879.

12. *Chicago Tribune,* March 2, 1879; *Buffalo Express,* March 29, 1879; *Albany [NY] Evening Journal,* April 3, 1879.

13. *Utica [NY] Daily Observer,* April 23, 1879; *New York Clipper,* May 3, 1879.

14. https://www.peachridgeglass.com/wp-content/uploads/2014/01/Flag1.jpg.

15. *Buffalo Express,* February 20, 1879; *New York Clipper,* April 19 and 26, and May 3, 1879.

16. *New York Clipper,* May 17, 1879.

17. *Boston Globe,* May 10, 1879; *Rochester [NY] Democrat and Chronicle,* May 10 and 12, 1897; *Buffalo Express,* May 12, 1879; *Springfield [MA] Republican,* May 10, 1879; *St. Louis Globe–Democrat,* May 14, 1879; *Chicago Tribune,* May 18, 1879.

18. *Brooklyn Daily Eagle,* May 23, 1879.

19. *New Haven [CT] Register,* May 13, 1879.

20. *Syracuse [NY] Daily Standard,* May 17, 1879.

21. *Rochester [NY] Democrat and Chronicle,* May 12, 1897; *Buffalo Courier,* May 25, 1879.

22. *Springfield [MA] Republican,* May 10, 1879.

23. *St. Louis Globe–Democrat,* May 14, 1879, quoting a story in the *Albany Argus.*

24. *Chicago Tribune,* May 18, 1879, paraphrasing a story in the *Albany Morning Express.*

25. *Rochester [NY] Democrat and Chronicle,* May 10, 1897.

26. Sam Crane, "Arthur Cummings," *New York Journal,* January 8, 1912.

27. *New York Clipper,* May 24, 1879.

28. *New York Clipper,* July 5, 1879.

29. *Washington [D.C.] National Republican,* April 30, 1879.

30. *Worcester [MA] Daily Spy,* May 10, 1879; *New York Clipper,* May 3 and 31, and June 21 and 28, 1879.

31. *Chicago Tribune,* July 6, 1879, quoting from *Hudson [NY] Republican.*

32. *New York Clipper,* July 7, 19, and 26, and August 2, 9, and 16, 1879.

33. Francis C. Richter, ed., *The Reach Official American League Baseball Guide for 1918* (Philadelphia: A.J. Reach, 1918), 251.

Chapter 19

1. *Boston Globe,* December 12, 1880.

2. *Brooklyn Daily Eagle,* May 28, 1882; *New York Clipper,* June 10, 1882.

3. *New York Herald,* July 7, 1882; https://commons.wikimedia.org/wiki/Category:Palisades_Mountain_House.

4. Introduction by Editor of "*Cottager*" to Cummings, "The 'Curve' Ball. The Inventor Tells All About It," in the Cummings *Cottager* series; Lain's Brooklyn Directory 1884, 259.

5. 1880 U.S. Census, vol. 1, Statistics of the Population of the United States, Populations of Civil Divisions Less than Counties, Table 3–Massachusetts, 210.

6. History of Athol is from William G. Lord, *History of Athol, Massachusetts* (Athol, MA: William G. Lord, 1953) (available online at https://archive.org/details/historyofatholma00lord); Massachusetts

Historic Commission, *MHC Reconnaissance Survey Town Report—Athol* (1984)
(available online at https://www.sec.state.
ma.us/mhc/mhcpdf/townreports/Cent-
Mass/ath.pdf); www.starrett.com.
    7. 1880 U.S. Census, vol. 1, Table 3, pp.
209 and 210.
    8. Cummins, *Cummings Genealogy*,
xii, 90.
    9. *Millers River District Directory of
Athol [and several other towns, 1885]* (West
Gardner, MA: L.B. Caswell, 1885), 44, and
Athol directories for subsequent years;
1900 U.S. Census, Athol, Worcester County,
Massachusetts, ED 1582, sheet 10; 1910 U.S.
Census, Athol, Worcester, County, Massachusetts, ED 1695, sheet 6B.
    10. *Lain's Brooklyn Directory 1858*, 82,
and subsequent years.
    11. *Boston Herald*, March 13, 1884;
https://www.baseball-reference.com/
bullpen/Massachusetts_State_Association.
    12. *Boston Herald*, May 8, 1884.
    13. *Athol [MA] Transcript*, June 3,
1884.
    14. *Athol [MA] Transcript*, June 10,
1884.
    15. *Springfield [MA] Republican*, June
21, 1884.
    16. *Athol [MA] Transcript*, July 8, 15,
and 22, 1884.

Chapter 20

    1. *Sporting Life*, April 11, 1896.
    2. *Brooklyn Standard Union*, January
20, 1896; "He Pitched the First Curve Ball";
Kings County (New York) death certifi-
cate, 1896, certificate 919; *Cleveland Plain
Dealer*, July 25, 1900.
    3. Marriages Registered in the Town of
Athol [MA] for the Year 1896; *Athol [Mass.]
Directory, 1897* (New Haven, Conn.: Price
& Lee Co., 1897), 27; United States World
War I Draft Registration Cards, Connecti-
cut, New Haven.
    4. Christopher Devine, "Harry
Wright," SABR BioProject, https://sabr.org/
bioproj/person/eb17c14e.
    5. Bob Ruzzo, "The South End
Grounds," in Bob LeMoine and Bill Nowlin,
eds., *The Glorious Beaneaters of the 1890s*
(Phoenix: Society for American Baseball
Research, 2019), 235–243.
    6. *Boston Advertiser*, April 14, 1896;

Boston Herald, April 14, 1896; *Brooklyn
Daily Eagle*, April 26, 1896. A photo of the
memorial is at https://www.findagrave.
com/memorial/2471/harry-wright.
    7. Introduction to Cummings, "The
'Curve' Ball. The Inventor Tells All About
It."
    8. *Ibid.*
    9. Cummings, "How I Pitched the First
Curve"; "How I Invented the First Curve
Ball," *Pittsburg Press*, June 26, 1921.
    10. *Fitchburg Directory 1899* (Price
and Lee Co., 1899), 82, lists Cummings as a
paper hanger for G.Z. Page.
    11. *Fitchburg [MA] Sentinel*, January
27 and 30, 1897; *Athol Directory 1898–1899*
(New Haven, CT: Price and Lee Co., 1898),
27: *Fitchburg Directory 1899* (Price and
Lee Co., 1899), 82, 230, and 493; 1900 U.S.
Census, Athol, Worcester County, Mas-
sachusetts, ED 1582, sheet 10; *Athol [MA]
Transcript*, April 15, 1902.
    12. Dick Chaisson, *Hometown Chron-
icles* (Athol, MA: Millers River Publishing,
1985), 20.
    13. *Washington Post*, March 6, 1899.
    14. *Boston Globe*, March 2, 1899;
"Pitched First Curve"; *Waterbury [CT]
Democrat*, March 11, 1899.
    15. *Sporting Life*, August 3, 1907, July
31, 1909, August 13, 1910, and March 25,
1911; "When Good Fellows Meet," *Baseball
Magazine* 2, no. 1 (November 1908): 41–42;
Springfield [MA] Republican, May 3, 1914.
    16. *Sporting Life*, July 31, 1909, and
March 25, 1911.
    17. *Springfield [MA] Sunday Republi-
can*, May 3, 1914.
    18. "Cummings Tells Story of Early
Days of Curve Ball."
    19. *Brooklyn Daily Eagle*, May 20,
1888; *Springfield [MA] Union*, June 30,
1914.
    20. "Cummings Tells Story of Early
Days of Curve Ball."
    21. *Brooklyn Daily Eagle*, August 5
and September 3, 1895, April 26, 1896,
August 16, 1897, June 20, 1916, and June 23,
1918.
    22. William B. Cummings: New York
City certificate of death, 1918, no. 32015;
Mary P. Cummings: New York City certificate of death, 1922, no. 9029; *Brooklyn
Daily Eagle*, December 21, 1918, and April
21, 1922; 1920 U.S. Census, Queens, New
York, ED 370, sheet 7B.

23. World War I Draft Registration Card, Arthur Roberts Cummings; *Lansing [MI] City Directory 1919* (Lansing, MI: Chilson McKinley, 1919), 305; https://historicdetroit.org/buildings/grinnell-brothers-music-house; *Perrysburg [OH] Journal,* July 17, 1919; *Toledo Ohio Directory 1921* (Toledo: Toledo Directory Co., 1921), 357.

24. *Athol Directory 1920* (New Haven, CT.: Price & Lee Co., 1920), 64; *Toledo Ohio Directory 1922* (Toledo, OH: Toledo Directory Co., 1922), 353; Chaisson, *Hometown Chronicles,* 20.

25. *Cleveland Plain Dealer,* May 17, 1924; State of Ohio, Division of Vital Statistics, Certificate of Death, Wm. A. Cummings; Ware, Mass., Cemetery Commission, Interment Card for William Arthur Cummings, Aspen Grove Cemetery.

26. *Brooklyn Daily Eagle,* May 18, 1924.

Chapter 21

1. *Sporting News,* June 5, 1924.

2. *Boston Herald,* August 16, 1935; https://baseballhall.org.

3. https://baseballhall.org.

4. https://baseballhall.org/hall-of-famers. The Hall includes 235 players, plus 98 umpires, managers, and executives. It counts Cummings in the executive category. Thus, I have added him to the 235 players; there might be other players who are placed in other categories. The 19,700 figure was given during a Baseball Hall of Fame virtual program, "Virtual Field Trip: Plaques of the Gallery," on August 6, 2020.

5. Arthur J. Daley, "Baseball Pageant Thrills 10,000 At Game's 100th Birthday Party," *New York Times,* June 13, 1939; "Hall of Fame and Doubleday Field Fittingly Dedicated," *Otsego Farmer* (Cooperstown, NY), June 16, 1939.

6. *Ware River News* (MA), October 11, 2012.

7. http://valleybluesox.pointstreak sites.com/view/valleybluesox/community/western-massachusetts-baseball-hall-of-fame.

Chapter 22

1. *Sporting News,* June 5, 1924.

2. *Sporting News,* June 19, 1924.

3. David Nemec, *The Great Encyclopedia of Nineteenth Century Major League Baseball,* 2d ed. (Tuscaloosa: University of Alabama Press, 2006).

4. Cummings, "How I Pitched the First Curve."

Bibliography

Books, Scholarly Papers, Articles, Monographs

Abrams, Roger I. *Playing Tough: The World of Sports and Politics.* Boston: Northeastern University Press, 2013.

Alden, William C. *The Physical Features of Central Massachusetts.* United States Geological Survey, Bulletin 760–B. Washington, D.C.: Government Printing Office, 1924.

American Railway Guide for the United States. 3d ed. June 1856. New York: Dinsmore, [1856?].

Anson, Adrian Constantine. *A Ball Player's Career.* Chicago: Era Publishing, 1900.

Arcidiacono, David. "Ben Douglas." SABR BioProject, https://sabr.org/node/26039.

_____. "Fred Goldsmith: A Closer Look." *Base Ball: A Journal of the Early Game* 6:2 (Fall, 2012): 70–82.

_____. "The Hartford Dark Blues." *Hog River Journal* 1:3 (Spring, 2003): 26–31.

_____. *Major League Baseball in Gilded Age Connecticut.* Jefferson, NC: McFarland, 2010.

_____. "The 'Model' Game: Hartford vs. Chicago." In *Inventing Baseball: the 100 Greatest Games of the Nineteenth Century,* edited by Bill Felber, 93–94. Phoenix: Society for American Baseball Research, 2013.

_____. "Return to Conventional Wisdom on Candy Cummings." *Baseball* 8 (Fall, 2014): 35–46.

"The Art of Pitching." In Patten, William, and J. Walker McSpadden, eds., *The Book of Baseball; The National Game from the Earliest Days to the Present Season.* New York: P.F. Collier, 1911, 59–78.

"Arthur Cummings Talks Over His Discovery of Curve Ball." *Springfield [MA] Republican,* March 9, 1919.

"Arthur Cummings Tells How He Discovered the Curve Ball." *The Mixer and Server: Official Journal of the Hotel and Restaurant Employees International Alliance and Bartenders International League of America"* 21:10 (October 15, 1912): 61.

Barber, John Warner. *Historical Collections, Being a General Collection of Interesting Facts, Traditions, Biographical Sketches, Anecdotes, &c., Relating to the History and Antiquities of Every Town in Massachusetts.* Worcester, MA: Warren Lazell, 1844. Available online at https://archive.org/details/historicalcolle00barbuoft.

The Base Ball Player's Pocket Companion. Boston: Mayhew & Baker, 1859. Available online at https://archive.org/stream/TheBaseBallPlayersPocketCompanionContainingRulesAndRegulationsFor/Baseball.

"Base Ball Science." *Scientific American* 37:20 (November 17, 1877): 312.

"Baseball Really Does Curve According to Measurements." *Science News Letter,* June 20, 1942, 399.

"Baseball's Curve Balls." *Life* 11:11 (September 15, 1941): 83–89.

Bergen, Ferris G. "The Department of Public Education." In *Civil Political, Professional and Ecclesiastical History and Commercial and Industrial Record of the County of Kings and the City of Brooklyn, NY from 1683–1884,* edited by Henry R. Stiles. Vol. 1, 609–618. New York: W.W. Munsell, 1884. Available online at https://archive.org/details/cu31924088998046.

Block, David. *Baseball Before We Knew It.* Lincoln: University of Nebraska Press, 2005.

Bolton, Charles Knowles. *Scotch Irish Pioneers in Ulster and America.* Boston: Bacon & Brown, 1910. Available online at https://archive.org/details/scotchirish00boltrich.

Brancazio, Peter J. "The Physics of a Curveball." *Popular Mechanics* 174:4 (April, 1997): 56–57.

Brooklyn, NY, Department of Public Administration. Department of Public Instruction. *Sixth Annual Report of the Superintendent of Schools of Brooklyn, New-York, for the Year Ending January 31, 1861.* Brooklyn: L. Darbee, 1861.

_____. *Twelfth Annual Report of the Superintendent of Schools for the Year Ending January 31, 1867.* Brooklyn: L. Darbee, 1867.

Brooklyn Scrapbooks. At Brooklyn Historical Society. Various volumes.

Brooklyn/Queens Waterfront. "Wallabout Bay/Navy Yard." https://sites.google.com/site/brooklynqueenswaterfront/neighborhood-histories/wallabout-bay-navy-yard.

Brown, Randall. "1837.1 The Evolution of the New York Game—An Arbiter's Tale." *Base Ball: A Journal of the Early Game* 5:1 (Spring, 2011): 81–84.

Burr, Harold. "Candy Cummings." *The Sporting News,* November 19, 1942: 5.

Butt, Richard. *Map of the City of Brooklyn, and the Village of Williamsburgh, showing the Size of Blocks and Width of Streets as Laid Out by the Commissioners, the Old Farm Water Line, and All Recent Changes in Streets.* 1846.

Byard, John. "Fulton, NY—Home of the First Curve Ball." *Oswego [NY] Valley News,* March 17, 1994: 14.

Caillault, Jean-Pierre, comp. *The Complete New York Clipper Baseball Biographies.* Jefferson, NC: McFarland, 2009.

"Carroll Gardens Brooklyn History." http://carrollgardenshistory.blogspot.com/2009/03/bergen-hill.html.

Caylor, O.P. "Caylor's Ball Gossip." Various newspapers and dates.

Chadwick, Henry. *American Base Ball Manual.* London: George Routledge, 1874.

_____. *The American Game of Base Ball.* Philadelphia, 1888.

_____. *The Art of Pitching and Fielding.* Chicago: A.G. Spalding & Bros., 1885. Available online at https://archive.org/details/artofpitchingfie00chad.

_____. "The Art of Pitching in Baseball." *Scientific American* 55:5 (July 31, 1886): 71–72.

_____. *The Base Ball Players' Book of Reference.* New York: J.C. Haney, later Peck & Snyder. Various years.

_____. *Beadle's Dime Base-Ball Player.* New York, Beadle, various years. Links to online volumes are available at http://www.seanlahman.com/2014/08/20/index-of-online-baseball-guides.

_____. ed. *DeWitt's Base-Ball Guide.* New York: DeWitt, various years.

_____. *The Game of Baseball.* New York: George Munro, 1868.

_____. *How to Play Base Ball.* New York: A.G. Spalding, 1889.

_____. "Old Time Baseball," *Outing* 38:4 (July 1901): 420–422.

_____. Scrapbooks. In the *Spalding Baseball Collection, 1845–1913, bulk (1860–1900),* microform reel 8, New York Public Library, Manuscripts and Archives Division.

Chaisson, Dick. *Hometown Chronicles.* Athol, MA: Millers River Publishing, 1985.

Chamberlain, General Joshua L., ed. *Universities and Their Sons.* Vol. 5. Boston: R. Herndon, 1900. Available online at https://archive.org/details/b2900035x_0005.

Chase, Arthur. *History of Ware, Massachusetts.* Cambridge, MA: University Press, 1911. Available online at https://archive.org/details/historywaremass00chasgoog.

Chase, Rev. W. Dempster, ed. *History and Reunion of Falley Seminary.* Fulton, NY: Morrill Brothers, 1890. Available online at https://babel.hathitrust.org/cgi/pt?id=mdp.39015075902927.

Churchill, John C., ed. *Landmarks of Oswego County, New York.* Syracuse, NY: D. Mason, 1895. Available online at https://archive.org/stream/landmarksofosweg00chur.

Citizens for New York City. *The Neighborhoods of Brooklyn.* 2d ed. New Haven, CT: Yale University Press, 2004.

City of New York. Landmark Preservation Commission. *Carroll Gardens Historic District: Designation Report.* 1973. http://s-media.nyc.gov/agencies/lpc/lp/0696.pdf.

Clark, Marietta, et al. *Isaac Cummings of Topsfield, Mass., and Some of His Descendants.*

Topsfield, MA: Topsfield Historical Society, 1899. Available online at https://archive.org/details/isaaccummingsoft00clar.

Commonwealth of Massachusetts. Massachusetts Historic Commission, *MHC Reconnaissance Survey Town Report.* Reports for Athol (1984) and Ware (1982).

_____. Department of Conservation and Recreation. Ware Reconnaissance Report. June, 2009.

Connole, Dennis A. *The Indians of the Nipmuck Country in Southern New England, 1630–1750: An Historical Geography.* Jefferson, NC: McFarland, 2000.

Constitution and By-Laws of the New England Association of National Base Ball Players. Boston: Wright & Potter, 1866. Available online at https://www.google.com/books/edition/Constitution_and_By_laws_of_the_New_Engl/0bwVAAAAYAAJ?hl=en&gbpv=1&dq=%22Constitution+and+By-Laws+of+the+New+England+Association+of+National+Base+Ball+Players.

Cooper, James F. *Tenacious of Their Liberties: The Congregationalists in Colonial Massachusetts.* New York: Oxford University Press, 1999.

Crane, Sam. "Arthur Cummings." *New York Journal,* January 8, 1912.

Cummings, David Butler. "Isaac Cummings (1601–1677 of Watertown, Ipswich, and Topsfield, Massachusetts, and His Ancestry." *New England Historical and Genealogical Register* 165 (January, 2011), 35–41.

Cummings, William Arthur. "How I Invented the First Curve Ball." *Pittsburg Press,* June 26, 1921.

_____. "How I Pitched the First Curve." First published in *Baseball Magazine* 1 (September, 1908), and reprinted in various places since then, including *Classic Baseball Stories,* edited by Jeff Silverman. Guilford, CT: The Lyons Press, 2003, 69–73.

_____. Series of articles about his career, and his invention of the curveball, in *The Cottager* (Athol, MA), in 1897–1898, referred to herein as the "Cummings *Cottager* series." Copies of the articles are in Arthur Cummings: Pitcher: Scrapbook, 1909–1939, BA SCR 175, National Baseball Hall of Fame Library, Cooperstown, NY. Article titles include: "Base Ball in 1864–1865. The Games for the Silver Ball"; "Baseball in the Sixties and Seventies. A Tour with the Star Club of Brooklyn"; "Baseball in the Sixties. Experience in Junior Clubs"; "Baseball in the Sixties. With the Excelsiors"; "Close of Mr. Cummings' Reminiscences"; "The 'Curve' Ball. The Inventor Tells All About It."

_____. "Story of the Curve Ball." In Elwood A. Roff, *Base Ball and Base Ball Player.* Chicago: E.A. Roff, 1912. Available online at https://babel.hathitrust.org/cgi/pt?id=loc.ark:/13960/t56d6ps7d&view=1up&seq=5.

"Cummings First Pitcher to Hurl a Curve Ball." *Duluth News Tribune,* January 17, 1920.

"Cummings of Brooklyn Fired First Curve." *Brooklyn Daily Union,* May 25, 1918.

"Cummings Tells Story of Early Days of Curve Ball." *The Sporting News,* December 29, 1921.

Cummins, Albert Oren. *Cummings Genealogy. Isaac Cummings 1601–1677 of Ipswich in 1638 and Some of His Descendants.* Montpelier, VT.: Argus and Patriot Printing House, 1904. Available online at https://archive.org/details/cummingsgenealog00cumm.

"The Curve Ball. The Discoverer of the Art of Curve Pitching." *Sporting Life,* May 4, 1895.

"The Curve Ball. Why the Battery has Grown Superior to the Skilled Pounders." *New York Times,* August 22, 1883 (reprinted from *Philadelphia Press,* August 20, 1883).

Daley, Arthur J. "Baseball Pageant Thrills 10,000 At Game's 100th Birthday Party." *New York Times,* June 13, 1939: 1.

Devine, Christopher. "Harry Wright." SABR BioProject, https://sabr.org/bioproj/person/eb17c14e.

Discover Smith Street: A Walking Tour and Guide Book—A Joint Project of the Merchants' Association of Smith Street, NYC. Board of Education, and Prospect Park Environmental Center. Booklet in the files of the Brooklyn Historical Society.

Dow, George Francis. *History of Topsfield, Massachusetts.* Topsfield, MA: Topsfield Historical Society, 1940. Available online at https://archive.org/details/historyoftopsfie00dowg.

Duffy, Donald. "Ne Namas Eck Or The Place of Fish." In *History of Ware, Massachusetts, 1961–2011.* Ware Historical Society. Salem, MA: Higginson Book Co., 2012.

Dyte, David. "1845.4 Baseball in Brooklyn, 1845–1870: The Best There Was." *Base Ball: A Journal of the Early Game* 5:1 (Spring, 2011): 98–102.

Early, Frank J., and Kenneth Mosher. "Fulton Man is Claimed Inventor of Curved Ball, Now Feature of Pitching." Fulton ed., *Syracuse Herald*. Newspaper image from website www.fultonhistory.com. Date unknown.

Economic History Association. "History of the U.S. Telegraph Industry." https://eh.net/encyclopedia/history-of-the-u-s-telegraph-industry.

Edwards, J.E. "The House Painter Who Discovered the Curve Ball." *Deseret Evening News* (Salt Lake City), March 12, 1910, and several other newspapers.

Egan, Casey. "The Surprising Irish Origins of Baltimore, Maryland." https://www.irishcentral.com/roots/history/the-surprising-irish-origins-of-baltimore-maryland.

Ephemeral New York. "The Piece of Plymouth Rock in a Brooklyn Church." https://ephemeralnewyork.wordpress.com/2015/07/20/the-piece-of-plymouth-rock-in-a-brooklyn-church.

Erie Canal. "Boats on the Erie Canal." http://eriecanal.org/boats.html.

Faber, Charles F. "Doug Allison." SABR BioProject, https://sabr.org/bioproj/person/dc86c546.

Falley Seminary. *Catalogue of the Officers and Students of Falley Seminary, Fulton, Oswego County, NY, for the Academic Year Ending June 29, 1865*. Fulton, NY: Patriot and Gazette Caloric Power Press Print, 1865. Ditto for the Year Ending June 28, 1866.

Farmer, John. *A Genealogical Register of the First Settlers of New England*. Baltimore: Genealogical Publishing, 1829.

Fast, Mike. "What the Heck Is PITCHf/x?" In Alan Nathan's "The Physics of Baseball" website, http://baseball.physics.illinois.edu/FastPFXGuide.pdf, reprinted from Distelheim, Joe, et al, eds., *The Hardball Times Baseball Annual, 2010*. Skokie, IL: Acta Sports, 2010.

Field, Thomas W. *Historical Sketch of the Public Schools and Board of Education of the City of Brooklyn*. Brooklyn: R.M. Whiting, Jr., 1873.

"The First Pitcher to Throw Curves—His Fancy Wrist Action." *Arizona Republican*, June 5, 1911.

"The First to Curve. How Arthur Cummings Made the Discovery." *Sporting Life*, April 11, 1896.

Fleitz, David. "Candy Cummings." SABR BioProject, http://sabr.org/bioproj/person/99fabe5f.

_____. "Fred Goldsmith." SABR BioProject, https://sabr.org/bioproj/person/99c4a5f5.

_____. *Ghosts in the Gallery at Cooperstown*. Jefferson, NC: McFarland, 2004.

Frommer, Harvey. *Old-Time Baseball: America's Pastime in the Gilded Age*. Lanham, MD: Taylor Trade Publishing, 2006.

Ganot, A., and William G. Peck. *Introductory Course of Natural Philosophy for the Use of Schools and Academies, Edited from Ganot's Popular Physics by William G. Peck*. New York: Barnes and Burr, 1865. Available online at https://babel.hathitrust.org/cgi/pt?id=nyp.33433069107732.

Goddard, Ives. "The 'Loup' Languages of Western Massachusetts: The Dialectical Diversity of Southern New England Algonquian." In *Papers of the Forty-Fourth Algonquian Conference*, edited by Monica Macaulay, *et al*. Albany: SUNY Press, 2016, 104–138.

Goldfarb, Irv. "Morgan Bulkeley." SABR BioProject, https://sabr.org/bioproj/person/73d7237a.

Goldsmith, Fred. "Fred Goldsmith, Star Hurler of '80s, Reminisces." *The Sporting News*, March 3, 1932: 5.

Goldstein, Warren. *Playing for Keeps: A History of Early Baseball*. Ithaca, NY: Cornell University Press, 1989.

Gould, Cornelia A. *Genealogy of the Descendants of James Breakenridge, Who Emigrated from Ireland, July, 1727*. Ware, MA: Charles W. Eddy, 1887. Available online at https://archive.org/details/genealogyofdesce1887goul.

Gruber, John H. "The Development of the Playing Rules." *Sporting Life*, January 8, 1916.

"Hall of Fame and Doubleday Field Fittingly Dedicated." *Otsego Farmer* (Cooperstown, NY), June 16, 1939.

Harrison, Fred H. *Athletics for All. Physical Education and Athletics at Phillips Andover Academy, 1778–1978*. Andover, MA: Phillips Academy, 1983.

Haupert, Michael. "William Hulbert and the Birth of the National League." SABR BioProject, https://sabr.org/research/william-hulbert-and-birth-national-league.

"He Pitched the First Curve Ball." *Brooklyn Daily Eagle,* April 26, 1896: 17.

Helander, Brock. "The League Alliance." https://sabr.org/bioproj/topic/league-alliance.

Hershberger, Richard. "The Antebellum Growth and Spread of the New York Game." *Base Ball: A Journal of the Early Game* 8:134 (2014): 134–149.

_____. "Baseball and Rounders." *Base Ball: A Journal of the Early Game* 3:1 (Spring, 2009): 81–93.

_____. "Did New York Steal the Championship of 1867 from Philadelphia?" In *The National Pastime: From Swampoodle to South Philly: Baseball in Philadelphia and the Delaware Valley,* edited by Morris Levin. Phoenix, Ariz.: Society for American Baseball Research, 2013, 22-27. Available online at https://sabr.org/research/did-new-york-steal-championship-1867-philadelphia.

_____. "A Reconstruction of Philadelphia Town Ball." *Base Ball: A Journal of the Early Game* 1:2 (Fall, 2007): 28–43.

Hinckley, David. "Flight of Ball. The Cummings Curve. Chapter 31." *New York Daily News,* March 31, 2003.

Hitchcock, Mrs. Edward, Sr. *The Genealogy of the Hitchcock Family.* Amherst, MA: Carpenter and Morehouse, 1894. Available online at https://archive.org/details/genealogyofhitch00hitc.

Holbrook, Jay Mack. *Massachusetts Vital Records to 1850: Ware 1735–1893* 3, "Births, Marriages, Deaths, 1844–1852, Births in Ware 1848–1849."

Hurd, Richard M. *A History of Yale Athletics.* New Haven, CT: R.M. Hurd, 1888. Available online at https://archive.org/details/historyofyaleath00hurduoft/.

Hyde, William. *An Address, Delivered at the Opening of the New Town-Hall, Ware, Mass., March 31, 1847.* Brookfield, MA: Merriam and Cooke, 1847. Available online at https://archive.org/details/addressdelivered00hyderich.

"Inventor of Curve Tells of Old Times." *Duluth Herald,* February 17, 1912.

Iorizzo, Luciano. *Al Capone: A Biography.* Westport, CT: Greenwood Press, 2003.

Jeanes, Jeanette. "A History of Carroll Gardens" (1970). Unpublished manuscript in the files of the Brooklyn Historical Society.

Jefferson, Charles E. *Congregationalism.* Boston: Pilgrim Press, 1910. Available online at https://archive.org/details/congregationali00jeffgoog.

Johnson, Crisfield. *History of Oswego County, New York.* Philadelphia: L.H. Everts, 1877. Available online at https://archive.org/stream/historyofoswegoc00john#page/n5/mode/2up/search/George+F.+Falley.

"Journalist Who Scooped the World Is Vindicated After Being Branded A 'Faker' for Twenty-five Years." *Washington [D.C.] Herald,* September 24, 1917.

Kadinsky, Sergey. *Hidden Waters of New York City.* New York, NY: Countryman Press, 2016.

Kagan, David. "The Physics of the Curveball—A Short History" (March 3, 2014), https://www.fangraphs.com/tht/tht-live/the-physics-of-the-curveball-a-short-history.

Katz, Stephen R. "The Story of the Portraits of Mr. and Mrs. William Brackenridge Cummings of Ware, Massachusetts, and Brooklyn, New York," *MASSOG: A Genealogical Journal for the Commonwealth of Massachusetts* 41:2 (Massachusetts Society of Genealogists, 2016–2017): 50–61.

Kepner, Tyler. *A History of Baseball in Ten Pitches.* New York: Anchor Books, 2019.

Kofoed, J.C. "Early History of Curve Pitching." *Cleveland Leader,* August 22, 1870. Reprinted in *Baseball Magazine* 15:4 (August, 1915): 55–57.

Lancaster, Clay. "Carroll Gardens/Brooklyn /Long Island/New York. An Architectural Evaluation" (23 May 1970). Unpublished manuscript in the files of the Brooklyn Historical Society.

"Letter of Mr. Isaac Newton, Professor of the Mathematicks in the University of Cambridge; containing his New Theory about Light and Colors." Reproduced at the website of The Newton Project, http://www.newtonproject.ox.ac.uk/view/texts/normalized/NATP00006.

Lewis, Clarence O. *The Erie Canal 1817–1967.* Lockport, NY: Niagara County Historical Society, 1967.

Light, Steve. "Baseball Came of Age During American Civil War." https://baseballhall.org/discover/baseball-came-of-age-during-civil-war.

Lord, William G. *History of Athol, Massachusetts.* Athol: William G. Lord, 1953. Available online at https://archive.org/details/historyofatholma00lord.

Magnus, G. *Über die Abweichung der Geschosse; Über eine auffallende Erscheinung bei Rotierenden Körpern.* Berlin: Ferd. Dümmler's Verlags–Buchhandlung, 1852. Available online at https://reader.digitale-sammlungen.de/en/fs1/object/display/bsb10909033_00001.html.

Martin, Alphonse C. "McSweeney of Mutuals First to Pitch Curve." *New York Sun,* March 17, 1918.

McCray, Larry. "1829.2. The Rise and Fall of New England-Style Ballplaying." *Base Ball: A Journal of the Early Game* 5:1 (Spring, 2011): 69–72.

McCue, Andy. "Branch Rickey." SABR BioProject, https://sabr.org/bioproj/person/6d0ab8f3.

McKenna, Brian, "Asa Brainard." SABR BioProject, http://sabr.org/bioproj/person/a151ac94.

_____. "Bob Ferguson." SABR BioProject, https://sabr.org/bioproj/person/df8e7d29.

_____. "Bobby Mathews." SABR BioProject, https://sabr.org/bioproj/person/e7ad641f.

_____. "Steve Bellàn." SABR BioProject, https://sabr.org/bioproj/person/78dbf37d.

McMahon, Bill. "Al Spalding." SABR BioProject, https://sabr.org/bioproj/person/b99355e0.

Melville, Tom. *Early Baseball and the Rise of the National League.* Jefferson, NC: McFarland, 2001.

Miner, Dorothy, et al. "Gowanus Canal Corridor." Columbia University Historic Preservation, Studio II, Spring, 2008. Available online at https://semspub.epa.gov/work/02/122510.pdf.

"Modern Stars Wonderful, But They Have Nothing on Old-Timers in His Opinion." *Rockford [IL] Morning Star,* July 14, 1912.

Mooar, Rev. George. *The Cummings Memorial: A Genealogical History of the Descendants of Isaac Cummings, an Early Settler of Topsfield, Massachusetts.* New York: B.F. Cummings, 1903. Available online at https://archive.org/details/cummingsmemorial00inmooa.

Morris, Peter. *Base Ball Founders: The Clubs, Players and Cities of the Northeast that Established the Game.* Jefferson, NC: McFarland, 2013.

_____. *But Didn't We Have Fun.* Chicago: Ivan R. Dee, 2008.

_____. *Catcher: How the Man Behind the Plate Became an American Folk Hero.* Chicago: Ivan R. Dee, 2009.

_____. *A Game of Inches: The Story Behind the Innovations that Shaped Baseball.* Chicago: Ivan R. Dee, 2010.

Murnane, T.H. "The Curve Ball." *Sporting Life,* March 25, 1911.

Nathan, Alan M. "The Physics of Baseball," http://baseball.physics.illinois.edu/nathan-papers.html.

Nathanson, Mitchell. *A People's History of Baseball.* Champaign: University of Illinois Press, 2012.

"A National Association of Amateur Base Ball Players Established." *New York Clipper,* March 25, 1871: 5.

National Association of Base Ball Players. *Rules and Regulations of the Game of Baseball.* Various years.

National League of Professional Base Ball Clubs. *Constitution and Playing Rules.* Chicago: A.G. Spalding. Various years.

"National League of Professional Clubs: A Startling Coup d'Etat." *New York Clipper,* February 12, 1876.

Nemec, David. *The Great Encyclopedia of Nineteenth Century Major League Baseball.* 2d ed. Tuscaloosa: University of Alabama Press, 2006.

_____. "Jack Manning." SABR BioProject, https://sabr.org/bioproj/person/fbd233f7.

New England Congregational Church and Society, Brooklyn, NY *Manual of the New England Congregational Church and Society, Brooklyn (Eastern District), NY.* Brooklyn: L. Darbee & Sons, Printers, 1859. In the Brooklyn Historical Society's Baptist Churches of Brooklyn publications and ephemera collection 1986.013.

New England Society in the City of Brooklyn. *Centennial Handbook.* Available online at http://newenglandsociety.org/images/NES_PDFs/newenglandsocietyhistory.pdf.

_____. *Constitution and By-Laws of the New-England Society in the City of Brooklyn.* Brooklyn: E.B. Spooner, Printers, 1847.

New Railway Map of the United States. New York: G.W & C.B. Colton, 1867. Available online at https://www.loc.gov/resource/g3701p.rr000480.

North Presbyterian Church (New York, NY). *Church Records and General Register, North Presbyterian Church.* New York: Nathan Lane, 1854.

_____. *Manual of the North Presbyterian Church in the City of New York.* New York: John A. Gray, 1858. Available online at https://archive.org/stream/manualofnorthpre00nort_0.

Nowlin, Bill, and Emmet R. Nowlin, eds. *20-Game Losers.* Phoenix: Society for American Baseball Research, 2017.

O'Hara, Philip N. "Survivor of Pioneer Days on Diamond Describes Game and Players of Five Decades Ago for Fans of Modern Age." *Detroit Free Press,* November 23, 1924.

Orem, Preston D. *Baseball (1845–1881): From the Newspaper Accounts.* Altadena, CA: Preston D. Orem, 1961.

"Origin of Curves," *Current Literature, A Magazine of Record and Review* 23 (January–June, 1898): 557–558.

"Oswego's Crack Baseball Team of the Sixties, The Ontarios." *Syracuse Herald,* May 19, 1912.

Palmer, A. Emerson. *The New York Public School. Being a History of Free Education in the City of New York.* New York: Macmillan, 1905.

Park Church, Elmira, New York. *Thomas K. Beecher, Teacher of the Park Church at Elmira, New York.* Boston: George H. Ellis, 1900. Available online at https://www.archive.org/stream/thomaskbeecherte00park.

Perris, William. *Maps of the City of Brooklyn* 2, 2d ed. (1855 and 1860–1861).

Pestana, Mark. "Candy Cummings Debuts the Curve." In *Inventing Baseball: The 100 Greatest Games of the Nineteenth Century,* edited by Bill Felber, 60–62. Phoenix: Society for American Baseball Research, 2013.

Peverelly, Charles A. *Book of American Pastimes.* New York: Charles A. Peverelly, 1866. Available online at https://babel.hathitrust.org/cgi/pt?id=nyp.33433082423470.

Pietrusza, David, et al, eds. *Baseball: The Biographical Encyclopedia.* New York: Total/Sports Illustrated, 2000.

"Pitched First Curve." *Washington Post,* March 6, 1899: 8.

Plymouth Church, website of, http://www.plymouthchurch.org/history.

"Plymouth Church of the Pilgrims," https://www.atlasobscura.com/places/plymouth-church-of-the-pilgrims?utm_source=atlas-forum&utm.

Porter, David L., ed. *Biographical Dictionary of American Sports.* Westport, CT: Greenwood Press, 2000.

Presbrey, Frank, and James Hugh Moffatt, comps. *Athletics at Princeton: A History.* New York: Frank Presbrey, 1901. Available online at https://archive.org/details/athleticsatprin00presgoog.

Princeton University. *Record of the Class of Eighteen Hundred and Seventy-Six,* Princeton: 1876–1911.

Prindle, Edward J. *The Art of Curved Pitching.* Philadelphia: A.J. Reach, 1886.

"The Proceedings at the Grand Central." *New York Clipper,* February 12, 1876.

"The Professionals in Council." *New York Clipper,* March 25, 1871: 2.

"The Profits of Ball Tossing." *West Meriden [CT] Daily Republican,* September 25, 1872.

Puff, Richard. "Douglas L. Allison." In *Baseball's First Stars,* edited by Frederick Ivor-Campbell, 2. Cleveland: Society for American Baseball Research, 1996.

Quigley, Martin. *The Crooked Pitch: The Curveball in American Baseball History.* Chapel Hill, NC: Algonquin Books, 1984.

Rainey, Chris. "Tommy Bond." SABR BioProject, https://sabr.org/bioproj/person/c0089818#sdendnote1anc.

Reach's Official Base Ball Guide. Various years. Philadelphia: A.J. Reach Co.

"Reminiscences of a Ball Player." *New York Times,* June 2, 1900: BR12–13.

Richter, Francis C. *Richter's History and Records of Baseball.* Philadelphia: Francis C. Richter, 1914.

Rosenberg, Eric. "The National Association of Professional Base Ball Players. The Origins of Professional Baseball and the American Identity." *Vanderbilt Undergraduate Research Journal* 8 (Spring, 2012), doi: 10.15695/vurj.v8i0.3522.

Ruzzo, Bob. "The South End Grounds." In *The Glorious Beaneaters of the 1890s*, edited by Bob LeMoine and Bill Nowlin. Phoenix: Society for American Baseball Research, 2019.

Ryczek, William J. *Baseball's First Inning: A History of the National Pastime Through the Civil War*. Jefferson, NC: McFarland, 2009.

_____. *Blackguards and Red Stockings*. Jefferson, NC: McFarland, 2016.

_____. "The 1867 Nationals of Albany, Part 2." August 5, 2013. Website of the National Pastime Museum, https://www.thenationalpastimemuseum.com/article/1867-nationals-albany-0.

_____. *When Johnny Came Sliding Home*. Jefferson, NC: McFarland, 1998.

Schiff, Andrew. *"The Father of Baseball." A Biography of Henry Chadwick*. Jefferson, NC: McFarland, 2008.

_____. "Henry Chadwick," SABR BioProject, http://sabr.org/bioproj/person/436e570c.

Seymour, Harold. *Baseball: The Early Years*. New York: Oxford University Press, 1960.

Shatzkin, Mike, ed. *The Ballplayers: Baseball's Ultimate Biographical Reference*. New York: Arbor House, 1990.

Smith, J. Calvin. *Smith's Rail Road, Steam Boat & Stage Route Map of New England, New-York and Canada*. New York: J. Calvin Smith, 1858.

South Brooklyn Network. "Carroll Gardens." https://www.southbrooklyn.net/neighborhood/carroll-gardens.

South Congregational Church, Brooklyn, NY. *Manual of the South Congregational Church, Brooklyn, NY*. New York: Blakeman and Mason, 1859. In the Brooklyn Historical Society's South Congregational Church of Brooklyn collection 1986.020.

_____. *Ninetieth Anniversary: South Congregational Church, Brooklyn, NY*. In the Brooklyn Historical Society's South Congregational Church of Brooklyn collection 1986.020.

Spalding, Albert G. *America's National Game*. New York: American Sports Publishing, 1911.

_____. *Spalding's Official Base Ball Guide*. Various years. Chicago: A.G. Spalding & Bro., or New York: American Sports Publishing. Links to online volumes are available at http://www.seanlahman.com/2014/08/20/index-of-online-baseball-guides.

Spink, Alfred H. *The National Game*. St. Louis: National Game Publishing, 1910.

Sutton, Richard M. "Baseballs *Do* Curve *And* Drop!" *American Journal of Physics* 19 (August, 1942): 201–202.

Syrett, Harold Coffin. *The City of Brooklyn, 1865–1898*. New York: Columbia Univ. Press, 1944. Available online at https://archive.org/details/cityofbrooklyn180000syre.

Terry, James L. *Long Before the Dodgers: Baseball in Brooklyn, 1855–1884*. Jefferson, NC: McFarland, 2002.

Thirteen/WNET. "History of Brooklyn." http://www.thirteen.org/brooklyn/history/history3.html.

Thorn, John, and Pete Palmer. *The Hidden Game of Baseball*. Garden City, NY: Doubleday, 1984.

Thorn, John. *Baseball in the Garden of Eden*. New York: Simon & Schuster, 2011.

_____. "George Wright." SABR BioProject, https://sabr.org/bioproj/person/5468d7c0.

_____. "Jim Creighton." SABR BioProject, http://sabr.org/bioproj/person/2d2e5d16.

_____. "1791 and All That: Baseball and the Berkshires." *Base Ball* 1:1 (Spring, 2007), 119–126.

_____. "Pitching: Evolution and Revolution." Our Game blog, https://ourgame.mlblogs.com/pitching-evolution-and-revolution-efd3a5ebaa83.

Treese, Joel D. "Baseball and the White House in the Nineteenth Century." https://www.whitehousehistory.org/baseball-and-the-white-house-in-the-nineteenth-century.

United States Environmental Protection Agency (EPA). "Gowanus Canal, Brooklyn, NY." https://cumulis.epa.gov/supercpad/SiteProfiles/index.cfm?fuseaction=second.Cleanup&id=0206222#bkground.

_____. "Record of Decision: Gowanus Canal Superfund Site, Brooklyn, Kings County, New York." Available online at https://casedocuments.darrp.noaa.gov/northeast/gowanus/pdf/GowanusROD.pdf.

United States Patent Office. Patents no. 149,376 and 194,996, issued to William A. Cummings.

Vacarro, Frank. "Origin of the Modern Pitching Win." https://sabr.org/journal/article/origin-of-the-modern-pitching-win. Originally Published in *Baseball Research Journal*, Spring, 2013.

Verwiebe, Frank L. "Does a Baseball Curve?" *American Journal of Physics* 10 (April, 1942): 119–120.

Waff, Craig B. "1860.60 Atlantics and Excelsiors Compete for the 'Championship,' July 19, August 9, and August 23, 1860." *Base Ball: A Journal of the Early Game* 5:1 (Spring 2011): 139–142. Available online at https://ourgame.mlblogs.com/atlantics-and-excelsiors-compete-for-the-championship-1860–55b9bfb89217.

_____. "No Gentlemen's Game, Excelsior of South Brooklyn vs. Atlantic of Bedford." In *Inventing Baseball: The 100 Greatest Games of the Nineteenth Century*, edited by Bill Felber. Phoenix: Society for American Baseball Research, 2013, 28–31.

Ward, John Montgomery. *Base-Ball: How to Become a Player*. Philadelphia: Athletic Publishing, 1888.

Warnick, Bernice Amsden. *Ancestors and Descendants of Jonathan Nichols Amsden and Amelia Jane Smith*. Santa Maria, CA: Bernice Amsden Warnick, 1978.

Waters, Thomas Franklin. *Ipswich in the Massachusetts Bay Colony*. Ipswich, MA: Ipswich Historical Society, 1905.

"When Good Fellows Meet." *Baseball Magazine* 2:1 (November, 1908): 41–42.

Wiley, Edwin, and Irving E. Rines. *Lectures on the Growth and Development of the United States* 9. New York: American Educational Alliance, 1915.

"William Arthur Cummings." *New York Clipper*, July 8, 1871: 3.

"William Arthur Cummings, the Inventor of the Curve Ball Tells About its Early Use." *Denver Post*, August 17, 1912.

Williams, Frank J. "All the Record Books are Wrong." https://sabr.org/journal/article/all-the-record-books-are-wrong/ (1982). Originally published in *The National Pastime: Premier Edition*, 1982.

Wright, Marshall D. *The National Association of Base Ball Players, 1857–1870*. Jefferson, NC: McFarland, 2000.

Yale University. *Fifty-Five Yale, Supplementary Record, 1889–1895*.

Selected Newspapers

Innumerable newspaper articles, in addition to those listed above, were read in researching this book. Many concerned games during the years in which Candy Cummings played. My objective was to review accounts of all his games. Inevitably, however, some were missed. Most of these were games that were not reported, which was more common before 1872. It is possible that there were a few games that were reported but for which accounts could not be found with the resources used. Below is a list of the principal newspapers consulted; there were many others.

Baltimore Sun	*Hartford Courant*
Boston Globe	*Hartford Times*
Boston Herald	*New Haven Register*
Boston Journal	*New York Clipper*
Boston Traveler	*New York Herald*
Brooklyn Daily Eagle	*New York Sun*
Buffalo [NY] Commercial Gazette	*New York Sunday Mercury*
Buffalo [NY] Courier	*New York Times*
Chicago Inter-Ocean	*New York Tribune*
Chicago Tribune	*New York World*
Cincinnati Commercial Tribune	*Philadelphia Inquirer*
Cincinnati Gazette	*Rockford [IL] Gazette*
Cincinnati Inquirer	*Rockford [IL] Morning Star*
Cleveland Leader	*St. Louis Globe-Democrat*
Cleveland Plain Dealer	*St. Louis Republican*
Connecticut Courant	*Spirit of the Times*

Sporting Life   *Washington [D.C.] Capital*
Sporting News   *Washington [D.C.] Evening Star*
Springfield [MA] Republican   *Washington [D.C.] National Republican*
Springfield [MA] Union   *Washington [D.C.] Post*

Selected Other Sources

Certificates of birth, marriage, death, from various locations and dates.
City Directories for Athol, MA; Brooklyn, NY; Lansing, MI; Newark, NJ; New York City;
    Toledo, OH. Various years.
New York State Census: various locations and years.
United States Census: various locations and years.
www.ancestry.com: various genealogical data and documents.
www.baseball-reference.com.
www.baseballhall.org.
www.brooksbaseball.net.
www.espn.com/mlb/stats/team: various seasons.
www.familysearch.org: various genealogical data and documents.
www.protoball.org.
www.mlb.com.
www.retrosheet.org.
www.threadsofourgame.com.

Index

Numbers in *bold italics* indicate pages with illustrations